Full-Size FORDS
1955-1970

David W. Temple

CarTech®

CarTech ®

CarTech®, Inc.
39966 Grand Avenue
North Branch, MN 55056
Phone: 651-277-1200 or 800-551-4754
Fax: 651-277-1203
www.cartechbooks.com

Edit by Paul Johnson
Layout by Christopher Fayers

ISBN 978-1-61325-070-9
Item No. SA176P

Library of Congress Cataloging-in-Publication Data

Temple, David W.
 Full size Fords : 1955-1970 / by David Temple.
  p. cm.
 ISBN 978-1-934709-08-5
 1. Ford automobile—Pictorial works. 2. Ford automobile—History. I. Title.

 TL215.F35T46 2010
 629.222—dc22

2009012636

Printed in USA
10 9 8 7 6 5 4 3 2 1

Dedication

To Mom,
who supported my writing career

Front Cover:
This 1964 Galaxie 500 carries a 427 R-code V-8 with a 4-speed transmission and 4.11 rear end gears. The 427 features a forged-steel crankshaft, cross-bolted main bearing caps, forged-aluminum pistons, a lightweight valvetrain, and a solid-lifter cam for producing 425 hp and 480 ft-lbs of torque.

Title Page:
The pictured Galaxie 500 7-Litre convertible is one of just two examples ordered with the 425-hp 427 V-8. That is not the only factor making this car special. It is also painted special-order Sapphire Blue, a color used by Lincoln.

Back Cover Photos

Top Left:
Ford's SOHC (single overhead cammer) was created to beat the Chrysler Hemi. It utilized the 427 cylinder block, single overhead camshaft with two rocker shafts per bank, roller follower type rocker arms, a lightweight chain and sprocket type valvetrain drive mechanism, and hemispherical combustion chambers.

Top Right:
The 1958 Sunliner featured audacious flairs and lots of chrome. The quad headlight system or as Ford dubbed it, "Safety-Twin Headlights," was one of the styling updates for 1958. A 265-hp 332-ci with a three-speed automatic transmission propelled the car. Four-wheel drum brakes provided the stopping power.

Bottom:
Dearborn Steel Tubing built this 1963½ Galaxie 500 as one of a reported 212 lightweight cars built for Ford. Hundreds of pounds were shaved from the standard Galaxie 500 through the use of fiberglass panels, the lighter Ford 300 frame, aluminum bumpers and other modifications.

CONTENTS

ACKNOWLEDGMENTS

I gratefully acknowledge the cooperation of the car owners who allowed me to photograph their car(s) and the contributions made by others who provided information and/or photography for this book. Many thanks go to the following individuals: Ronald Anderson, Charles D. Barnette, Jimmy Blackburn, Chuck Carter, Adrian Clements, Dave Cline (Dave's Classic Limousine Pictures), John Craft, Colin Date (*Legendary Ford* Magazine), Robert and Darlene Davidson, Steve Drake, Jim Duffack, Sr., Nelson Bates, Russell Chandler, David Flack, Mitch Frumkin (Chicago Automobile Trade Association), Sue Gooding (Texas State Fair), Gale Halderman (Ford Executive Director of Design, ret.), Thomas Heidenfelder, Carl Hilliard, Paul Hobbs (1962 Ford Galaxie registry), Stu Marshall, Kevin Marti (Marti Auto Works), Scotty and Mary McCally, Tom Meadows, Leroy and Sharon Meints, Dick Nelson, Russ Owens, Mike Patak (Mike's Classic Cars; Blair, Nebraska), Z. T. Parker, Dick and Marjorie Peach, Ward Plauché, Doug Pollock (SMS Auto Fabrics), Mark Reynolds (president, Ford Galaxie Club of America), Dick Rozum (*Legendary Ford* Magazine), John Rotella (Lovefords.com), Carl Sable, Joe Shields (chief judge, Crown Victoria Association), Martin Siemion (Ford Galaxie Club of America), Gary Spracklin, James Stanchfield (www.mercury stuff.com), Cody and Betty Stollan, Frank Stubbs, Doug Swanson (Swanson Ford; Ceresco, Nebraska), Tommy Taylor, Jack Telnack (Global Vice President of Design, Ford Motor Co., ret.), Bill Warner, Bob Weenink (www.1964ford.com), Ron White, Scott Wiley, Darren Will, Carl Wimberly, Maurice Wright, and Tom Yanulaytis (1966 Ford Full-Size Registry).

FOREWORD

The 1950s, 1960s, and 1970s were an exciting time to be an automotive designer. Big, bold, and different was "in" and management was usually very agreeable to what we designers were doing.

Each model had its own character and each company had its own look. All General Motors' vehicles had a soft, rounded appearance while Ford's had a crisp, angular look. Every car in the line was different, yet maintained a family resemblance. Higher-priced models all had distinguishing features to separate them from the lower-priced cars. Full-size, six-passenger models had long hoods, bold front ends, and were ornamented with chrome, though each series had its own distinguishing amount of trim.

Every shape was taken into consideration. For instance, the cars were designed so a driver could see all four corners, making parking easier. Roofs were shaped with a fast slope to suggest sportiness or given a formal look to suggest luxury.

Complexity in production was awesome! Each nameplate had a two-door, four-door, convertible, and station wagon in several series. Furthermore, if your car was red you could select a red interior to match, or any one of a great variety of other schemes. A buyer could select from many accessories such as wheel covers, hood ornaments, outside mirrors, radio, and even antennas. Bold two-tone colors were offered, too.

Interior design was also bold and striking during these years. Stylists used a lot of chrome on the instrument panel and door panels. Seats were two-toned and coordinated with the exterior. Steering wheels were designed with a deep-dish center and all controls were arranged near the instrumentation.

Stylists were not afraid to suggest something different. Sometimes the results were even shocking at first glance. During those years, stylists were always trying to improve the overall appeal of their designs and were never deterred from being aggressive in their approach. Yes, it was a very exciting time to be an automotive designer!

Gale Halderman
Ford Motor Company, retired

PREFACE

Why a book about full-size Fords, 1955–1970? Well, for one reason, it hasn't been done until now. Yes, plenty of books about Ford's cars have been written, but none to date have focused specifically on these models with the exception of some compilations of contemporary road tests. Second, some of the most collectible full-size model Fords come from this range of years. Some of these that are not yet seriously collected appear to be gaining notice. They should be noticed!

In 1945, Henry Ford II was given an early discharge from the U.S. Navy so he could take over the company created by his grandfather. The elder Ford created a gargantuan and highly successful company, but as time marched onward, he began leading his empire into ruin. Debt was high, accounting standards were poor, and along the way, Ford had lost its number-one position in the auto industry to Chevrolet and it was up to its financial ears in debt— about $700 million worth.

By 1952, Ford's fortunes had reversed, though it would not regain the number-one spot except sporadically over the years. Profits meant money for modernization,

Ford produced a separate brochure detailing its line of station wagons. On the cover was the new Parklane two-door wagon.

This banner hung in Ford dealerships and prompted potential buyers to "Action Test" the new 1957 Fords.

Economy was emphasized heavily in Ford's advertising for 1958. Ford claimed that the new Interceptor V-8s and Cruise-O-Matic automatic transmission saved "up to 15 percent on gas."

We'd do anything to prove our beautiful '67 Ford is strong. After two bone-jarring championship leaps on Lake Placid's Olympic Ski Jump, this brand-new Ford was still new-Ford quiet. That's strong!

That's our 1967 Ford. Quieter because it's stronger...stronger because it's better built. FORD

Total Performance was a major advertising theme for Ford in 1964. This is the cover of the brochure for the full-size lineup that year.

including overhead-valve V-8s, automatic transmissions, and fresh styling every one to two years. That led to some promotional gimmicks such as the Skyliner, first with a plexiglass sunroof and later with a retractable steel top. Ultimately, the rescue of Ford Motor Company led to the Total Performance years featuring such engines as the dual-quad 427. The adage, "Success breeds success" comes to mind.

My father bought and drove Galaxie 500s in the 1960s. Pictured (top to bottom) are a Pagoda Green 1964 model with a 390-ci, a triple-black 1965 Galaxie 500 powered by a 289-ci and fitted with dealer-installed air conditioning, and a Wimbledon White 1966 model, also with a 289-ci.

With the release of the two-seater Thunderbird for 1955, Ford had two differently sized cars to offer simultaneously. By 1962, Ford had a

This advertisement must have convinced at least a few people that the 1967 Ford Galaxie 500 was well-built! It was driven off the Lake Placid Olympic Ski Jump fitted with snow tires, a standard suspension, and the addition of a skid plate to protect the oil pan.

lineup consisting of full-size, intermediate-size, compact, and the "personal luxury" Thunderbird. Full-size Fords included the Fairlane Victoria, Custom, Galaxie 500, Galaxie 500/XL, and the LTD. These cars offered family transportation, sportiness, and even luxury to their owners and sold very well. During the 1961 model year, the Galaxie reached one million unit sales since its release in 1959.

Today, models such as the Crown Victoria, Skyliner, Starliner, and Galaxie 500/XL are among the most desirable to Ford fans. Those with big-block V-8s are especially so.

With that said, fasten your seatbelt and take a thrill ride with Full Size Fords, 1955–1970!

In the foreground is a Custom 500 powered by a 315-hp 390-ci and 4-speed. Two Galaxie 500 7-Litres are in the background. The 7-Litre convertible is one of only two ordered with the 425-hp 427-ci. All are from Mike Patak's fine collection of full-size Fords.

1955–1956: Y-BLOCKS, A CROWN, A SUNROOF AND SAFETY

Horsepower ratings had long been a selling point when the post-World War II horsepower race commenced. However, the span of 10 years following the U.S. victory over the Axis powers in 1945 offered improved technology, higher-octane fuel, and thus better performance.

The first few years of automobile production presented mild reworks of 1942 models powered by the old engines such as Ford's respected Flathead V-8. Once the pent-up demand for new cars began to be met, manufacturers had to offer fresh styles and features including, of course, modern engines. So, while buyers were snatching up warmed-over pre-war models, there was much work being done within the various engineering and styling departments in the Motor City.

Cadillac startled the automotive world with its new 1948 models featuring the first of the Lockheed P-38 (a World War II fighter) inspired tail fins, which would capture the hearts of many car buyers and stylists for years to come. Oldsmobile and Cadillac took the lead in the modern V-8 race with new over-head-valve engines for 1949. Hudson soon followed with a powerful straight-eight.

Chrysler Corporation unleashed the fabled Hemi in 1951. Hudson's engine was a fine performer and proved tough to beat in the emerging sport of stock car racing. (By the way, "stock" meant essentially that. Except for a few safety medications, the rules restricted factory stock cars to factory equipment.)

Straight-eights had become passé—the public wanted V-8s. The V-8 offered superior characteristics, such as improved cooling and valve-train, which enhanced horsepower and torque. The relatively compact V-8 design made lower hood lines possible, leading to sleeker styling. At times, however, engineering compromises had to be made in the design of the air cleaner and/or carburetor to allow a hood to close over the engine. In the case of the 1955–1957 Ford Thunderbirds, a hood scoop was employed to gain the necessary clearance.

This 1955 Sunliner is painted in Golden Rod Yellow and Raven Black, one of 18 colorful two-tone paint schemes offered for this model year. It is also equipped with a 272-ci, Fordomatic, power steering, wheel covers, wide whitewall tires, fender skirts, and stone shields. (Photo by Dick Rozum, Legendary Ford Magazine)

Ford's 1955 model year lineup of 6- and 8-cylinder engines was advertised as delivering Trigger Torque Power. Displacement of the inline 6-cylinder measured 223 ci, while the Y-Block V-8s came in 272- and 292-ci displacements.

More Power

Ford Motor Company's first V-8, of course, was the Flathead, made available in 1932. It stayed in production for many years, but as the 1940s came to a close, its days were numbered. The revered Flathead was no longer practical to upgrade in a manner to keep it competitive with the competition's V-8s.

For 1952, Ford Motor Company (FoMoCo) began offering its replacement, known as the Y-Block V-8. That model year, the Lincoln and some Ford trucks became the first to receive the new V-8 (or Y-8 as it was sometimes advertised). Lincoln's version displaced 317-ci and had hydraulic valve lifters. Mercury and Ford got the Y-block for 1954 in 256- and 239-ci displacements, respectively, and received solid valve lifters, though they trailed Lincoln in horsepower.

Ford's Y-block is a big-bore, short-stroke design, often referred to as "over-square." The concept was relatively new at the time. One persistent myth about the Y-block series is that its Y-shaped cross-section provided strength to the main bearings. What the deep skirted design actually did was to give support to the transmission mounting points, which had been a week point on the previous flathead engine. The Y-block's valve guides were integral with the head, and the joint between the guide and the head acted as a barrier to heat transfer. This reduced the valve-stem running temperature about 125 degrees Fahrenheit, while valve-head running temperatures dropped well over 200 degrees. The Y-blocks and heads also handled the higher compression ratios—up to 12:1, in fact—expected to come during the 1950s.

For 1955, FoMoCo planned to offer the 256-ci V-8 as an option in Ford models, but once managers learned of Chevrolet's plan to release their new V-8 with 265 ci, the 256-ci was dumped in favor of a 272-ci displacement. The Thunderbird 292-ci was also an option for the big Fords.

The 272-ci with a Holley 2-barrel carburetor and 7.6:1 compression ratio provided 162 hp. The 4-barrel "Power Pack" version with 8.5:1 compression and dual exhausts gave 182 hp. Both 272s were equipped with a manual choke and an oil bath air cleaner.

The next step up in V-8 power was, of course, the Thunderbird 292-ci 4-barrel Thunderbird Special, which was rated at 193 hp when coupled to the standard 3-speed manual transmission, or 198 hp with the optional Ford-O-Matic. Both the 6-cylinder and Y-block engines were newly equipped with tapered-seat spark plugs with an 18-mm base. The Thunderbird Special received an automatic choke and a dry-type air filter.

Late in the model year, an Interceptor kit was offered. It boosted horsepower to 205 for the base 292-ci. Issuing the kit made it legal for National Association for Stock Car Racing (NASCAR) competition. Ford Motor Company backed two drivers in NASCAR, Curtis Turner and Joe Weatherly. But the kit did not arrive in time for the Southern 500 in Darlington, South Carolina, and both cars experienced front end problems and failed to finish. Herb Thomas, driving a Chevrolet, finished first.

By the end of the season, it was clear that Ford did not have a dominant package. In fact, Chevy and Ford were tied with two Grand National victories each; neither at the time could seriously compete on the racetrack with the Chrysler 300s, Oldsmobile 88s, and Buick Centurys. Still, it was the start of a major rivalry that would captivate racing fans for some time to come.

Late in the 1955 season, Ford hired ex-Indy car racer Pete DePaolo to help direct factory-backed efforts. Ford officials saw racing as an effective means of promoting their cars, and it led to the Total Performance years the following decade. Furthermore, the popularity of the Y-block among performance enthusiasts resulted in aftermarket companies, such as Edelbrock and Weiand, offering three-deuce and dual-quad setups, adjustable rocker arms, and other high-performance equipment.

While the new Ford V-8 was certainly big news to car buyers, it was not the only new engine from FoMoCo. The 6-cylinder of 223-ci was released the same year and continued in service until 1965, when it was replaced with a newly designed straight-six.

"These engines," according to Ford, "coupled with any of Ford's three transmissions and Torque-Tailored Rear Axle Ratios deliver mighty Trigger-Torque Power." The three transmission choices to which Ford's literature referred were a standard-issue 3-speed "Conventional Drive" manual transmission, "Ford Overdrive" with a lock-out feature, and the "Fordomatic" 3-speed automatic transmission. All had a column-mounted shifter for gear selection. The manual transmission used helical gears and its clutch was a single, dry-plate, cushion-disc type. Overdrive reduced engine RPM by about 30 percent. The Fordomatic employed an air-cooled torque converter.

Features and Models

The 1955 model year brought forth an all-new-appearing Ford line that included a smaller, sporty car dubbed Thunderbird, which shared a significant number of components with the big Fords. While the big Fords looked all-new, they were in reality heavily reworked versions of the 1952–1954 body design. Ford's ball-joint front suspension debuted in 1954, and carried forward for 1955, though the chassis and suspension were new.

The front suspension, called "Angle-Poised Ball Joint Front Suspension," was angled 3 degrees forward for better handling. In back was a leaf spring suspension employing five leaves on the Mainline, Customline, and Fairlane models, while station wagons had seven. These leaves were longer than those used on the 1955 models. This, too, was for improved handling.

There were 16 different big Ford models for 1955. The top-level Crestline moniker used during the three prior model years was replaced with the Fairlane tag. There were two Fairlane Crown Victorias atop the hierarchy, one of which had an all-steel roof, while the other featured a 1/4-inch-thick, blue-green tinted plexiglass insert in the roof over the front passenger compartment. The latter is often mistakenly referred to as the

As can be seen in this factory illustration, the Fairlane Crown Victoria with the transparent roof section had a 1/4-inch-thick, blue-green-tinted plexiglass insert in the roof over the front passenger compartment.

Skyliner, but that name did not appear on the car or in factory sales literature. Instead, it was called the Crown Victoria with the transparent roof section or skylighted top. A Lincoln show (or experimental) car dubbed XL-500 inspired the transparent insert.

The Crown Victoria's body with the skylighted top sat on a convertible X-type frame to increase frame and body stiffness. Both the plexiglass and steel-topped Crown Victoria models wore a decorative stainless steel band or "Crown of Chrome," which began at the B-pillar location and arched over the roof. This, too, was an idea lifted from the XL-500. Blacked-out recesses in the wide molding gave the impression of air vents. A stainless spear met the base of the crown and swept back atop the quarters all the way to the taillights.

The stainless band was mimicked on the inside of the top. Also, bright trim traveled the perimeter of the rear interior side panels and the top of the rear-seat back rest before meeting at the dip in the middle to form a "V" shape. The molding did not substantially increase the strength of the roof itself, but a steel bar welded to the inner roof, along with B-pillars, added some rigidity to the body and provided attachment points for the crown molding assembly. Furthermore, both Crown Victoria models benefitted from a more graceful rear slope for the roof.

The Crown Victoria with the plexiglass insert was not very popular; only 1,999 were sold for 1955, making it the least-produced model. Over 20,000 were sold the prior year, though that model was dubbed the Crestline Skyliner. Interior heating is often cited as the main cause of the sharp decrease in sales. The blue-green tint supposedly blocked 60 percent of the sun's heating rays and testing revealed only a five-degree increase in interior temperature. Of course, five degrees can be the difference between comfortable and uncomfortable. Air conditioning was an option, but expensive.

In addition, the Crown Victoria with the transparent panel and V-8 was the highest-priced car in the big Ford lineup at $2,443—nearly $50 more than the Sunliner. Ford made available a nylon curtain, which could be zippered in place to block the sunlight. That may have prompted potential buyers to ask, "What's the point of the plexiglass roof?" The concept stayed in production for 1956, this time labeled Crown Victoria Skyliner. Only 603 were built, though, making it the lowest-production Ford model that year. Incidentally, Mercury offered a similar car (sans the crown molding) for the 1954 and 1955 model years. It was dubbed Sun Valley and also sold in low numbers.

Even the "non-Crown" Fairlane Victoria two-door hardtop, and the three other models in the Fairlane series—the Sunliner (the sole con-

Regency Purple and Snowshoe White was one of many optional two-tone arrangements offered. This 1955 Fairlane Victoria two-door hardtop is one of 113,372 built, making it the third-most-ordered model behind the four-door Town Sedan (254,437) and the two-door Club Sedan (173,311). (Photo by Colin Date, Legendary Ford Magazine)

The Fairlane Victoria Town Sedan was the sales leader for 1955. It accounted for about 17.7 percent of the 1,435,002 big Fords built for the model year.

vertible offering among all series), the two-door Club Sedan, and the four-door Town Sedan—had plenty of bright trim. In fact, the side molding on these models became known as the "Fairlane Sweep." The stainless Fairlane Sweep began as a narrow strip at the top of the front fender at the headlight rim and arched downward at an increasing slope while gradually gaining in width all the way to the door, where it reached its maximum dip. It then became a narrow molding again arching upward steeply for a short distance forming a check-mark shape, and then sweeping straight back across the quarter panel to the taillight.

This trim provided a break for the optional 12 conventional two-tone combinations and 18 unique two-tone combinations. Conventional two-toning resulted in sedans and coupes having the area from the drip rails and below one color and the roof another color. Unique-type two-toning meant the area below the body side moldings, headlight rims, and across the body beneath the deck lid were one color, while the area between the belt-line and drip rails on sedans were the other color. The Victoria's contrasting color was applied above the body side molding. However, Crown Victorias had the area beneath the body side molding, headlight rims, below the deck lid, and roof all one color with the balance the contrasting one.

Two-tone schemes that were offered for 1955 models included Sea Sprite Green/ Snowshoe White, Waterfall Blue/Aquatone Blue, Tropical Rose/Snowshoe White, Golden Rod Yellow/Raven Black, etc.

Later, the two-tone Style-Tone option became available for Crown Victorias. Convertibles could be had with black, dark blue, or tan rayon tops. The lower series Customline (composed of the Business Sedan, which had no back seat, Tudor Sedan, and Fordor Sedan) and the Mainline (composed of the Tudor Sedan and Fordor Sedan) could be ordered in two-tone colors; however, the roof and entire lower body wore the respective colors. Customline cars were fitted with a narrow strip of bright trim on their body sides, while the Mainline carried no body side moldings.

Thirteen standard monotone body colors were also offered for the big Fords this model year:

- Raven Black
- Snowshoe White
- Banner Blue
- Aquatone Blue
- Waterfall Blue
- Pinetree Green
- Sea Sprite Green
- Neptune Green
- Buckskin Brown
- Torch Red
- Goldenrod Yellow
- Tropical Rose
- Regency Purple

Some of these colors were not normally available on certain models. For instance, monotone Goldenrod Yellow and Regency Purple were reserved for the Sunliner.

In addition to the body side sweep molding, other standard equipment for the 1955 Fairlane models included chrome window and A-pillar moldings (hardtops and Sunliner), chrome "eyebrows" on the headlight doors, plus standard features of the Customline—two sun visors, an armrest for all doors, and rear passenger assist straps on the B-pillars (Sedan models only). Both Crown Victoria models featured an exclusive fold-down center armrest for back seat passengers. Mainline versions received only a sun visor and armrest for the driver plus rubber window moldings. Dog dish hub caps were standard on all models. Tubeless tires became standard for all models this year.

This year Ford added another station wagon model, the eight-passenger Country Sedan, to bring the total to five available in the line, which was now considered its own series. In addition to the eight-passenger Country Sedan, the other four models were the two-door six-passenger Ranch Wagon, two-door six-passenger Custom Ranch Wagon, four-door six-passenger Country Sedan, and eight-passenger Country Squire. The Ranch Wagons represented the base trim level, six- and eight-passenger Country Sedans represented the intermediate level, and the Country Squire served as the top trim level. Trim for each paralleled that of the Mainline, Customline, and Fairlane series. All were offered with 6-cylinder power as standard equipment or with a V-8 at extra cost.

Incidentally, Ford also offered a Courier, a sedan delivery model

based on the station wagon body. However, it was considered part of Ford's truck line.

The Country Squire, which debuted for the 1950 model year, had its styling based on the woody wagons of the past, but instead of real wood the Country Squire was given a steel body with wood panel attachments and framing. Wood-bodied cars required substantial maintenance to preserve the wood. They developed squeaks and rattles over time, too.

The solution to both problems was a steel body. The wood attachments were no longer structural, but still required periodic attention. By 1952, Ford replaced the wood panels with Di-Noc woodgrain transfer, though real wood continued to be used for framing. The wood framing was replaced with fiberglass covered with a maple-grain transfer for 1955. The simulated woodgrain was altered in appearance in the following years. Replacing the wood with decals and fiberglass significantly cut material and production costs.

Interior Design

All 1955 models featured an Astra-Dial speedometer, another component carried over from 1954, said to be easier to read because it reduced reflection. The semi-circular 120-mph speedometer rested within a pod atop the dash with a small window on the upper surface allowing for daylight illumination. A set of gauges for fuel quantity and coolant temperature was mounted just beneath the speedometer; warning lamps for low oil pressure and generator output sat inboard of these gauges.

Clustered to the left of the steering column on the dash were the switches for the ignition, headlights, and vacuum-operated windshield wipers. To the right side were the cigarette lighter and manual choke adjustment control (when applicable). A little farther to the right (when ordered) were the optional MagicAire heater/defroster, AM-radio, and clock (all with round dials). The MagicAire system incorporated the right air vent control.

The glove box was ahead of the passenger's position. "Ford" script was fitted on its door, along with an "I-6 or Y-8 emblem, depending on whether the car was powered by an inline six or optional Y-block V-8.

When the MagicAire heater/ defroster was not ordered, the fresh-air vent controls were still included. Regardless of how they were incorporated into the car, opening either or both allowed air through screened scoops flanking the radiator into the interior. Supposedly, air circulation through this ram-air system and the rectangular push-out vent windows, which had to be only slightly opened in wet weather, inhibited window fogging. In reality, they leaked "excessively" when open, according to one 1955 road test report.

Color-coordinated upholstery choices were plentiful. Upholstery came in Craftweave, Random Twist, Flake Pattern, Vinyl, and Styletex types. Ford literature described Craftweave as "an unusually durable material of combined nylon, rayon, and cotton." It was offered on the Mainline and Customline series, though the stitch pattern varied depending on the model. Random Twist was "a distinctive new pattern for Fairlane Club Sedan and Town Sedan" models. It was a "luxurious, long-wearing nylon-cotton-metallic yarn combination" offered in three

colors: brown, green, and blue. Flake Pattern was a "fabric of nylon, rayon, and cotton mixture. With both brown and black, the irregular snowflake motif is in white. Brown or black Flake Pattern is available in the Fairlane Victoria, and black is also available in the Crown Victoria," according to Ford's literature.

In addition to the black Flake Pattern nylon-rayon-cotton fabric, three all-vinyl schemes combining quilted and smooth grains were offered for the Crown Victoria models: red-quilted/white, green-quilted/white, plus rose-quilted/white.

The Country Squire and Country Sedan shared upholstery choices of woven plastic in blue and white, green and white, plus red and white. Red and white vinyl was an additional option for these models. Ranch Wagon and Custom Ranch Wagon models also could be upholstered with woven plastic, but in the case of the base version, just one color combination, brown and beige, was offered; Western Brown vinyl was the only other upholstery choice. The Custom Ranch Wagon was offered with the same colors of woven plastic as found in the Country Squire and Country Sedan models, as well as the Western Brown vinyl available for the base level station wagon.

The Sunliner could be had with any one of five all-vinyl combinations: red-quilted/white, green-quilted/white, blue-quilted/white, rose-quilted/white, and yellow-quilted/black.

Seat inserts were sewn with lateral pleats. Styletex interiors combined vinyl and a woven plastic. Regardless of the upholstery scheme chosen, it covered newly designed seat frames. Ford declared the front

seat as "strong, resilient non-sag cushion springs," having rubber-coated tension wires directly attached to a box-section steel frame. The cushion padding of Mainline and Ranch Wagon models used rubberized hair between heavy cotton pads. Other models had thick foam rubber over cotton felt.

In all, 200 exterior and interior combinations were available, which certainly should have been enough to satisfy the most demanding Ford customer!

1956: Lifeguard Design

Production of 1956 Fords began October 17, 1955. The basic styling of the big Fords, this time consisting of 18 models, did not change very much. Up front, a new grille and a wraparound parking light arrangement were distinctive differences. The roof panels were altered to reduce overall height (by 1½ inches in Victoria models and 1 inch in sedans) yet retain the same amount of headroom. The 1955 Crown Victoria's sleeker roof slope was applied to all two-door hardtops. A less noticeable change was the removal of the chrome "eyebrows" from the headlight doors.

In back, the deck lid molding and Ford crest were deleted from the Fairlane series. A new trunk handle appeared on the Fairlane sedans while Fairlane hardtops got a new "V" molding incorporating the trunk lock and Fairlane nameplate.

A revised Fairlane sweep was used to update the profile of the Fairlane series. This trim was also used on the new two-door station wagon model, the Parklane, and the eight-passenger Country Sedan. The Style-Tone paint option was expanded to

For 1956, Ford added the Customline Victoria two-door hardtop to the lineup. It brought 33,130 orders. This unrestored example has just 82,000 actual miles, still wears most of its original paint, and is equipped with a 292-ci 4-barrel and Fordomatic.

This Customline Tudor Sedan is equipped with the extra-cost two-tone paint, wheel covers, wide whites, left and right rearview mirrors, radio, and rear-mount antenna.

A 223-ci inline 6-cylinder produced 120 hp at 4,000 rpm and was standard issue on the Customline series. The air/fuel mixture was delivered via a Holley 1-barrel carburetor.

This Customline Victoria has green wave nylon cloth with green vertically striped gros-grain vinyl upholstery and the optional padded dash. Clear seat covers have been fitted to preserve the original factory-installed material. Customlines also got an arrowhead-pattern, black rubber floor covering.

include the eight-passenger Country Sedan as well as the Parklane. The six-passenger Country Sedan received the Customline body side molding. A two-door hardtop joined the Customline series.

At mid-year Ford added one more model to the Fairlane line, the Town Victoria Fordor. This was a four-door, pillarless hardtop model offered to counter the 1956 Chevrolet Bel Air four-door pillarless hardtop.

Various improvements were made in the Y-block to keep in stride with the horsepower race. These included additional cubic inches, better breathing through enlarged passages in the heads and intake manifold, and a higher-lift camshaft.

The Thunderbird Special this year had the 312-ci engine rated at 215 hp when coupled to a manual transmission and 225 hp with the Fordomatic. A dual-quad 260-hp 312-ci became available later in the model year as a dealer-installed option. Horsepower ratings went up in the 6-cylinder and the 272-ci 2-barrel thanks to a small boost in compression ratios. The 272-ci 4-barrel was dropped. The 292-ci 4-barrel gained a few additional horsepower, now rated at 200 hp with the manually shifted transmission or 202 hp with the automatic.

Minor revisions to the carburetors, distributors, and differentials were made in the interest of improved fuel economy, and in some models, the transmission was modi-

fied to withstand higher torque. All V-8s now had an automatic choke. Upholstery patterns were altered and the instrument panel was redesigned.

Upholstery choices were again in abundance. Standard for Mainline series were gray lattice nylon cloth and gray vinyl. Customline interiors were upholstered in a choice of blue checker cloth and green or gray

A four-door hardtop was released for 1956, dubbed the Fairlane Town Victoria Fordor. It was a four-door pillarless hardtop model offered to counter the 1956 Chevrolet Bel Air four-door pillarless hardtop.

woven nylon cloth with vinyl. Styletex interiors combining vinyl and a woven plastic were optional for the Mainline and Customline series. Brown or blue scroll cloth, green or gray random dot cloth, and red shadow cloth with vinyl were the standard selections for the Fairlane Club and Town Sedans.

Fairlane Victoria models offered buyers blue, green, black, and peacock tree pattern nylon cloth and vinyl upholstery choices at no extra cost. However, the Fairlane Victoria Fordor offered two additional choices: red mosaic cloth and white vinyl or

One of the four standard upholstery combinations was peacock tree pattern nylon cloth and white vinyl offered for the 1956 Fairlane Crown Victoria. The Crown Victoria came with a rear-seat fold-down armrest.

red mosaic cloth and black vinyl.

Standard issue for Crown Victoria models was green, black, and peacock tree pattern cloth, as well as red mosaic cloth with white or black vinyl.

Sunliner upholstery was all-vinyl in two-tones of white-quilted and blue, white-quilted and red, white-quilted and black, plus orange-quilted and white. A single tone of green-quilted and green was also available.

For the Ranch Wagon, the choices were quite simple: brown woven plastic and Western Brown vinyl. Choices were expanded a bit for the Custom Ranch Wagon, available with Western Brown all-vinyl or Western Brown vinyl with woven plastic in red/white, blue/white, and green.

The fancier Parklane in standard form had three choices of woven plastic and vinyl in blue, green, and tan. Four interior offerings for buyers of the eight-passenger Country Sedan and Country Squire wagons were: woven plastic and vinyl in red/white, blue/white, and green as well as Western Brown all-vinyl. The vinyl grain type and stitch pattern varied by model as well as location (i.e., back of front seat and lower seat cushion). Design of the door panels varied by model, too.

Paint colors were revised for 1956. The shades listed were:
- Raven Black
- Colonial White
- Nocturne Blue
- Bermuda Blue
- Diamond Blue
- Peacock Blue
- Pine Ridge Green
- Meadowmist Green
- Platinum Gray
- Buckskin Tan
- Fiesta Red
- Goldenglow Yellow
- Mandarin Orange

The Astra-Dial instrument panel was replaced with a conventional arrangement. Rectangular-design heater/defroster controls, radio, and clock took over for round units. Other updates included replacing the six-volt electrical system with a 12-volt setup (which was happening industry-wide over the preceding few years) and a new Signal-Seek radio.

For the 1956 model year, Ford managers decided to emphasize safety features under the banner Lifeguard Design, as well as performance. Some of the Lifeguard features were standard and others composed an option group.

The Lifeguard equipment resulted from a two-year study conducted by Ford Motor Company in cooperation with Cornell Medical College, the American College of Surgeons, the National Safety Council, and other groups. Test crashes were conducted with crash-test dummies, instrumentation, and cameras to record the reactions of the "occupants" and the behavior of the test car.

As a result of these tests, the steering post was recessed from the steering wheel a little more than 3 inches and the steering wheel itself was designed to bend away from the driver. Furthermore, the door latches were redesigned to reduce the possibility of doors opening during a collision. The double-grip door latch employed an interlocking striker plate made of high-tensile chrome-molybdenum steel to overlap the door latch rotor. The inside rearview mirror was given a special backing to prevent the glass from shattering, too. Optional safety equipment was composed of webbed nylon seat belts plus a padded dash and sun visors.

Safety did not sell, and few people ordered the optional Lifeguard package. Even so, Ford continued to market safety for another dozen years. By then, the federal government had made such equipment mandatory.

Options and accessories for the 1955 and 1956 big Fords were numerous and included:

- seven-tube Super Range or five-tube Console Range AM-radio
- rear-mount antenna
- rear-seat radio speaker
- back-up lights
- turn indicators (where not already required by state law)
- rear window defroster
- air conditioning
- power steering
- power brakes

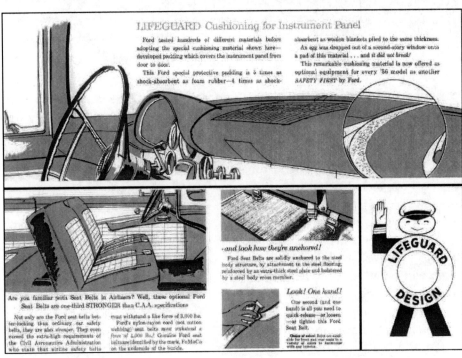

In addition to performance, Ford managers decided to emphasize safety features under the banner Lifeguard Design, for the 1956 model year. Some of the Lifeguard features were standard and others composed an option group.

Monotone paint was standard, but seeing one of these Fords without two-tone paint seems unusual. This Diamond Blue Fairlane Victoria is equipped with numerous accessories, including the Sports Spare Wheel Carrier, backup lights, bumper wing guards, rear deck guard, rear fender shields, wire wheel covers, rocker molding, and front fender gravel shield.

Ford's Lifeguard safety campaign included producing this flicker button reading "Ford Lifeguard Design... Have You Heard About It?" (Button courtesy of Doug Swanson; photo by author)

The all-steel-top Crown Victoria sold in far greater numbers than the Skyliner variant, with 9,209 finding buyers versus just 603 for the plexiglass-top car. This example is painted Colonial White and Peacock Blue and has several options and accessories. The wire wheels, however, are later-model Kelsey-Hayes units.

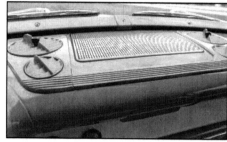

Adjustable outlets for the optional SlectAire air conditioning were on the top of the center dash. A padded dash was offered, but this car is not so equipped.

Controls for the SelectAire air conditioner were located in the lower central dash. SelectAire employed a new magnetic clutch and was integrated with the heater/defroster.

- power seat
- power windows
- electric clock or hand-wind clock
- deluxe steering wheel
- floor mats
- engine compartment light
- spotlight with mirror
- portable spotlight
- outside rear-view mirrors
- outside visor
- window side shades
- locking gas tank cap
- rocker panel trim
- fender skirts
- exhaust deflectors
- Coronado Deck (a.k.a. Continental kit)
- grille guard
- rear deck guard
- wide white sidewall tires
- engine dress-up kit
- and more

One other especially interesting option was Rain Guard for the Sunliner. This gadget would automatically raise the convertible top when it sensed rain. A moisture-sensitive control grid operated an actuator under the hood through an electrical circuit. The top would automatically rise when a 2 x 3-inch grid on top of the left front fender was struck with moisture and the ignition was off, so the owner did not have to worry about an unexpected rainfall while away from the parked car. (Presumably the owner was instructed to leave the boot off. How the top locked in place was not explained in the dealer's book.) Whether or not the option was ever ordered would be interesting to learn. It was not listed in Ford's literature for 1956.

These five dials housed the speedometer/odometer; gauges for the generator, fuel quantity, and coolant temperature; and the optional clock. The gear indicator shows the optional automatic transmission is present.

The chrome band of the Crown Victoria was repeated inside the car. It swept down the pillars, across the upper side panels, and continued over the top of the back seat.

1955–1956 Road Tests

Contemporary road test reports revealed a general satisfaction with the 1955–1956 full-size Fords. The February 1955 issue of *Motor Trend* had praise for the Astra-Dial instrument panel. As they explained, "When you climb into your new Ford, you face what is in our opinion the top instrument panel in the 'popular' price field. We say this not from an esthetic appreciation alone, but due to its exceptional readability,

night and day. The eerie bits of ecto-plasm that floated across the 1954 windshield have now been laid to rest by lowering and flattening the speedometer's bubble top."

On the negative side, *Motor Trend* noted, "Not so good are Ford's windshield wipers, which cover so little area that any advantage of the new wraparound windshield is less than useless on a wet and dirty day." *Motor Trend* also found fuel mileage had dropped with the increase in horsepower over 1954. Its Custom-

line Fordor test car equipped with the 162-hp V-8 and Fordomatic achieved 14 miles per gallon at a steady 60 mph and managed a standing start quarter mile time of 19.4 seconds at 74 mph. Handling was evaluated as comfortable at "posted speeds with emphasis being placed on "posted." Braking via the car's 11-inch drums was judged as above average with stops from 60, 45, and 30 mph taking 178, 82, and 33 feet correspondingly.

Motor Trend concluded the report with, "Overall, the Ford Customline sedan was designed and built to satisfy the day-to-day needs of your family, and we wouldn't be at all surprised if it turned out to be your choice with just that purpose in mind."

Tom McCahill, reporting in his unique style for *Mechanix Illustrated* in their January 1955 issue, said, "The 1955 Ford is loaded! Like a well-equipped bride, it has something new, something borrowed and even something blue, if you happen to want one in that color. The 'old,' which is not very old at that, is the still-great ball-joint suspension that grooves the turns like a well-sharpened ice skate. The 'new' department includes an engine that's giant-sized for this price car, power everything, 100 mph performance and optional air conditioning. And for 'borrowed' Ford now has the GM goldfish bowl-type wraparound windshield... The 1955 Ford will prove very rough for its competition, as it is loaded with more salable angles than a shipload of Marilyn Monroes."

The July 1955 issue of *Popular Mechanics* detailed some of the comments of 1,000 owners of 1955 Fords and found 64 percent rated their car

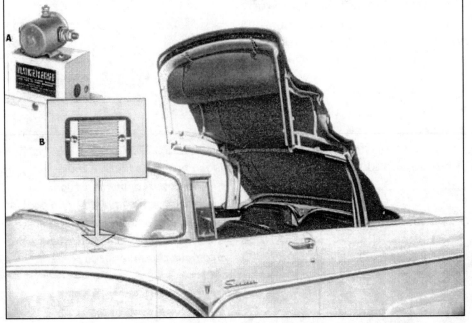

New Ford Sunliner RAIN GUARD automatically raises the top at the first splash of a raindrop!

A. SWITCH—Control box with automatic actuator of regular top-raising motor, mounts under the hood on the left side of the engine compartment. Rain Guard system can be installed in as little as 60 minutes.

B. GRID—Moisture-sensitive control grid operates actuator under hood, through electrical wiring circuit. A drop of moisture on the 2" x 3" grid, top of left front fender, raises car top automatically, when ignition is off.

While the owner's away, Ford's automatic top-raising Rain Guard raises the Sunliner top the moment moisture touches the wet-sensitive cell, to protect the car's upholstery and interior from rain. Unit will not operate, however, when ignition is turned on, thereby eliminating any danger of top attempting to raise while car is under way. Rain Guard takes the worry out of parking the Sunliner top-down, anywhere.

An unusual option for the 1955 Sunliner, dubbed Rain Guard, was illustrated in All the Facts About the 1955 Fords, *a book supplied to Ford salesmen. With the ignition off, this gadget would automatically raise the convertible top on a parked car when rain was sensed by a moisture-sensitive control grid.*

as excellent and 33 percent judged it as average. Performance and styling were the top two appreciated qualities, and 87 percent approved of the new color combinations. Rattles were among the more frequent complaints (29 percent) followed by poor gas mileage (18 percent), door operation and fit (17 percent), and careless body work (14 percent). Others noted faults such as leaks around the doors, quickly corroding screws holding park and taillights, and engine problems involving the carburetor or valves. However, in the matter of engine problems 73 percent said they had no trouble at all; only 3 percent experienced considerable engine trouble.

In the same issue, publisher and auto enthusiast Floyd Clymer reported on his test results of a Fairlane Fordor with a 182-hp V-8 and Fordomatic. His test drive of over 400 miles left him with the opinion, "This model is definitely a sensational performer that handles and performs like a car in the high-price range. It really 'scats' away from traffic signals and up hills. Roadability and handling are better than any other Ford I have ever driven and compare favorably with any car I have tested regardless of price." His written evaluation went on to praise the car's brakes, suspension, and interior comfort.

Road tests on the 1956 models were similar. Writing for the July 1956 issue of *Popular Mechanix*, Tom McAhill once again praised the new Ford with more metaphors than a politician has promises: "For 1956, Ford is fielding a family car that'll be a real high-performance, high-powered bomb. The horsepower race has invaded the low-price field with all the fury of a starved wildcat thrust

The two-door Parklane station wagon was a new model for 1956. This one has the Style-Tone paint option, Diamond Blue and Bermuda Blue. A total of 15,186 were built. The wire wheels on this example are later-model Kelsey-Hayes units.

into a cage of Easter bunnies... The Fairlane I tested had a 292-ci engine with enough torque to yank an elephant through a keyhole by the tail."

With all seriousness, he noted, "Bill France, the president of NASCAR, said to me, 'Tom, the one thing you can't take away from the Ford is that they have the best steel in the entire industry regardless of price.' He was referring to the fact that under the terrible beatings of stock car racing, Ford cars break fewer axles, wheels, frames, and front-end assemblies than any other make."

Motor Life reported 0-60 mph average times of "just a shade over 9.5 seconds" in the November 1955 issue.

As for racing results, the 1956 Fords performed significantly better in NASCAR competition than they did in the previous year. Ford hired John Holman to manage its 1956 racing program and also hired two more drivers, Glenn "Fireball"

Roberts and Ralph Moody. Together they helped Ford win 14 Grand National races and the company's first NASCAR Manufacturer's Championship. In doing so, it established an intense rivalry with Chevrolet, which, by the way, strongly advertised as major achievements its two wins during the 1955 race season.

1955–1956 Sales Summary

Total sales figures represent another measure of success. Ford's passenger car production numbers (excluding Thunderbird totals) for model years 1955 and 1956 were 1,435,002 and 1,392,847 units respectively. Output for 1955 was Ford's best to that point of the post-World War II years, and second only to 1923.

However, the model year was a good one for most of the American auto industry, especially Chevrolet

The second seat on the Country Sedan was split. Each portion could be folded for extra cargo storage. The eight-passenger version's two-piece rear seat could be lifted out for even more load space.

Standard upholstery for the Parklane station wagon was two-toned; in this case, two-tone blue. Ford offered three standard color schemes of woven plastic and vinyl. Seat belts were an option.

Optional equipment on this Parklane includes a 312-ci V-8, engine dress-up kit, power steering, and power brakes.

division of GM. Chevy continued to outpace Ford thanks to its attractive all-new 1955 line consisting of the One-Fifty, Two-Ten, and Bel Air. This was also the first year in which Chevy offered a modern OHV V-8, the 265-ci Hot One.

Like Ford, Chevy only mildly updated styling for 1956. Chevy out-sold Ford by over 277,000 and by nearly 182,000 units in 1955 and 1956, respectively. Ford, though, bested Chevy in station wagon sales. Moreover, a newly designed lineup of Fords would drastically close the sales gap with their arch rival in 1957.

This Bermuda Blue and Colonial White 1956 Country Sedan 8-passenger station wagon was one of six wagons offered for this model year. A total of 60,256 Country Sedans were ordered, with most having an optional V-8. This example has the 292-ci 2-barrel with a Fordomatic transmission.

1957: *FINS, SUPERCHARGING AND A FLIP TOP*

Ford's 1957 model year, which officially began on October 3, 1956, offered a dramatically new big-car lineup with even the model names getting revised. Gone from the ranks were the Mainline and Customline nameplates. Their replacements were the Custom and Custom 300. The Fairlane remained above these two models, with the new Fairlane 500 as the top-trim-level car. Neither Fairlane series had a Crown Victoria, though such a model was considered.

The station wagon ranks were altered again, too. The Parklane was dropped, leaving five instead of six station wagons from which to choose. The Del Rio Ranch Wagon replaced the Custom Ranch Wagon.

In all, buyers could choose from 20 full-size Fords, including the new "flip top" Skyliner, a true hardtop convertible. Ford's new design also served as the platform for their Ranchero, a car-like truck.

Ford completely redesigned the body of their big cars for 1957, rather than perform a heavy rework as they did for the 1955–1956 models. Styling was based in part on Ford's show car, dubbed *Mystere*. From front

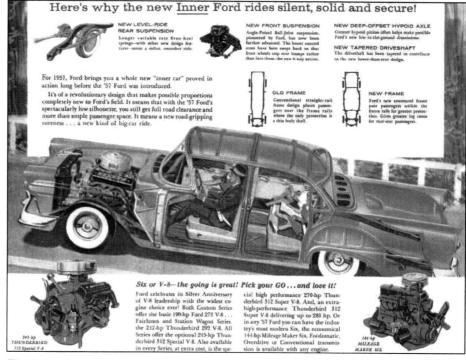

The inner Ford was illustrated in one of Ford's sales catalogs. It showed how the new frame allowed for a lower profile body, and a lowered rear floor pan allowed rear seat passengers to sit more fully within the chassis perimeter. This permitted a 2-inch reduction in overall height without sacrificing interior space.

to rear, the 1957 big Ford's styling was clearly inspired by the lines of the show car, especially the fins, though in a subdued fashion.

Station wagons got a wraparound liftgate "for increased visibil-ity and greater accessibility plus sleek modern styling," according to Ford's brochure. Ford was the only one in the low-price field to offer the feature. The floor offered up to 85.4 inches of depth for cargo storage. A

A total of 193,162 Fairlane 500 Town Sedans came off Ford's assembly lines for the 1957 model year. It was the highest-produced big Ford that year.

The Custom series was comprised of a two-door Business Sedan, a Tudor Sedan, and a Fordor Sedan. A Tudor Sedan is shown here. This austere model listed for $1,991 in standard form.

new "cow belly" frame allowed for a lower profile body. In addition, frame rails, which turned up farther back than the 1955–1956 frame, permitted a lowered rear floor pan. This feature allowed rear-seat passengers to sit more fully within the chassis perimeter, which in turn allowed for a 2-inch reduction in overall height without sacrificing interior space.

The redesign was very successful for Ford Motor Company—even more so than that of perennial rival Chevrolet, which featured a major sheetmetal rework. Ford even made quite an impression abroad this model year, especially in Moscow. According to the October 15, 1956, issue of *Life* magazine, the first 1957 Fairlane 500 built was crated and sent to the U.S. Embassy there after it was purchased for a "nominal fee of $1." The Town Sedan was shown to a fascinated public, where few owned an automobile.

The Lineup

The most affordable Ford, the Custom, offered the choices of a two-door Business Sedan, which lacked a back seat, a Tudor Sedan, and a Fordor Sedan. The austere Custom included the same 144-hp, 223-ci 6-cylinder coupled to a 3-speed man-

This early newspaper advertisement for the 1957 big Ford lineup summoned potential buyers to "See the new kind of Ford for '57," and explained, "Its new elegance comes from within... There are a thousand-and-one automotive lessons built into this New Kind of Ford. All of the changes are toward more rugged endurance, toward increased power, toward smoother operation."

ual transmission that was standard issue on any big Ford passenger car (with the exception of the Skyliner). It also featured chrome window moldings, thin "check-mark-style" side moldings on the quarter panels, driver's side sun visor and armrest, cloth upholstery, and Sof-Tred rubber floor mats instead of carpeting.

Distinguishing the Custom 300, composed only of Tudor and Fordor Sedan, from the Custom, was the

addition of a sun visor for the passenger side, a chrome horn ring instead of a horn button, armrests on all doors, chrome window moldings, and Fairlane 500-style side trim with an anodized gold insert. The model was composed of a two-door sedan and a four-door sedan.

As was the case with the Custom, the Custom 300's wheelbase spanned 116 inches; 1/2 inch more than that of the 1955–56 Fords.

Loads of newly built 1957 Fords are seen in this photo taken at Ford Motor Company's Dearborn Assembly haulaway yard. The River Rouge Plant is in the background.

Take an extra week's vacation on what you save

It costs less to go first in the new kind of

FORD

The Fairlane 500 Town Victoria depicted in this advertisement had a price tag of $2,357 less options. Ford's ad explained that the low cost of the car allowed the owner to save enough money to "take an extra week's vacation." A total of 68,550 were built. The Town Victoria was also offered in the Fairlane series, and it accounted for 12,615 sales.

The mid-level Fairlane series, composed of two- and four-door hardtops and two- and four-door sedans, had unique side moldings. Two-tone paint, whitewall tires, and wheel covers as shown here were extra-cost options.

Overall length of the Custom and Custom 300 models measured 201.6 inches. Both the Custom and Custom 300 used a station wagon rear bumper, while the upscale cars had their own heavier-style bumper. Four-door sedans had six side windows while four-door hardtops got a small triangular insert between the C-pillar and the rear door.

The Fairlane series was composed of two- and four-door sedans christened Club Sedan and Town Sedan, respectively, along with two- and four-door hardtops correspondingly dubbed Club Victoria and Town

Victoria. Fairlanes received the longer 118-inch wheelbase shared with the top-of-the-line Fairlane 500. Overall length for the series, as well as that of the Fairlane 500 lineup, was 207.7 inches, or 6.1 inches longer than the Custom and Custom 300.

Standard equipment on the Fairlane model included front fender mounted "Fairlane" script, Fairlane crest on the trunk lid, unique "bullet" style side trim, two sun visors, an armrest on all doors, chrome-plated horn ring, combination cloth and vinyl upholstery, and Luxury-Loom carpeting.

The Fairlane 500 came standard with the same equipment listed for the Fairlane, with the exception of the so-called Fairlane sweep side trim. This incorporated an anodized gold insert in place of the Fairlane's bullet molding, and Fairlane 500 script on the quarter panels. Both the Fairlane

and Fairlane 500 received a V-type crest on the deck lid, similar to that of the 1956 Fairlane, as well as carpeting. Also included was additional chrome trim on the C-pillars of closed models and Sunburst wheel covers.

Body styles in the series were the same as the Fairlane lineup with the additions of the Sunliner convertible and the Skyliner. All of these Fords came standard with the Bulls-Eye hood ornament on the forward-opening hood. Pricing for the Fairlane 500s added approximately $50 to the base prices of the comparable Fairlane series. Choosing the base V-8 engine added $100 to the base price of any model, with the exception of the Skyliner, which came standard with the 190-hp, 272-ci V-8.

Ford wagons were described in company literature as "long, lean and loaded with room" offering a "cavern of space" for hauling cargo.

The six-passenger Country Sedan accounted for 135,251 sales during the 1957 model year, but extremely few had the supercharged 312-ci, which powers this Willow Green and Colonial White example. (Photo courtesy of Frank Stubbs)

Ford offered this brochure to prospective station wagon buyers. It boasted, "Big as they come... Loaded they go... really GO!" The five new "Glamour Wagons" consisted of the Ranch Wagon, Del Rio Ranch Wagon, six- and nine-passenger Country Sedan, and the nine-passenger Country Squire.

All models featured a wraparound liftgate, which could be locked partially open for ventilation. The tailgate was noted for having support arms rather than flexible cables.

Ford's wagon lineup consisted of the six-passenger Ranch Wagon, six-passenger Del Rio Ranch Wagon, six- and nine-passenger Country Sedans, and the nine-passenger Country Squire. Standard equipment for each paralleled that for the Custom, Custom 300, Fairlane, and Fairlane 500, respectively.

However, external trim did not quite follow this rule. The Country Squire wore simulated wood paneling and framing. Country Sedans and Del Rio Ranch Wagons got the same style of side molding used for the Fairlane 500 series. The Ranch Wagon wore the Fairlane type "bullet" side molding.

A True Hardtop Convertible

Ford's Skyliner, a.k.a. retractable or flip top in collector lingo, was one of the biggest automotive stories of the year. Billed as the "Miracle Car of This Generation" and as "Two Cars in One", the Skyliner was certainly a very different car. Simply described,

the metal top folded into the trunk area, where a rear-hinged deck lid closed to conceal it via a maze of links, wiring, motors, and relays.

The Skyliner name was not new of course; it was first used on Ford's two-door models with the plexiglass roof insert (see Chapter 1). However, the new Skyliner was a very different car. When General Motors introduced the first hardtop models, they were sometimes referred to as "hard-

top convertibles," because their appearance was similar to that of a convertible with its top in the up position. Of course, these hardtops had a fixed roof. Ford's Skyliner was an actual hardtop convertible.

Patents on the retractable steel top go back to the 1930s in this

Ford's new Skyliner was one of the biggest automotive stories of 1957. Its metal top folded into the trunk area, where a rear-hinged deck lid closed to conceal it via a maze of links, wiring, motors, and relays.

With the top down on the Fairlane 500 Skyliner, luggage space was limited to this small enclosure in the trunk. The top and mechanisms consumed the remaining volume.

country. In England, Grimston Hartley had a one-piece roof that slid back over the deck on an experimental vehicle. Peugeot built a two-passenger prototype retractable in 1934, and the production Eclipse from 1935 through 1939. Chrysler's Thunderbolt show car, built in 1940–1941, had a retractable roof. Kaiser-Fraser considered such a model for production for 1946, but the idea failed to get past the drawing-board stage. The small independent, Playboy, actually did offer a retractable for 1948. Still, these were all either foreign or small-scale production retractables. Ford Motor Company was willing and able to produce an American version on a significantly larger scale.

The retractable hardtop program at FoMoCo officially began in 1953, when $2.19 million was authorized for the study of the concept and construction of a prototype. Gil Spear with the Ford Advanced Styling Studio built a scale model with a roof that slid back over the trunk. He had convinced Special Products and Continental Division head William Clay Ford and Chief Engineer Harley Copp that the concept was practical and should be pursued. Spear's boss suggested the roof be stored within the

trunk, and later, a 1952 Lincoln Capri convertible was modified into a working retractable. During the early stages of the Mark II project, a retractable model was seriously considered for the lineup, which was to include a two-door hardtop and a convertible.

The task of producing a workable Mark II retractable was far from a simple one, with many technical obstacles to overcome. The design required the roof to fit within the confines of the trunk, lock in place when in the up position, be practical to mass produce, work reliably, be leak-proof, etc., etc. To give you some sense of the complexity involved, here is an excerpt from *Skyliner: The Birth of the Retractable*, written for the International Ford Retractable Club by Ben Smith, one of the engineers involved in the program:

"We were having some trouble with the travel of the roof with our parallel linkage. When the roof retracted, the front flipper, as it folded under, would cut off the rear passenger's heads (on the layout, that is). I really don't think that would have been one of the features we would have liked our future customers to experience. Other options were to have the passengers duck at just the right time or get out of the car while the roof was in motion. Obviously, something had to be done!

"By putting the lower pivot of the rear link on a slide, we could get the exact travel we needed... during the next few weeks, the slide became a simple link. The long cantilever spring became a compression spring that would cushion the fall of the roof into the trunk, but at the same time, assist the roof as it was being raised.

"During this period, we were working overtime to try to keep up with our self-imposed schedule...

"The prototype Continental had an integral high-pressure hydraulic system to lock the roof and deck in place. A bayonet-type plunger with a ramp effect, operated by a small-diameter hydraulic cylinder, was used. This had some design limitations and was somewhat costly, and also, eventually could be a source of maintenance problems. I could see a little old lady in a nice mink coat being sprayed by hydraulic oil.

"By the end of 1953, which was about six months into the program, we knew about a lot of things that would not work. On the other hand, we had a fairly good idea where our major problems were and what needed to be done."

Problems were solved and new ones appeared. Those, too, were solved over time only to find that the solutions themselves sometimes presented new problems! Eventually, a fully functional prototype dubbed blandly, Mechanical Prototype 5, or simply MP-5, was constructed. This prototype was a mechanical marvel, but the decision as to whether or not to include a production version in the Mk. II line vacillated between yes and no. Cost would finally settle the matter.

At the start of the Mark II program, the price of the two-door hardtop was projected to be approximately $7,500. However, the projected price quickly soared to a stratospheric $10,000. (For comparison, a 1956 Ford Fairlane Crown Skyliner sold for a base price of $2,507 and a Lincoln Premiere convertible listed for $4,747. The two prices added together fell far short of the price for a single Mark II hardtop—in fact, the difference left room for the purchase of another Fairlane Crown Skyliner with more than $300 remaining for a down payment on another car!) The retractable model would have added substantially to that figure, so the Mk. II retractable simply could not be produced in quantity at any remotely reasonable price. Prior to the decision to terminate the concept, planners began considering a way to make use of the R&D invested in it. Perhaps, they reasoned, a Fairlane could be offered as a retractable.

The 1957 Ford Fairlane retractable program got underway in early 1955. The roof panel had to be shortened 3¾ inches to make the retractable roof function properly on the Fairlane, and the roof panel was also flattened to get the rear deck as low as possible. The rear panel was blunted, the belt-line reshaped, and the rear overhang was extended 3 inches. In addition, the rear seat was moved forward 2½ inches and positioned more upright as compared to the fixed-roof, two-door hardtop model.

To create space for luggage, the spare tire had to be relocated to an area normally reserved for the fuel tank. The fuel tank, in turn, had to be relocated to a saddle position in front of the rear axle. This solution made fuel flow from the tank to the engine more difficult. However, the frame was revised to wrap around the repositioned fuel tank and remedied the problem.

After another $18 million had been spent to adapt the design to the new Ford, a 1957 Fairlane retractable-hardtop prototype was built and ready for review about one month ahead of schedule. It appeared at the New York Auto Show during December of 1956. (Also shown at this venue was a two-door version of the Country Squire.) Needless to say, it received much attention from onlookers. A short time later, production models with the already

familiar name Skyliner started appearing at dealerships across the country.

The electrical system consisted of approximately 600 feet of wiring attaching ten power relays, eight circuit breakers, ten limit switches, three drive motors, four lock motors, a dashboard warning light, and a safety interlock to prevent operation without the transmission set to neutral. Despite the complexity, the flip top typically worked well. However, because the system was sequential, if one component failed, the entire process came to a stop. Engineers realized this was a problem, and therefore a manual override crank was included.

To lower the top, a switch on the steering column was activated to begin the operation of energizing the two (three on the 1959 model) switches, which started the deck motor that lifted the long, rear-hinged lid via twin shafts at each side. As the deck locked into the full-open position, it triggered the switch on the motor to raise the package shelf to deck level. That, in turn, activated another switch to energize a motor to unlock the roof. At that point, two more motors (one on the 1959) moved the top upward and rearward into the trunk compartment (making the luggage container inaccessible). A separate servo folded the flipper panel under the roof. Once down, the lid closed. The process could be reversed at any point.

The Skyliner generated a lot of publicity for Ford Motor Company, justifying the expense involved in producing it. A total of 20,766 flip tops were sold for the 1957 model year. Sales dropped dramatically to 14,713 during the recession-marred 1958 model year, but the recession

could not be completely to blame, as just 12,915 were sold for 1959.

Even with the sluggish sales for the last two years of production, Ford's president Robert S. McNamara, according to Ben Smith's *Skyliner: The Birth of the Retractable*, wanted to continue with the model for the redesigned 1960 lineup. He believed the continued publicity generated by the Skyliner justified its production—it was free advertising worth as much as $25 million

Unfortunately, the members of the same engineering team who developed the 1957–59 design had disbanded and been given other assignments. The new team assembled to design the system for the 1960 model went over budget. As a result, the Product Planning Committee voted to discontinue the project. McNamara fought to get it reinstated for 1961, but lost that battle.

Some years ago, both Peugeot and Mercedes revived the retractable concept. Most people likely believed it to be a new idea!

Harmonizing Colors

While the Skyliner generated much fanfare, most buyers opted for a conventional hardtop or sedan. Regardless of which model was purchased, Ford offered a variety of paint colors in single tones, two-tones, and Style-Tone combinations, such as Flame Red/Raven Black, Dresden Blue/Starmist Blue, and Inca Gold/Colonial White. The roof and lower body were painted contrasting colors with the two-tone option. Cars with the Style-Tone option still used two colors, but on the Fairlane 500s the portion of the body below the body side molding and the roof were one color while the body area

This Inca Gold and Raven Black 1957 Fairlane 500 Club Sedan is powered by the 340-hp 312-ci with a Phase 2 blower. Production of this model totaled 93,753, but very few had an F-code engine.

Gold basket-weave fabric combined with black sculptured fabric was one of five standard schemes offered for the Fairlane 500 Club Sedan.

beneath the roof and above the body side molding were the other. Custom 300s, which also had a Fairlane Sweep molding, could also be had with two-tone or Style-Tone paint. The Fairlane's side trim allowed for single or two-tone paint, as did the Custom series.

A wide selection of new harmonizing upholstery choices was offered for the restyled interior, which was further freshened with a revised instrument panel. Standard issue for the Custom was gray random block fabric combined with a silver and gray shantung vinyl bol-

ster. The Custom 300 received either gray, green, or blue flying dart fabric combined with a chain grain vinyl bolster in Woodsmoke Gray, Willow Green, or Starmist Blue, respectively.

Fairlane Town and Club Sedans offered a choice of Woodsmoke Gray chain grain bolster and gray-silver dash fabric, Willow Green chain grain bolster with green-silver dash fabric, Starmist Blue chain grain combined with blue-silver dash fabric, and Doeskin Tan chain grain bolster with brown-silver dash fabric.

Fairlane Club and Town Victorias differed with Colonial vinyl bolsters

paired with tropical leaf fabric in gray, green, blue, or brown. The Fairlane 500 Club and Town Sedans came with gray, green, blue, and brown basket weave fabric combined accordingly with a similar shade of gray, green, blue, or brown sculptured fabric, as well as gold basket-weave combined with black sculptured fabric. Fairlane 500 Club and Town Victoria models were equipped with the same Colonial White bolster as the Fairlane series in combination with shadow fabric of green-silver, blue-silver, brown-silver, black-silver, and red-silver or with a Raven Black vinyl bolster paired with

Flame Red and Raven Black was one of many two-tone choices offered. However, typically it was applied reversed from what is seen here. The paint code is blank on this car's VIN. Furthermore, it is equipped with the rare E-code 312-ci featuring twin 4-barrel carburetors.

This red-silver and black-silver fabric upholstery was not one of the five standard arrangements offered, thus it was an extra-cost option. However, this combination was a standard choice for Fairlane 500 Club and Town Victorias.

gold ripple-wave fabric. Colonial White vinyl bolsters with embossed vinyl in Cumberland Green, Dresden Blue, Flame Red, or Raven Black were the choices for the Sunliner.

The Skyliner got a Colonial White vinyl bolster sewn to either red, brown, or black airweave vinyl, a Starmist Blue vinyl bolster combined with blue airweave vinyl, or a Willow Green vinyl bolster with green airweave vinyl.

The Ranch Wagon was upholstered with a Doeskin Tan bolster with tan sharkskin woven plastic or a Colonial White vinyl bolster with a blue French-stitch vinyl. Del Rio and six-passenger Country Sedan wagons had several choices: Colonial White bolsters attached to either tweed woven plastic in blue-silver or tan-silver or embossed vinyl in Cumberland Green or Flame Red. The Country Squire had still other combinations of a Colonial White vinyl bolster stitched to blue-silver or tan-silver tweed puff woven plastic or pleated Cumberland Green or Flame Red vinyl. Incidentally, the Sunliner convertible top colors were black, white, tan, or blue. These were standard issue upholstery choices; however, other combinations were available to customers.

Options and Accessories

Among the many options and accessories offered for the 1957 Fords were:

- SelectAire air conditioning
- MagicAire heater/defroster
- Signal-Seek radio
- rear speaker
- rear deck antenna
- power windows
- power seat
- electric clock
- spotlight with mirror
- tissue dispenser
- auto/home electric shaver
- Aquamatic windshield washer
- back-up lights
- visored outside rearview mirror
- Swift-Sure power brakes
- Lifeguard package
- turbine-style wheel covers
- chromed exhaust deflector
- rocker panel trim
- grille guard
- Sports-Spare wheel carrier (Continental kit)

Engines

Engine choices were similar to those of the previous model year, but there were important changes and upgrades. The 6-cylinder received a compression boost for a gain of 7 hp; the 272-ci 2-barrel got a more productive increase in output to 190 hp. The 292-ci, optional on Fairlanes and wagons, gained 6 hp when coupled to the manual transmission and 10 hp with the automatic via a compression increase. The 2-barrel carburetor was upgraded with venturi area greater than that of the 4-barrel from 1956. The single-exhaust system was also changed to a Y-type, which replaced the cross-over pipe setup.

The changes were even more significant for 312-ci V-8s, with outputs ranging from 245 hp to 340. The 245-hp Y-block Thunderbird Special received dual exhausts, a 4-barrel carb, and 9.7:1 compression. Next in the hierarchy was the twin-4-barrel-carb version of the famous E-code engine in 270- and 285-hp versions. The F-code supercharged engine topped the heap with 300- and 340-hp variants, but those figures were conservative and realistically were 325- and 360-hp, respectively.

A longer duration cam (290 degrees versus 256 from the previous year) created more horsepower for the E- and F-code Y-blocks. The F-code 312-ci, with its Paxton VR-57 supercharger, had a compression ratio of 8.6:1. One could order any of the transmissions Ford offered with the E and F engines.

In the mid-1950s, rumors began circulating that rival Chevrolet might offer a supercharged Corvette. McCulloch had tested a VS-57 supercharger on a 1953 Corvette and then offered the kit to retrofit Chevy's fiberglass sports car, as well as Ford's Thunderbird.

Ford hired Pete Depoalo, an ex-race car driver, to make its cars competition ready, and he recommended building a supercharged 312 ci. Ford's engineers experimented with fuel injection, but reliability issues forced Ford officials to act on Depoalo's advice. Furthermore, the E-code cars could not compete with the fuel-injected Chevys on the race track.

Ford inked a deal with Paxton Products to supply the new VR-57 variable ratio planetary drive superchargers. The supercharged 312-ci became available in January 1957, on any Ford passenger cars including Skyliners and station wagons, as well as on the new car-based truck, the Ranchero. The earliest examples were equipped with the Phase I supercharger, which was soon found to have unreliable control valves. A Phase II unit solved the problems encountered with the first design and had a ribbed case and a large clamp (rather than screws) to hold it together. The 285-hp 312-ci was dropped with the introduction of the supercharged version.

The F-code supercharged engine came conservatively rated in 300- and 340-hp variants (realistically 325 and 360 hp, respectively). Ford used the Paxton VR-57 supercharger on this Y-block.

The E-code 312 was initially offered in 270- and 285-hp versions. In early 1957, the latter was dropped when the supercharged version was released.

Road Testing

A road test performed on a 245-hp, four-door sedan Fairlane 500 for the January 1957 issue of *Hot Rod* showed the car to be a relatively good handling vehicle. Pushing the car into some serious turns at 55 mph at "near-full power in the Ford's intermediate gear" resulted in the car going "around as if on rails." At 60 mph, chassis roll "reached its limit" and at 70 mph "the car rounded the turn way wide despite the fact the front wheels were fully cramped into the turn." The article

referred to the improved (compared to 1956) front ball-joint suspension, the more rigid one-piece upper and lower A-arms, and improved weight distribution.

The testing did show there were faults in the Fairlane, though. Changing the sway bar from the standard 5/8-inch type to the 11/16-inch version used on station wagons or to a 3/4-inch bar was recommended. Also, stiffer shocks and torque dividing differential were mentioned as other desirable upgrades for the chassis.

In analyzing the steering, the same *Hot Rod* report stated, "It is both light and accurate... but the overall steering ratio of 27:1 is entirely too slow for quick and easy-made corrections." The report did note the Ford-Bendix power steering unit had "a reassuring feel" and "is responsive though slow, and continues as one of the very best power steering units available."

Braking was evaluated and considered to be good during normal operation, but when things became livelier, brake fade took place "sooner than expected." The brake system was carried over from 1956.

The final observation in the *Hot Rod* report was, "Mechanically, the '57 Ford is a very sound automobile. It isn't without faults, but it contains

a minimum of bad ones and most of these were due to compromises made for the sake of styling. It performs well, is quite roadworthy and driving it can be a real ball... I'll bet they'll sell a jillion of 'em."

Racing and the AMA Ban

Hot Rod's "jillion" estimate was about right. Production amounted to 1,653,068 units—a total which surpassed Chevrolet's 1957 model year production by about 170,000 units.

Ford's success on the race track translated to sales success. By the time the 1957 Fords appeared, racing was becoming an increasingly popular sport, and auto manufacturers were using it to promote their cars. As noted in an article from the 1958 annual issue of Motorspeed, "If the car wins frequently, there is publicity that follows naturally. That publicity is often better than advertising, so dealers sell more cars."

During the mid 1950s, some in authority began to notice the rising highway death-toll. Politicians sought an issue to capitalize and began to criticize the way cars were being made and advertised. Such publicity got the attention of NASCAR's rule-making body. In April 1957, NASCAR prohibited the use of fuel injection, multiple carburetors,

A 1957 Ford Custom, probably powered with a supercharged 312-ci, is shown here at the start of a timed run on the sand of Daytona Beach. The event was the annual Daytona Speedweeks.

and supercharging—all of which were in use on the speedways. But this action proved too little, too late.

NASCAR wanted to avoid the kind of scrutiny the Feds were giving the auto manufacturers. Hence, the Automobile Manufacturers Association (AMA) banned factory-backed racing the following June. (Perhaps another factor involved in getting GM to at least give lip service to the new ruling was the suggestion by some in the U.S. Congress for the big company to be broken into smaller ones. General Motors had about half the U.S. car market and some politicians thought such success suggested a monopoly.) The auto makers seemingly complied with their professional association's pledge.

Another reason for the AMA edict was the tremendous cost involved in staying competitive. The same 1958 *Motorspeed* article stated this opinion:

"Stock car racing was a highly expensive venture. It diverted the interest of the engineers, the public relations people and the sales executives away from their principle reason for existing—selling automobiles. "To be kept in its true perspective auto racing should have been one of the sales aids, but it became an all consuming monster."

The "all consuming monster" did not go away, in spite of the AMA ban. Pontiac basically ignored the ban. Chevy went a bit further by disguising its performance equipment under the banner of "for police use only." Chrysler had already dropped out of NASCAR Grand National racing, but continued to be involved with events, such as Daytona Speed trials. Ford actually took the ban seriously and sold all of its racing related equipment to race team Holman-Moody.

Fireball Roberts is shown behind the wheel of this supercharged 1957 Custom at a NASCAR event early in the 1957 season. Ford cars managed to win 27 of 53 Grand National races this year, giving them their second consecutive Manufacturer's Cup.

Even without factory involvement in the last part of the race season, the Ford teams managed to win 27 of 53 Grand National races and a second consecutive manufacturers cup. In contrast, runner-up Chevrolet succeeded in winning 18 races.

In Unites States Auto Club (USAC) competition, the supercharger setup was legal for the entire season, and Ralph Moody drove one to victory in four races. Overall, Ford managed 12 USAC wins for 1957. This season had been the best to date for Ford, greatly exceeding the 14 NASCAR wins of the previous year and the lowly 2 victories achieved in 1955.

To show off the new 1957 Fairlane's performance capabilities, a blown version lapped the Indianapolis Speedway at an average speed of 117 mph in the Stephen Trophy Trials. In addition, for 22 days starting September 9, 1956, two Fairlanes were run continuously at 110 mph at the Bonneville Salt Flats in Utah. Pit stops lasted an average of 17 seconds. The cars ran day and night until the 28th, when the 50,000-mile mark was reached, thus proving the car's superior durability. Prior to this event, the same Fairlanes broke 458 national and international performance records.

The results at the annual Daytona Speedweeks event were impressive, too. Fran Hernandez drove a supercharged Fairlane to a third-place finish at 130.058 mph in Class 7 (two-way flying-mile speed runs). Class 7 was the over-350-ci-displacement category, so the 312-powered Ford had to compete with a 392-ci Hemi-equipped Chrysler 300 C, a 364-outfitted Buick, and a Dodge with a 354-ci V-8. The top five results were as follows:

Place	Car	Speed (mph)
1st	1957 300 C	134.128
2nd	1957 Buick	130.766
3rd	1957 Ford	130.058
4th	1957 Dodge	129.753
5th	1957 Buick	129.683

In the Class 7 acceleration, 1-mile, standing-start event, the same blown Fairlane managed an average speed of 85.066 mph, placing it behind a 1957 300 C and 1957 Mercury (equipped with a 368-ci engine) with average speeds of 86.873 and 85.511 mph, respectively.

Bud Wilcox drove a twin-carb 312-ci Fairlane to fifth place in Class 6 competition. The top five finishers were:

Place	Car	Speed (mph)
1st	1957 Pontiac	131.747
2nd	1957 Pontiac	131.531
3rd	1957 Pontiac	128.434
4th	1957 Plymouth	126.205
5th	1957 Ford	125.239

The charged-up Fords proved to be just as fast as the fuelie Chevrolets. Both were capable of 130 mph top speeds. The Fords seemed to have the advantage on the fast speedways while the Chevy did better on the short tracks.

Jerry Unser drove a supercharged Fairlane in the 1957 Pike's Peak Hill Climb held in July and won with a record time of 15 minutes, 39.2 seconds. Another supercharged Fairlane finished in second place 9.6 seconds later.

Production breakdown for the two 4-barrel (E-code engine) and supercharged (F-code engine) cars is not available. Hinting at the numbers, though, is the fact that NASCAR rules of the day required an automaker to advertise the engine and have 100 to 125 units delivered to dealers by January 1, 1957. Additionally, 1,500 units had to be scheduled for production by January 15.

Production of supercharged T-Birds is known to have totaled between 208 and 211. If this figure is included with the 1,500 required units, then less than 1,300 full-size, supercharged Fords were needed to meet NASCAR rules. The NASCAR ban in April, along with the AMA agreement in June certainly precluded such a production total. In fact, the actual figure probably did not approach anywhere near 1,292, and is most likely a number in the hundreds (approximately 300 has been reported).

The same would apply to the E-code engine, although they were probably more common due to the lower cost of the option. Regardless of the number built, E- and F-code 312s were uncommon when new and are quite uncommon today.

Mystere

The Ford *Mystere* show car, completed in late 1954, influenced the styling of the 1957 full-size Fords. The one-of-a-kind car was originally intended to be placed on the 1955 show circuit with its first public appearance scheduled for the 1955 Chicago Auto Show held in January. But by the time it was completed, many of its features had been adopted for the production 1957 Fords. Therefore, management decided not to unveil the car at that time because it would give away the 1957 styling to the competition, which was about two years away from release.

The *Mystere* was finally revealed to the public in the fall of 1955. The hood and scalloped front fender design was taken virtually unaltered from the unique show vehicle. Its wheel cover design, check-mark side molding, fins, and large round tail lamps appeared as well, though in much subdued fashion. The show car's quad headlight arrangement had to wait until the 1958 model year because states across the country were changing their laws to allow the setup.

Its cockpit featured an aircraft-inspired steering wheel with push-button automatic transmission controls across the top, four bucket seats, and a TV mounted at the front end of a console positioned between the rear seats. Bucket seats would be placed into production with the four-passenger T-Bird and later the Galaxie 500/XL. The push-button gear selectors mounted on the steering wheel would find their way onto the Edsel.

But not everything about the *Mystere* appeared in production. Certainly bubbletop cars never went into production, nor did the proposed turbine engine intended for the show car. No engine, in fact, was installed in that car. According to *Ford Design Department Show Cars, 1932-1961*, by Jim and Cheryl Farrell, the *Mystere* survived at Ford until the early 1970s when it was finally scrapped.

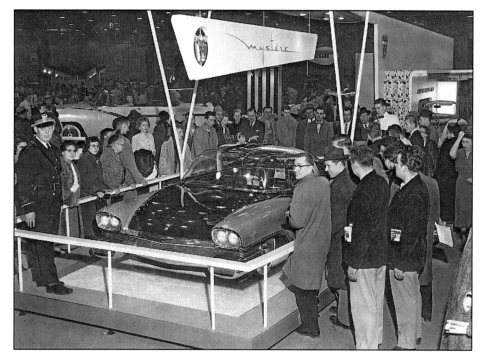

Ford's **Mystere** *show car provided the inspiration for the styling of the new 1957 production models. This photo was taken at the 1956 Chicago Auto Show.* (Photo courtesy of Chicago Automobile Trade Association)

1958–1959: THE FE-ENGINE, CRUISE-O-MATIC AND THE THUNDERBIRD LOOK

Ford's Y-block had been in production a very short time before the company's engineers went to work on a more advanced V-8, dubbed the FE (Ford/Edsel) engine.

The New FE

In 1958, the FE series of engines debuted in 332- and 352-ci displacements (361 ci for Edsel). Its design evolved from Ford's Y-block, and the two overhead-valve cast iron V-8s shared the Y-shaped cross-section, thick-wall, over-square design. The FE's thick wall added weight, as did the rather wide intake manifold. Because of its width, the heads were narrow, causing the pushrods to go through the intake manifold. Intake ports were much larger than those of the Y-block and valve lift was higher. The valvetrain was substantially lighter and less complex for the FE as well.

Gasket sealing near the corners of the intake manifold that met the heads was a source of problems. There

A total of 80,439 Fairlane 500 Club Victorias were built. The one seen here is painted Desert Beige and Colonial White and is equipped with a 332-ci V-8, automatic transmission, wheel covers, fender skirts, radio, and clock.

was a water passage, intake port, and opening into the lifter chamber of the engine at these points. Improper gasket sealing on some engines allowed water to leak into the intake port or mix with the engine oil. To solve the problem, Ford made improved replacement gaskets.

The new FE engines featured a nodular cast-iron, precision-molded

crankshaft, forged steel rods, and aluminum alloy pistons with solid skirts and flat tops. Early 1958 FE engines had machined combustion chamber heads, but this was soon changed to cast chambers. Machined chambers reduced possible hot spots and, therefore, pre-ignition, but the quality of premium gasoline at the time was inconsistent. The cast

The 332-ci V-8 was offered with a 2- or 4-barrel carburetor; advertised horsepower was 240 and 265, respectively. This car has the 4-barrel with dual exhausts.

The 352-ci 4-barrel was advertised as providing a peak horsepower of 300, but dynamometer testing revealed it fell well short of that figure. Early engines had a 10.2:1 compression ratio, but this was subsequently dropped to 9.6:1.

For 1958 Ford offered the first of its long-running FE-series engines in 332- and 352-ci displacements. The FE engine was based upon lessons learned from the Y-Block.

chamber heads had the virtue of being cheaper to manufacture. Together these factors evidently justified the modification. A new cooling system of 13 psi was also provided, which permitted as much as a 33-degree increase in the coolant temperature without loss of coolant and allowed a faster engine warm-up, and longer engine life.

The 332-ci FE V-8 was offered for the 1958 and 1959 model years only, with 2- and 4-barrel carburetors in 1958 and only a 2-barrel the next.

Output was rated at 240 hp with the 2-barrel and 265 hp with the 4. Dual exhausts were standard with the 265-hp engine. The bore and stroke measured 4.00 x 3.32 inches, and the compression ratio was 9.5:1. For 1959, the compression ratio was decreased to 8.9:1.

A longer stroke, 3.50 inches, resulted in a 352-ci displacement for the FE block. Its compression ratio measured 10.2:1, but this was reduced to 9.6:1 when the combustion chambers were enlarged. Dual exhausts were standard or better breathing. Advertised horsepower remained at 300, though it was later shown to be a much exaggerated figure. Tests conducted by *Hot Rod* magazine (August 1958) revealed the true output was much closer to 200 hp.

Also offered was the 292-ci Y-block with a 2-barrel carburetor; its horsepower rating was advertised as 205 early in the model year. However, head chamber size increased

from 69 to 72 cc, lowering the compression ratio from 9.1:1 to 8.8:1 and reducing the rating to 200 hp. This engine burned regular gasoline.

All V-8s were extra-cost options, as the Mileage-Maker Six remained the standard engine for all series of big Fords. The 6-cylinder received some tweaks leading to a trivial 1-hp gain, but as much as a 10-percent increase in fuel mileage.

Cruise-O-Matic

Ford also released its new Cruise-O-Matic 3-speed automatic transmission for this model year; its evolutionary design derived from the 3-speed Ford-O-Matic (which remained available). Designed by Borg-Warner, the Cruise-O-Matic featured a torque converter, a planetary gearset, and two "DRIVE" positions (D1 and D2) allowing the driver to start in either low or second gear. Ford's advertising stated,

"In combination with a gas-saving axle ratio (2.69:1) you get real 'built-in' overdrive economy..." The Cruise-O-Matic was an optional transmission and the 3-speed manual was standard issue on all models; overdrive remained as an option.

The AMA ban on racing prevented the new FE engine from going into any factory-backed stock cars. However, Holman-Moody managed to build several of the new four-passenger Thunderbirds powered with the Lincoln 430-ci. They finished second, eighth, and tenth in the inaugural Daytona 500. It marked the genesis of Ford's return to factory-backed racing a couple of years later.

Performance was officially being downplayed, though sales catalogs still mentioned power: "These newest of all Fords give you GO like no other Ford cars have ever given you before," said one brochure. Fuel economy was also stressed: "For 1958 Ford presents three engines that are new from fan blade to flywheel—the matchless Interceptor V-8s. These new engines feature the most important advance in V-8 design in 25 years—an advance that gives you more power on less gasoline—Precision Fuel Induction!"

After each V-8 was assembled, it was electronically balanced while running under its own power before being installed in a car. Ford claimed it was the first in the low-priced field to undertake this advance in engine testing.

Road Testing

Dynamometer testing at the time revealed the 352 Interceptor fell considerably short of Ford's advertised 300-hp rating.

This Silvertone Green and Colonial White 1958 Fairlane is either a Springtime Special or was fitted with the anodized gold trim and quarter panel ornaments as accessories. **(Photo courtesy of Stu Marshall)**

The April 1958 issue of *Hot Rod* reported on a test of three Interceptor-equipped Fairlanes (Club Victoria, Club Sedan, and Sunliner) and judged the engine to be "well designed." The Victoria had a Cruise-O-Matic and a 2.69:1 rear axle ratio; the Club Sedan had the 3-speed with overdrive and a 3.56:1 axle ratio; the convertible had the Ford-O-Matic and 2.91:1 gearing.

Hot Rod noted that, "We weren't particularly taken by surprise when the Ford-O-Matic with 2.91 axle or the Cruise-O-Matic with the 2.69 axle didn't accelerate too well. This is the price you pay for so-called economy gears. We were a bit surprised, however, to discover that the stick shift model with the big engine didn't go."

The final conclusion was, "After a couple of weeks behind the wheel of the new Ford we were undecided on only one item and this was the rear axle ratio. These high gears are fine for the highway, but it is a bit maddening to have to stomp on the throttle for a kickdown gear to get around a car traveling 40 miles per hour when your car is supposed to have 300 horses under the hood. Maybe the horsepower race isn't over yet. Looks as though Ford needs some more to pull those high gears."

Incidentally, after Paxton Products' contract with Ford expired, they continued to market their superchargers and offered the VR-57B kit for Ford's 352. That was one way an enthusiast could get the additional power the *Hot Rod* magazine writer believed was needed.

The *Hot Rod* editors did not just find faults, but also discovered favorable aspects to the 1958 Fords. They judged the 1958 Ford to be "a comfortable automobile with good wheel position and good location of instruments and dash panel knobs. Steering is easy even without power and naturally easier with, and the brakes can be described in the same manner. Body fit, chrome trim, interior molding and general workmanship in the 1958 Fords is very good."

The February 1958 issue of *Motor Life* reported findings similar to those found by *Hot Rod* regarding fit and finish as well as performance. However, *Speed Age* magazine gave a different report after testing a Fairlane 500 four-door sedan with a 332-ci Interceptor and Ford-O-Matic. The analysis, which appeared in the March 1958 issue, said, "The Fairlane 500, even with the second-most-powerful engine, can keep up with any kind of traffic, and pass most." As for fit and finish, the *Speed Age* editors found "a little more orange-peel than we would like to see on a car. Characteristically, the side accent panel was misaligned at the doors."

Exterior Styling

Side accents varied depending on the model. The Fairlane 500 received a modified version of the 1957's design, incorporating a longer sweep for the anodized gold insert and surrounding trim, which spanned nearly three-fourths of the overall length of the car. It provided a break for any of several two-tone paint combinations.

A narrow molding distinguished the Fairlane. It looped from the headlights to the forward end of the rear wheel opening and back to the trailing side of the front wheel opening. This molding provided an area for a contrasting color for two-tone paint. Custom 300 Tudor and Fordor Sedans were equipped with a unique treatment, too, again allowing for a two-tone paint treatment. These models could be had with an optional anodized gold spear or Style-Tone trim, which replaced the standard horizontal stainless molding with a double strip with the gold insert.

The low-level Custom received a simple check-mark-type body side molding, which dropped downward from the belt-line then swept forward to the headlights. However, the Custom was dropped early in the

"There's nothing newer in the world than the '58 Ford," proclaimed Ford Motor Company. The 1958 models did offer updated styling, new engine choices, and a new automatic transmission.

Ford compared its 1958 full-size models to the new, upscale Thunderbird. "There's a lot of Thunder-bird in the way Ford moves," said this advertisement.

model year, and the Business Sedan migrated to the Custom 300 line from the deleted model series.

Station wagon models, except for the Country Squire, Ranch Wagon, and the Fordor Ranch Wagon, shared the side trim design with the Custom 300 series. Of course, the Country Squire maintained the woody-look paneling. The Ranch Wagon and

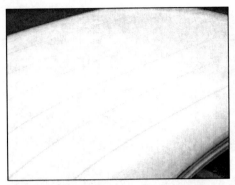

Seven longitudinal grooves added some styling to the Slipstream roof panel of the 1958 Fords. All models with the exception of the Skyliner, and of course, the soft top, received this treatment.

A nonfunctional hood scoop with a chrome inlet on the Power Flow hood was a prominent part of the new styling for 1958.

This Torch Red and Colonial White 1958 Skyliner is one of 14,713 built for the model year. The total was about a 6,000-unit decrease from the 1957 figure. However, this decrease was nearly proportionate with the overall drop in Ford's sales for 1958.

Side accents varied depending upon the model. The Fairlane 500 received a modified version of the 1957's design incorporating a longer sweep for the anodized gold insert, which spanned nearly three-fourths of the overall length of the car. It provided a break for any of several two-tone Style-Tone paint combinations.

Fordor Ranch Wagon each received a long check-mark-style molding like that of the Custom series.

Other distinguishing characteristics of these models included chrome headlight trim for the Fairlane 500 and Fairlane models. Custom 300s received painted trim, though the chrome pieces were available as an extra-cost accessory. Other standard equipment for each model basically paralleled that of the 1957s. However, the Fairlane 500s now came standard with "Fashion Ray" wheel covers instead of hub caps.

Other details of the styling of the 1958 Fords included a frontal design based on the new four-passenger Thunderbird. Unfortunately, the bumper and grille were controversial because these body pieces were not nearly as well executed as on the T-Bird.

Incidentally, according to Doug Swanson of Swanson Ford, the oldest Ford dealership in Nebraska, the earliest 1958 Fords were refitted with the crossbar over the honeycomb grille and the chromed headlight trim (for the Fairlane) via a service

order and at the request of customers. Paint on the pot-metal headlight bezels did not adhere well, which may have been the reason for the change being made for the top-level cars. Evidently the crossbar was a last minute styling change. Ford provided a template so the service department personnel could properly drill the mounting holes for the bar into the bumper.

The quad headlight system, or as Ford dubbed it, Safety-Twin Headlights, had only become legal in all states some months prior to the release of the 1958 models and represented another update for this model year. A nonfunctional hood scoop with a chrome inlet on the Power Flow hood was a prominent part of the styling as well as was an elliptical recess in the center of the deck lid.

The traditional round tail lamps of the past were replaced by a set of four oblong lenses. Back-up lights were optional, but no longer contained within the taillights. Instead (when ordered), the back-up lights were placed in the gap between the paired taillight lenses. Another distinctive new feature was the longitudinal grooves (numbering seven) stamped into the Slipstream roof of all big Ford models.

Ford's Global Tour

From early July 1957 through the first half of October, a fleet of Ford vehicles including two of the first 1958 Fords (both blue and white Fairlane 500 Town Sedans), began a long journey from Michigan to New York where the caravan boarded a ship to England.

These Fords were beginning an around-the-world trip, which took them through Paris, Geneva, Rome, Trieste, Dubrovnik, Athens, Istanbul,

Prior to the launch of the 1958 model year, Ford took two blue-and-white Town Sedans on an around the world journey to test the ruggedness of the design. This advertisement showed one of the test cars on the rough, winding roads of Turkey and a Sunliner on the steep hills of San Francisco.

FoMoCo produced a booklet detailing the around-the-world experiences with two new 1958 Fords. The long journey began in Detroit, continued to New York and resumed in England. These Fords traversed France to Vietnam before being shipped to the Philippines, Guam, Honolulu, and San Francisco. The two cars continued across country all the way back to Detroit.

Teheran, Kyhber Pass, Lahore, New Delhi, Calcutta, Penang, Bangkok, Saigon, Manila, Guam, Honolulu, San Francisco, Salt Lake City, Kansas City, Chicago, and back home to Detroit. The Fords endured extreme temperatures, unpaved roads, mountain terrain, and dust storms. Where there was no road the cars were transported by either ship or rail.

In one instance while coming around a hairpin curve along the Adriatic, one sedan ran into a fresh-fallen rock with no time to stop or go around it. The large rock jammed underneath the car, striking the rear engine mount and moving the engine about 1½ inches. The decision was made to push on rather than stop for repairs, and the car arrived in Detroit this way.

Ford Motor Company produced a booklet about the grueling test drive in which they summarized its purpose and results: "The '58 Ford was sent around the world for just one purpose... to prove itself to you. It was given the most merciless test ever put to a new automobile before its public announcement. The results speak for themselves. The soundness of the new 1958 Ford's design, the enormous strength of its construction, the complete dependability of all its working parts have been proved." And in conclusion, "There's nothing newer, nothing finer on any road in the world today than the 58 Ford." The statement was a slight exaggeration; the basic bodies and the suspension with only minor revisions were carried forward from 1957.

Air Suspension and Other Goodies

One more notable option on the 1958 Fords was the "Ford Aire" air suspension available for Fairlane 500, Fairlane, and wagon models equipped with a 332- or 352-ci V-8.

The standard rear-leaf-type suspension required considerable modifications to install the air suspension. Each leaf spring was discarded and a trailing arm put in its place. This required several additional brackets to be attached to the frame rails and the rear axle housing.

Despite the intention of giving a "cloud soft ride" and handling "curves with a minimum of swing and sway" it did not work very well and was withdrawn after only about 100 cars were so equipped. (The new Thunderbird, which was delayed, was also designed with the option in mind, but none were ordered with the system because it was dropped prior to the availability of the T-Bird. Lincoln and Mercury were also meant to have this option.)

When it did function properly, the opening of the driver's side door activated the system, triggering solenoids connected to the courtesy light switches. A 300-psi compressor and an air storage tank on the right side of the engine compartment pressurized four rubberized domes or air springs, while three leveling valves went into action and leveled the car according to load. The leveling valves adjusted for the road surface and braking. Leaky air bags and water condensation or freezing water in the air lines kept the system from working reliably.

One of the three test cars used for the aforementioned April 1958 *Hot Rod* magazine road test was equipped with the system. The report said,

"Our limited experience of riding and driving a car with Ford-Aire did not impress us enough with riding improvement over conventional springs to warrant the extra cost involved. Within a few years there might be enough refinements in air-suspension systems to make them vastly superior to steel, but not now."

Other options and accessories were similar to those previously offered and included:

- power steering
- Swift-Sure power brakes
- four-way manually adjusted front seat
- I-Rest tinted safety glass
- Turbine wheel covers
- Sunburst wheel covers
- fender skirts
- deluxe rear deck antenna
- bumper-mounted exhaust deflectors
- license plate frames
- tissue dispenser
- luggage rack (for station wagon models)
- Sport Spare Wheel Carrier
- SelectAire or the new PolarAire air conditioning with tinted glass for V-8 powered cars. The PolarAire was a stand-alone unit that hung underneath the dash.

Interiors and Paint

Custom 300 upholstery patterns were:

- silver lattice-patterned nylon cloth with silver shantung-grained vinyl bolsters
- medium gray box-striped nylon with light gray vinyl bolsters
- medium blue box-striped nylon with light blue vinyl bolsters

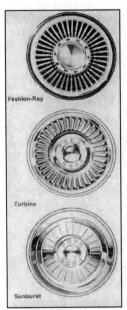

Three designs of wheel covers were listed in the 1958 Ford accessories brochure. The Fashion-Ray type was standard on Fairlane 500s. The Turbine and Sunburst wheel covers were carried over from 1957.

- medium green box-striped nylon with light green vinyl bolsters

The gray and blue versions were extra-cost options.

Fairlane Club Sedan and Town Sedan nylon/vinyl interior combinations also numbered four: medium blue/light blue, medium green/light green, medium brown/light brown, medium gray/light gray.

Fairlane Club Victoria and Town Victoria models had almost the same interior options with the one difference being black nylon with white vinyl bolsters in place of medium gray and light gray.

The Fairlane 500 Club and Town Sedans offered the same color combinations in nylon as the comparable Fairlane series, plus gold and black but in damask upholstery with a shadow block pattern bolster.

Club and Town Victorias used a Royal Scot tweed pattern in several pairings:

- medium blue nylon with light blue vinyl bolsters
- medium green nylon with light green vinyl bolsters

A Sport Spare Wheel Carrier added 10 inches of length to a 1958 Ford; here, a Fairlane 500 Skyliner. Other extra-cost features in this view are Style-Tone paint, backup lights, rocker panel trim, and exhaust deflectors.

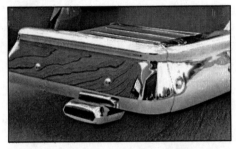

Bumper-mounted, chrome-plated exhaust deflectors were said to "add dash and 'personality' to your new Ford." Shown here is one of two types offered for 1958; the other was the so-called Delta-wing type carried over from 1957.

- medium brown nylon with light brown vinyl bolsters
- black nylon sewn to either white, red, buff, or turquoise vinyl bolsters
- black nylon with gold vinyl bolsters

Interior selections for the Sunliner were vinyl: medium blue/light blue, black/white, red/white, buff/white, and turquoise/white. The second member of the pairing was the color of the bolsters.

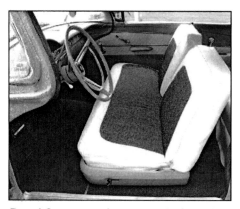

Royal Scot tweed pattern cloth and vinyl upholstery was standard issue for Fairlane 500 closed models.

The instrument panel layout for the 1958 Fords was little changed from the previous model year. The arcing speedometer was flanked by fuel and coolant temperature gauges.

Skyliner upholstery offered combinations of cloth and vinyl. Upholstery was of Royal Scot tweed in linen-patterned, all-weather nylon in a choice of six colors highlighted with gold Lurex. Bolsters were leather-grained vinyl. The choices were:

- medium blue/light blue
- medium brown/light brown
- black/white
- red/white
- buff/white
- turquoise/white

Inside the Ranch Wagon was a limited selection consisting of medium brown shadow pattern woven plastic with light brown vinyl bolsters or medium blue embossed-stitch pleated vinyl and light blue

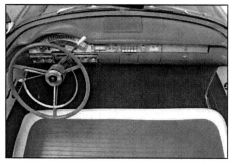

All-vinyl upholstery was standard issue for the Fairlane 500 Sunliner. The red-and-white combination shown here was one of five standard color schemes offered for the model.

vinyl bolsters. The Del Rio Ranch Wagon and six-passenger Country Sedan shared the same upholstery choices: medium blue basket-weave woven plastic and light blue vinyl bolsters, medium brown basket-weave woven plastic and light brown vinyl bolsters, medium green pleated whipcord embossed vinyl and light green bolsters, plus red-pleated-whipcord embossed vinyl and white vinyl bolsters.

The nine-passenger Country Sedan and Country Squire also shared upholstery patterns: medium blue thong-patterned Plasti-Fab woven plastic and light blue vinyl bolsters, medium brown thong-patterned Plasti-Fab woven plastic and light brown vinyl bolsters, medium green Sof-Textured vinyl with light green vinyl bolsters and seat backs pleated with white stitching, red Sof-Textured vinyl with white vinyl bolsters and seat backs pleated with white stitching.

Thirteen single tone colors were offered, along with Style-Tone and conventional two-tone options. Schemes for the latter included Sun Gold/Gunmetal Gray, Torch Red/Colonial White, and Silvertone Blue/Azure Blue.

Other colors offered were:
- Raven Black
- Palomino Tan
- Bali Bronze
- Desert Beige
- Gulfstream Blue
- Silvertone Green
- Seaspray Green

Sales Weaken

Sales for the 1958 model year were significantly lower than for 1957 despite a small price reduction for the Custom 300s and the around-the-world test drive. Part of the reason was an economic recession affecting all automakers that year. The less-than-dazzling styling certainly did not help Ford, either.

The March 1958 issue of *Speed Age* was not especially complementary of the styling updates: "We found the interior cheerful and bright, but the general effect was in keeping with the rest of the car. The object seems to be to make the car look as expensive as possible. To this end, simplicity is discarded in favor of maximum ornamentation and complexity of line. As a result, aside from a very handsome front-end treatment, the car has a cluttered, non-integrated look that is, frankly, more flashy than beautiful."

Nevertheless, these 1958 models were judged as mechanically better than those of the previous year. Ride and handling qualities improved thanks to alterations to the upper front control arms andadjustments to shock calibrations and rear springs rates. Ford's Magic-Circle recalculating ball-type steering said to be "the nearest thing to power steering" was made standard on all models as well.

Even so, styling meant a lot to buyers. An attempt to boost sales a

As stated in this newspaper ad, the sticker prices for the Custom 300 models decreased as much as $50 from 1957 levels. While a $50 savings on a new car is laughable now, it represented a significant percentage of the total price at that time.

The Fairlane 500 was the top-of-the-line model at the start of the 1959 model year. The Galaxie soon displaced it in that spot.

bit was made with a "spring time special" model—the Fairlane fitted with a narrow anodized gold molding positioned within the loop formed by the stainless steel molding. It probably did not help contribute much to Ford's output, as production for the model year totaled barely over 950,000 units (less the T-Bird). The next model year would be much better, though, thanks to an improved economy and styling updates, which were well-received.

1959: Gold Medal Winner

The 1959s had substantial inner and outer body component alterations. The end result was a car much different in appearance than the 1958. In fact, the redesign resulted in the 1959 Fords being awarded the gold medal of the Comitée Français de l'Élégance at the Brussels World's Fair "for exceptional proportioning and elegance of line." Ford, taking advantage of their good fortune, boasted it had "The World's Most Beautifully Proportioned Car."

Buyers must have agreed because Ford almost outsold rival Chevrolet for the model year. The dashboard also sported a redesigned instrument panel, which included a flattened speedometer.

In all, there were 17 models available in the big Ford lineup at the beginning of the model year, which officially began with the dealer introduction of the cars on October 17, 1958 (the public got to see them on the 27th.

However, a short time later, four more models bearing the name Galaxie were added: a Club Victoria, Town Victoria, Club Sedan, and Town Sedan. A Thunderbird-inspired formal roofline distinguished these cars from the Fairlane 500 series. The Skyliner and Sunliner also became a Galaxie basically by default, as they represented top-of-the-line models.

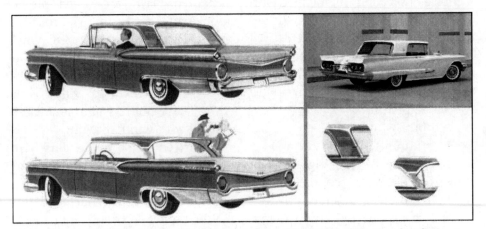

The new Galaxie's Thunderbird-inspired roofline differentiated the top-level car from the Fairlane 500, which had a narrow C-pillar post and wraparound backlight.

Interestingly, Galaxie script appeared on the quarters, but Fairlane 500 identification was mounted in back, technically making them Fairlane 500 Galaxies. Furthermore, all the closed cars wore a gold crest on the C-pillars.

Ford's revised sales catalog said of the new model, "Married in style to the Thunderbird!" It went on to tie the Galaxie with the Thunderbird through such phrases as, "Thunderbird in looks... Thunderbird in luxury... Thunderbird in everything but price," and, "If your family is too large for Ford's 4-passenger T-Bird, this 6-passenger, Thunderbird-like hardtop is for you!"

The Fairlane 500 series, with its narrow C-pillar and wraparound rear backlight, retained four of the same body styles (with the exceptions, of course, being the Skyliner and Sunliner) prior to the release of the Galaxie: Club Victoria, Town Victoria, Club Sedan, and Town Sedan. This year all of these models shared a 118-inch wheelbase. Prices increased this year and ranged from a low of $1,977 (Custom 300 Business Coupe) to $3,138 (Skyliner).

The pecking order for the rest of the line was the Fairlane and Custom 300, along with six station wagon models: Country Squire, nine-passenger Country Sedan, For-dor Country Sedan, Country Sedan, Fordor Ranch Wagon, and Ranch Wagon. The Fairlane was composed only of the Club and Town Sedans this time; the hardtops were dropped. Custom 300s continued with three offerings: Business Sedan, Tudor Sedan, and Fordor Sedan.

The differences in standard features were similar to past years. Custom 300s received bright-metal front and rear windshield moldings, a horn button rather than a ring, driver's side sun visor and armrest, and a single strip of trim on the body side. Fairlanes had a horn ring, passenger side sun visor, armrests for all doors, a two-piece body side molding (which could be had with an optional silver anodized insert), and chrome window frames. Before the release of the Galaxie, the Fairlane 500 line contained common Fairlane features and styling, such as the anodized silver insert along with ribbed aluminum panels on the rear quarters. It also had the three-tone upholstery until the Galaxie took the top spot on the roster. From that point, the Fairlane 500 got two-tone upholstery.

Galaxies were on view at the 1959 Chicago Auto Show. Models helped attract attention. A Town Sedan is in the background. (Photo courtesy of Charles D. Barnette collection)

The Skyliners roof mechanism and function was very complex. The Skyliner's roof function required an arrangement of approximately 600 feet of wiring connected to many power relays, circuit breakers, limit switches, drive motors, lock motors, a dashboard warning light, and a safety interlock to prevent operation without the transmission set to neutral.

This Ford dealership showroom reveals several new 1959 models including a pair of Country Sedans, a Sunliner, and a Custom 300 Tudor Sedan with a standard 6-cylinder engine. (Photo courtesy of Thomas Heidenfelder collection)

The Custom 300 series was composed of the Business Sedan, Tudor Sedan, and Fordor Sedan, which are shown here in clockwise orientation. Four chevron medallions mounted on the quarter panels were included on the latter two versions.

Quietly Impressive; No Buck Rogers

The January 1959 issue of *Car Life* magazine began their report on the new Ford's this way:

"The '59 Ford is a quietly impressive car. Although there's nothing wildly sensational about it in any given department, Ford delivers a very solid overall impression. First of all, the styling is sharp, clean and well balanced. Ford looks sleek and fast, yet the designers haven't been swept away by what you could call the 'Buck Rogers bit'—an attempt to make a car look like a TV set designer's conception of a space ship… The '59 Ford styling has swung back, and happily so in my book, to the functional. Gone are the useless and irritating quadruple tail lamps, the dummy air scoop and the dirt-catching roof grooves of the '58 model."

Not only was the writer comparing the new Ford's styling to that of the previous year model, but also to the competition from GM—probably directly to the new Chevrolet with its flared-out fins and deeply sculpted quarter panels. Some of the cars from GM were not necessarily viewed as the best styled at the time. That was quite a change, as GM had been viewed as the style leader for many years.

The writer also found favor with other attributes of his test car noting, "If early pilot production models are a good indication of what we may expect from the various Ford assembly plants this year, then the '59 Ford is going to be an outstanding solid and rattle-free car… Sound proofing, too, is unusually good… Although the suspension setup hasn't been changed much on the 59s, the ride seems a bit softer, yet at the same time better controlled on the bumps… Handling has improved by the addition of a link-type front stabilizer and is very good indeed."

Interestingly, the article noted the availability of the air suspension. Perhaps Ford was going to try it again, but nixed the idea prior to production since the option was not listed in Ford's brochures.

Another road test published simultaneously in *Motor Life* also had favorable remarks about the revised suspension, noting that the alterations "result in the softest ride Ford has ever offered, except perhaps that furnished in the relatively few air-suspended 1958 models built."

The *Motor Life* evaluation was a little less complimentary of the performance capability: "The performance picture, as might be expected, is not so bright. Lowered compression and use of a 2-barrel rather than a 4-barrel carburetor have reduced the horsepower rating of the 332-ci V-8 from 240 in 1958 to 225 as installed in 1959 models… When coupled to the two-speed automatic gearbox and 2.91 rear axle and saddled with a total weight of more than 4,000 pounds, including driver, it's obvious the engine is handicapped…" The writer went on to state the optional 3.10 rear axle "would probably be a better choice than the 2.91 ratio for most buyers." The optional 3.70:1 gear with the conventional stick shift offered for 352-powered cars was also recommended.

Another feature for the 1959 Fords was a new Ford-O-Matic automatic transmission. Though the name was the same as the previous years' automatic, this transmission was very different. It had two forward speeds and fewer parts. In fact, it weighed only 18 pounds more than the manual version, which was

The Skyliner was in its final year of production in 1959. A total of 12,915 were built, the least of its three-year lifespan.

A tri-tone interior was standard on Galaxies. Clear seat covers were dealer-installed accessories.

standard issue with the 6-cylinder engine. The optional Ford-O-Matic costs about $50 less than the older version and about $79 less than the top-of-the-line Cruise-O-Matic. The latter was available only with the 332- and 352-ci V-8s.

Interior and Paint Choices

Interiors were another characteristic used to set apart these series of models. The Custom 300 Tudor Business Sedan had one upholstery combination as standard issue: Gunsmoke Gray random block nylon with Gunsmoke Gray ribbed vinyl bolsters. The other Custom 300s also had that combination, along with blue and green random block nylon with ribbed vinyl bolsters.

Fairlane Club and Town Sedans had shadoweave nylon paired with bolsters in Sof-Textured vinyl. The respective color combinations were Gunsmoke Gray/radiant silver, blue/radiant blue, green/radiant green, and bronze/radiant bronze.

The Fairlane 500 Club and Town Sedans had another pattern: silver-flecked linen-pattern nylon with tweadweave nylon bolsters, with colors of gray/gray, gold/gray, blue/blue, green/green, bronze/ bronze, and turquoise/turquoise.

Fairlane Club and Town Victorias offered striped nub-fabric with silver strands sewn to bolsters of Sof-Textured vinyl. Respective color combinations numbered seven:

- blue/radiant blue
- green/radiant green
- bronze/radiant bronze
- Raven Black/radiant gold
- turquoise/radiant turquoise
- Geranium/radiant Colonial White
- Torch Red/radiant Colonial White

Thirteen Diamond Lustre paint colors were available:

- Raven Black
- Colonial White
- Torch Red
- Geranium
- Indian Turquoise
- Wedgewood Blue
- Surf Blue
- April Green
- Sherwood Green
- Inca Gold
- Fawn Tan
- Tahitian Bronze
- Gunsmoke Gray

Sun Ray wheel covers with the optional center dress-up kit adorn this 1959 Galaxie Fairlane 500 Skyliner.

Again, conventional two-tones were offered, as were Style-Tone paint schemes.

Options and accessories were mostly the same as those of 1958. New items included a dress-up package consisting of Tee-Ball fender ornaments, bright-metal darts on the quarter panels, and stainless steel fender skirts.

As mentioned earlier, Ford almost outsold rival Chevrolet for the model year. According to official records, Ford sold 1,394,687 big Fords, while GM's bow tie division is credited by various sources with anywhere from a 12,000-car margin of victory to as much as nearly 86,400 more full-size Chevys.

During the 1959 model year, Ford achieved an important milestone, building its 50-millionth car, a Colonial White Galaxie Town Sedan. It was sent on a transcontinental tour from New York City to Seattle. The car is now a part of the collection of the National Parts Depot in Florida. (Photo by Dick Rozum, Legendary Ford Magazine)

The 50-millionth Ford was equipped with a special black, gold, and white interior. (Photo by Dick Rozum, Legendary Ford Magazine)

The Galaxie proved to be highly popular with Ford buyers of 1959; well over 400,000 were built. This nameplate would stay in production into 1974.

La Galaxie

The 1958 *La Galaxie* was designed by David Ash (Advanced Studio), Bud Kaufman (Lincoln-Mercury Studio), Jim Powers (Advanced Studio), and Dick Noe (design engineer). According to authors Jim and Cheryl Farrell, Ash and John Najjar (head of the Lincoln studio) were studying astronomy in their spare time. Ash selected the name "La Galaxie" while looking through a telescope.

This unique styling exercise became a show car and appeared at the Detroit, Chicago, and New York Auto Shows and other venues, as well as being placed on display at the Ford Rotunda. Proposed features of the *La Galaxie* included Slide-A-Door parallel-action doors for entry/exit, though they were never actually built. Interior access was either through removal of the backlight and crawling inside or via a trapdoor underneath the car!

Another proposed feature was a small nuclear power plant to operate the *La Galaxie*; in reality, of course, no such nuclear system was installed and the show vehicle was a push-mobile. An additional gadget on the *La Galaxie* was a proximity warning device to alert the driver when he or she was too close to a car or other object in the path. This system probably was not functional either.

The *La Galaxie*'s interior, however, was functional. In fact, it was said to "look like a spaceship" when the interior lights were on. One of the many prominent styling features was the reverse-slant C-pillars similar to those of the 1958–1960 Continentals. One other feature of the show car was its flush-fitting glass—something that was eventually adopted by the auto industry. Its rear deck was a two-piece affair designed to be opened from the curbside.

In the end, the *La Galaxie* contributed little if anything to the design of Ford's production cars beyond its name. Ironically, many of the styling features were incorporated on Chrysler's 1963 Turbine Car! The headlight and taillight styling of both cars is very similar. (It was no coincidence. Elwood Engel, who headed the corporate advanced studio at Ford for a time, left the company in late 1961 to take charge of styling at Chrysler Corporation.) Just as notable, if not more so, was the definition of the name with its French spelling; Galaxie means "an assemblage of brilliant or noted people or ideas."

The *La Galaxie* was reportedly destroyed in late 1959 or early 1960 when being shown in Budapest, Hungary. According to Jim and Cheryl Farrell, authors of *Ford Design Department Concept and Show Cars, 1932–1961*, it was dropped from a forklift while being unloaded, cracking the fiberglass body.

1960: THE CONTROVERSIAL LOOK AND THE RETURN OF HIGH PERFORMANCE

Originally, Ford intended to build the 1960 full-size models on the one-year-old 1959 platform. However, after Ford's planning committee approved the design, arch rival Chevrolet unknowingly sent Ford scurrying to develop an all-new design.

According to writer Jim Farrell, Ford's marketing department had an arrangement with the General Motors' tool and die maker. After GM sent its plans to the tool and die maker, Ford immediately received a copy, too. When Ford's managers got a look at the plans, they did not believe them—they guessed GM had caught on to their scheme and sent bogus plans. Later, spy photographs of Chevrolet's clay mockups of their 1959 models confirmed the plans.

Concurrent with all of this activity was an unrelated project in the *Advanced Studio*, a show car eventually dubbed *Quicksilver*. When the spy photos were reviewed, the original planning was scrapped, and the Quicksilver eventually served as the archetype for the new car.

The Galaxie series included the Club Sedan shown here in Raven Black and Corinthian White. A total of 31,866 were built. **(Photo courtesy of Ronald Anderson)**

Ironically, Chevrolet's 1959 styling was not universally accepted. Some Chevy loyalists even switched to Ford. Even so, the flamboyantly styled Chevys outsold Fords in 1959 model year production, but Ford outpaced Chevrolet in calendar year output thanks in large part to the midyear introduction of the new Galaxie.

Despite being billed as "The Finest Fords of a Lifetime," Ford sales for this model year amounted to just 1,439,553 cars, which was slightly less than the 1,462,140 built the previous model year (with both figures including T-Birds). At a glance, that figure does not appear to be so bad, but closer inspection reveals that the 1960 output includes 435,676 compact Falcons, a car that did not exist one year earlier.

The meaning of the numbers was very clear to FoMoCo—sales of the 1960 full-size Fords were less than stellar, to put it mildly. Nevertheless, Ford's decision to use the *Quicksilver* design was probably the best option, as the original 1960 design featured an ungainly frontal area that probably would have been less popular than the 1958s.

This factory publicity photo shows a 1960 Galaxie Town Victoria equipped with the optional wheel covers and whitewall tires. It was the most popular of the Galaxie series, with 104,784 finding buyers.

Some states set a maximum width of 81½ inches for passenger cars, otherwise the offending vehicle was required to have side marker lamps. The 1960 Fords exceeded this limit by 1½ inches. Ford agreed to remedy the problem with the 1961s, and the law looked the other way.

This brochure showed the full line of Ford passenger cars for 1960, which included 15 full-size models such as the Galaxie, Fairlane, Fairlane 500, and station wagons. Engines ranged from the 223-ci inline 6-cylinder with 145 hp up to 360-hp 352-ci V-8.

The 1960 full-size Fords, priced from a low of $2,170 (Business Coupe) to $2,973 (Sunliner with base V-8), could be had in 15 versions. The new Starliner, a two-door hardtop with arching C-pillars "designed for those who yearn for a dashing sports car—for six passengers," according to Ford's sales literature. Five of the 15 models were station wagons.

Besides the addition of the Starliner, there were other changes to the lineup from the previous model year. The Skyliner was discontinued, the two-door version of the Country Sedan station wagon was dropped, as was the two-door hardtop Club Victoria. There were no Fairlane 500 hardtops, either. Therefore, the only hardtop models were the Starliner and the four-door Town Sedan in the Galaxie series.

The highest-selling car of the line was the Fairlane 500 Town Sedan with a production run of 153,234, followed by the Fairlane Fordor Sedan (109,801) and the Galaxie Town Sedan (104,784). On the other end of the scale, only 1,733 Business Coupes were built. The sporty Starliner brought 68,641 sales.

The newly designed full-size Fords were longer, lower, and wider than the 1959s. Overall length measured 213.7 inches and wheelbase grew to 119 inches. Height varied a bit by model, but the sedans and hardtop stood 55 inches high (54.5 inches for the Starliner), as compared to 56 for the 1959s.

The cars also swelled in overall width to enormous proportions; so much so, their width was illegal in some states! The rush to get the design completed in time perhaps caused the styling team to overlook that detail. Some states set a maximum width of 81½ inches for passenger cars, and the 1960 Fords exceeded this limit by 1½ inches. The over-wide vehicle would have to have side marker lamps. Edsel, in its last year, as well as Mercury, exceeded the limit, too. (Even Chevrolet and Oldsmobile slipped over the maximum allowed limit this year.) Ford was fortunate to get a one-year waiver on the side marker lamp requirement, and for 1961 its cars were under the 80-inch limit.

Front tread grew a full 2 inches to 61 and rear tread spanned 60 inches, up from 56.4. The so-called Wide-Tread Design, credited by Ford as offering greater stability, countered Pontiac's Wide Track theme begun one year earlier. The extra bulk did not cause a negative impression on those reporting for *Motor Life*. According to their February 1960 issue, the 1960 Ford was "one of the longest and is the widest of all 1960 models, yet it handles easy in town and is not difficult to park."

The cooling and exhaust systems also received updates. A cross-flow radiator replaced the older design, which was vulnerable to overheating in heavy traffic. As styling changed, radiators transitioned from tall and narrow to short and wide. Cooling fans had a limit on size and were not able to pull enough air through the radiator to cool it. Redesigning the radiator to allow coolant to flow across it solved that problem. The low height of the radiator allowed for the sloping hood (which was hinged at the back for the first time since 1956). Ford also included a 2-quart expansion tank mounted at the front of V-8 engines.

This Galaxie Club Sedan was ordered with the optional 352-ci 2-barrel advertised as producing 235 peak horsepower. Note the expansion tank, which was included on all V-8 engines. (Photo courtesy of Ronald Anderson)

Aluminized exhaust pipes and mufflers were standard this year. They resisted rust and permitted Ford's engineers to place the mufflers at the rear of the car where there is more room. Typically, engineers wanted mufflers as close to the engine as possible to use the hot exhaust to keep moisture out. As exhaust gases traveled the length of the exhaust system, the gases cooled, and therefore the front of the car was the ideal location for mufflers. However, with the ever-decreasing height and step-down floor design of cars muffler placement was made more challenging. Ford fixed that problem with their aluminized system.

The redesigned dashboard featured fuel and temperature gauges flanking the horizontal speedometer, which registered to 120 mph. To the right was the location for the clock. Below these, on either side of the steering column, were the various switches for the wipers, lights, etc. At the bottom of the arrangement was the ignition switch (on the left again) and the location for the heater/defroster. This was all housed within a flared, elongated oval

The new 1960 big Fords received a redesigned dashboard. The fuel and temperature gauges flanked the horizontal speedometer, which registered to 120 mph. All of the major gauges and controls were housed within a flared, elongated, oval-shaped opening.

shape. Further to the right was the location for the optional radio and the glove box.

Models and Trim

There was a long list of standard equipment for the Galaxie series, which encompassed the Starliner, Sunliner, Town Victoria, Club Sedan, and Town Sedan. This included stainless steel moldings for the A-pillars and windows, a horizontal body side molding, ribbed aluminum stone shields behind the rear wheel openings similar to those of the 1959 models, and another ribbed panel between the tail lamps. Also the "Galaxie" script appeared on the front fenders and deck lid, except in the case of the Starliner and Sunliner, which replaced the Galaxie script with the corresponding model name. In fact, the name "Galaxie" did not appear on these two models.

In addition to these features, the Starliner received three distinctive

External model identification for the Sunliner (and Starliner) was limited to a Ford crest on the hood and anodized gold script on the front fenders and deck lid. Half-moon taillights were a departure from the traditional round units.

four-point star ornaments on each C-pillar. Formal-roof cars had their lower C-pillars decorated with a ribbed molding. The 223-ci inline 6-cylinder with 145 hp and 3-speed-manual, column-shifted transmission were standard issue for the Galaxie series, as well as for the rest of the full-size line.

The intermediate series was the Fairlane 500, which consisted of the Club Sedan and Town Sedan. These models featured five chrome arrow-head moldings on the quarter panels, as well as bright work for the A-pillars and windows, and a ribbed molding for the base of the narrow C-pillars.

The Fairlane models, composed of the Club Sedan, Town Sedan, and Business Coupe, carried the least amount of bright exterior trim. A-pillars were left exposed, but window moldings were included all around, as was a ribbed molding for the C-pillars. In a step up from the past, this series came equipped

with two sun visors and armrests for all doors at no extra charge.

The Custom 300 was dropped as a model. However, it was an option for the Fairlane Club Sedan and Fairlane Town Sedan. Fleet buyers could purchase stripped-down versions of these cars for a $33 credit on each car bought. The option was ideal for taxi and police car applications. Deleted equipment included the chrome horn ring, armrests, passenger side

sun visor, and some cushioning in the seating. Of course, they could be ordered with additional equipment, such as the 352-ci Police Interceptor or other available options and accessories. Despite not being an official model, the body codes for cars with the Custom 300 option differed: Club Sedans were given the body code of 64H and Town Sedans, 58F. Only 302 Club Sedans and 572 Town Sedans had the Custom 300 option.

Standard equipment for station wagon models basically followed the hierarchy of the other passenger cars. The nine-passenger Country Squire, with its distinctive faux wood continued as the top-of-the-line station wagon model. Ford bragged that it "is truly the queen of the station wagon kingdom. It's perfectly at home on the grandest estates, in the best clubs... and the supermarket, too."

The mid-level wagons were the six- and nine-passenger Country Sedans. Lowest in price within the lineup was the Ranch Wagon in two-door and four-door forms. Ford's full-size station wagons offered 97 cubic feet of "bowling alley load space" and a loading entry claimed to be as much as 1½ feet wider than other stations wagons in the same price class.

"Nine Fit Fine," said Ford's station wagon literature in regard to the nine-passenger 1960 Country Sedan.

Upholstery and Paint

Upholstery selections varied by model. The Fairlane could be had with three combinations of black-stripe nylon cloth inserts and Morocco grain vinyl in green, blue, and gray, though the Business Coupe was restricted to gray. Fairlane 500s used the same cloth and vinyl, but added beige, bringing the choices to a total of four.

Galaxie sedans came with pleated tweed nylon cloth and Morocco grain vinyl bolsters in the following color schemes: green, blue, beige, turquoise, and a two-tone combo of white and black. The Galaxie Town Victoria and Starliner offered the buyer eight striped tweed nylon cloth/Morocco grain vinyl choices: green, blue, black, beige, turquoise, red, yellow, and lavender.

Galaxie Sunliner interiors could be purchased with any of six pleated Morocco grain vinyl color choices in two-tone or even three-tone patterns: blue/white, black/white/red, lavender/white, yellow/white/black, turquoise/white, and black/white. Convertible tops were in either black or white.

The Ranch Wagon came with three offerings of blue striped thong woven plastic inserts and ribbed Morocco grain vinyl in green, blue, and beige.

Country Sedan interiors were offered with three dash-pattern woven plastic inserts and ribbed Morocco grain vinyl with color selections of green, blue, and turquoise or two all-vinyl types with tweed print inserts and ribbed Morocco grain bolsters in choices of beige or a two-tone of white/red.

The Country Squire wagons were equipped with either pleated-thong nylon cloth inserts and ribbed

Galaxie Sunliner interiors could be purchased with any of six pleated Morocco grain vinyl color choices in two-tone or even three-tone patterns. In this case, the choice was black and white.

Morocco grain vinyl bolsters in choices of green, blue, and turquoise or with two all-vinyl combinations with pleated inserts and ribbed Morocco grain bolsters of beige or white/red.

Regardless of the upholstery chosen, the seating was advertised as being "chair high" with the seat backs front and rear positioned at a "posture perfect 23 degree angle for real living room comfort."

Exterior colors numbered 13, including Orchid Gray, a color limited to the Starliner, Sunliner, and Town Victoria models. The other 12 colors were:

- Meadowvale Green
- Platinum
- Sultana Turquoise
- Skymist Blue
- Corinthian White
- Belmont Blue
- Montecarlo Red
- Beachwood Brown
- Adriatic Green
- Raven Black
- Yosemite Yellow
- Aquamarine

Two-tone offerings, such as a Skymist Blue/Belmont Blue or Corinthian White/Montecarlo Red, were of the conventional type. Style-Tone patterns were discontinued.

Engines and Transmissions

Besides color choices, there were other considerations for the 1960 Ford owner to ponder: engine and transmission choices, along with a variety of options and accessories. Ford continued to offer the 292-ci Y-block for 1960. The engine was fed its air/fuel mixture via a 2-barrel carburetor, and with an 8.8:1-compression ratio, made 185 hp.

The 292-ci V-8 could be coupled to either the optional Ford-O-Matic or Cruise-O-Matic transmissions, but came standard with the column-shifted 3-speed manual. Overdrive continued to be an extra-cost option with the manual transmission.

Three 352-ci engines were available in 235-, 300-, and 360-hp guises. Either automatic transmission could be had with the 235-hp 352-ci; only

the Cruise-O-Matic could be purchased for the 300-hp engine. The high-performance 352-ci was offered only with the manual transmission because a high idle speed at 700 rpm was required for smooth operation. If the 352-ci had been equipped with an automatic, the driver would have to apply heavy brake pedal pressure at stop lights to keep the vehicle stationary. Furthermore, the Cruise-O-Matic's components as designed could not survive the stresses of high-performance driving.

Available Options

Some of the options and accessories listed for the 1960 Fords included:

- Equa-lock differential
- PolarAire (dealer-installed air conditioning) or SelectAire (factory-installed air conditioning), except with the 360 hp V-8
- MagicAire heater
- power steering (except with the 360-hp 352)
- power windows
- AM-radio
- rear speaker
- wheel covers
- rear-mounted antenna
- back-up lights
- clock (standard on Galaxies)

Ford advertising for many years tied the Thunderbird's mystique to the full-size line. This low-quality original advertisement depicting the 1960 Starliner declared, "The finest Fords of a lifetime bring you the Thunderbird's spirited performance." It listed the optional V-8s, including the Thunderbird 292, which had not been available in a T-Bird since the original two-seater version was built, and the 360-hp Thunderbird 352 Super V-8, also not available in a T-Bird.

The rare 360-hp 352-ci V-8 powers this restored 1960 Sunliner. This high-performance engine features 10.6:1 compression, a solid-lifter camshaft, heavier valvesprings adjustable rocker arm shaft, heavier crankshaft balancer, dual-point distributor without vacuum advance, 4-barrel Holley carburetor, aluminum intake manifold, cast-iron header-type exhaust manifolds, and dual exhausts.

- I-Rest tinted glass
- windshield washers
- electric windshield wipers
- rocker panel moldings
- remote deck lid release
- luggage rack for station wagons
- fender skirts
- bumper guards
- exhaust deflectors
- locking gas cap
- tissue dispenser

One other interesting accessory was red reflectors for the half-moon-shaped indentation at the ends of the rear bumper. These indentations were inverted mirror images of the taillight shape.

The 352-Powered Starliner

While the styling of the 1960 big Fords was not universally liked, the road test reporters had good things to write about their experiences driving the new car. The report published in the February 1960 issue of *Motor Trend* concluded, "For '60, Ford seems to be back to the good solid feel we used to like about their products years ago. Handling, brakes, and ride are vastly improved over the '59 and the fuel economy is good for such a big engine. Interiors are well detailed, and the bodies and doors have a real solid feel."

Other favorable comments included "legible instrumentation," "good heating and ventilation," and "uniform and convenient control knobs." The unfavorable commentary included "braking difficult without power assist... poor placement of spare tire," and "performance not up to advertised horsepower."

A 352-ci with an advertised 300 hp powered this particular *Motor Trend* test car. However, the magazine's next article in the same issue gave the details of Ford's new 360-hp 352-ci: "For those who want the ultimate in performance from their '60 Fords, there's an extra 'Go!' package that ups the output of the 300-hp engine to 360."

The so-called Go! package consisted of:

- cylinder heads that contribute to a 10.6:1-compression ratio
- solid-lifter camshaft
- heavier valvesprings with flat wound steel dampers to inhibit valve float
- adjustable rocker arm shaft
- oil pump with a different pressure relief spring to give 55 to 65 psi at 1,000 rpm
- heavier crankshaft balancer
- larger generator pulley for higher RPM operation
- solid pushrods
- dual-point distributor without vacuum advance
- Champion F83Y spark plugs
- 4-barrel Holley carburetor
- 3/8-inch gas line (3/16-inch on other engines)
- aluminum intake manifold with larger passages
- cast-iron header type exhaust manifolds
- dual exhausts

Tubular pushrods from the Falcon's 6-cylinder, as well as an oil cooler were also available, the latter was bolted to the block in place of the oil filter. The cast-aluminum oil cooler was itself cooled by water. Peak horsepower for this engine was achieved at 6,000 rpm, while peak torque of 380 ft-lbs occurred at 3,400 rpm.

The chassis also received some upgrades: new axle shaft, new differential, heavier stabilizer bar, stiffer front springs, and heavy-duty brakes with 3-inch shoes in front. Available over-the-parts-counter were 15-inch wheels, heavy-duty spindles with shorter steering arms giving a steering ratio of about 18:1, and heavy-duty steering linkage. Power steering was not available with the 360-hp 352-ci because of the high engine idle. The suspension, as in past years, employed coil springs in front and leaf springs in back.

A 3-speed manual transmission with or without overdrive was the only choice with the 360-hp engine. It used an 11-inch clutch with 1,710 pounds of spring pressure and 113 square inches of lining area. For comparison, the 3-speed issued with the 300-hp 352-ci had a spring pressure of 1,575 pounds. A 10.5-inch clutch with 2,495 pounds of spring pressure was available through Ford's parts department.

The story in *Motor Trend* revealed a 1960 Ford equipped with the 360-hp engine and 3.56:1 gearing could be pushed to 152 mph as shown at the Ford Proving Grounds. Motor Trend tested a prototype Starliner with this engine coupled to a 3-speed transmission with overdrive and 4.86:1 differential. Their 0–60 mph time was seven seconds flat, which was at least three seconds faster than the 300-hp engine could do. They also discovered their high-performance test car to be "remarkably docile in traffic" and "...the engine is reasonably smooth and quieter than one would expect with the wild cam." Handling was judged as "excellent, with a firm feel."

Hot Rod magazine also tested a 360-hp Starliner. Their December 1959 issue declared, "Here's the performer you've been waiting for—a 360 hp V8 capable of pushing a stock-bodied coupe over the 150 mph mark." They found a top speed of exactly 152.6 mph.

Ray Brock, writer for the *Hot Rod* report, recommended the Police Interceptor suspension and heavy-duty brakes. However, the test car had standard brakes, which were evaluated as "very good." (Even the standard brakes were larger than

those of the prior year. Ford advertised them as "truck size brakes... the biggest in Ford's field.") The car tested did have the Police Interceptor suspension and it was found to be "outstanding when pushed around the Ride and Handling section of the proving grounds." A "box top" Galaxie with the standard suspension was also given a comparison test and was said to be "almost as good."

The same prototype Starliner, equipped with the Police Interceptor suspension, was taken to the 2½-mile oval of the Daytona International Speedway in August 1959, where race car driver Cotton Owens tested the car's Firestone racing tires for 40 laps at an average speed of 142 mph. An additional five laps were run at an average speed of 145.5 mph. Instead of asking the Holman-Moody team to prepare the car, Ford hired the lesser-known Wood Brothers team, which hired Owens to do the driving.

Once the results of the testing became public, a lot of drivers wanted to race a Ford. Holman-Moody soon began offering to independent drivers a race-ready Starliner for $4,995. Chassis modifications for speedway racing included completely rewelded frame rails, heavier control arms, twin shocks per side in front and back, and stronger brakes.

Many buyers used their new Ford for common driving, but those who opted for the less lively 300-hp 352-ci with the Cruise-O-Matic could get remarkably good fuel mileage. *Motor Trend* reported 18.4 mpg at a constant 60 mph and found a maximum speed of 110 to 115 mph. The 300-hp cars provided 0–60 mph times of around 11 seconds during typical road tests.

Strangely, Ford assigned the Y code to both the 300-hp and 360-hp 352s, which makes identifying an

altered 300-hp car more difficult for enthusiasts. Three-inch-wide front brake shoes and a longer brake line running across the front frame crossmember were a couple of unique features of the 360-hp 352 Fords. The high-performance engine adds value to any 1960 Ford so equipped, especially the popular Starliner and Sunliner models.

Fords in Racing Competition

Ford honored the AMA agreement on banning factory-backed racing and promotion of high-performance driving from its inception. But by now, insiders at Ford realized everyone else was ignoring the ban. Ford soon began reconsidering its participation in the agreement.

In 1959, only one big Ford appeared on the speedways of the National Association for Stock Car Racing (NASCAR). For 1960, 32 cars entered the Daytona 500 and 24 qualified for the race. Fans, drivers, and mechanics soon learned Ford had more work to do to be competitive. Running at 145 to 150 mph for relatively short distances was not the same as doing it for 500 miles. In the 200-mile qualifying races, Fords finished third and thirteenth, but blown engines were a problem for several Fords in their first 500-mile race. Even so, Fords finished the prestigious race sixth, seventh, and eighth with drivers Ned Jarrett, Curtis Turner, and Fred Lorenzen, respectively. Three cars finishing in the top ten was definitely not a bad result for Ford drivers. Ford teams got better with experience and managed 15 wins—more than any other make—in NASCAR Grand National racing. (However, only ten of these wins were achieved with 1960 Fords.) Joe

Weatherly accounted for three of the wins for the Holman-Moody team. The sleek roofline of the Starliner certainly played a roll in these victories.

In USAC stock car competition, driver Norm Nelson won three of the nine events in a 1960 Fairlane sedan sponsored by Zecol-Lubaid, Inc. In so doing, he took the series championship. He and Don White (also sponsored by Zecol-Lubaid) finished first and third, respectively, in the final 250-mile race of the USAC season. Nelson Stacy won the Midwest Association for Race Cars (MARC) championship driving a 1960 Fairlane sedan, too.

On the drag strips, Ford had difficulty beating the Chevrolets, Dodges, Plymouths, and Pontiacs, but Ford drivers were able to set a few records. Since the Fords were rated at 360 hp, they were forced to compete in the Super Stock class. Furthermore, they also competed in only the stick shift class because an automatic transmission was not offered for the high-performance engine.

While some Ford personnel had a considerable amount of interest in the 1960 race season, the Blue Oval was not backing any racers at this point—a policy that changed for 1961. The change coincided with the departure of Ford President Robert McNamara to join the John F. Kennedy administration as Secretary of Defense. Lee Iacocca filled the vacancy.

Quicksilver

The 1960 full-size Fords came as the result of various factors that intersected and changed the design process almost at once. Initially, the 1960 Ford was to be built on the 1959 platform. That changed over a short time with the introduction of the 1957 Chrysler product line, the discovery of Chevrolet's plans for 1959, and a proposed concept car dubbed *Quicksilver.*

Chrysler's 1957 car lines startled the designers at GM and Ford, and the public responded very favorably to the styling. According to an article written by historian Michael Lamm, after his first peek at the 1957 Chrysler cars, GM stylist Chuck Jordan said, "They looked so clean and lean with that thin roof and nice proportions of glass, just the opposite of what we were doing at GM."

What no one realized early in the model year was that Chrysler's cars were highly rust-prone. Of course, that had nothing to do with the fabulous styling. When Jordan got a sneak peek at the 1957 Plymouths, he made sure his associates got a look. They all agreed GM was headed in the wrong direction for its 1959 models. Major changes occurred rapidly in regard to GM's styling for that model year. When Ford got its own sneak peek at Chevrolet's 1959 clay mockups, Ford's planners had to reconsider the direction they were taking. Luckily, they had a show car in progress, which could be readied for production for 1960.

Joe Oros, who headed the Ford studio, believed that Chrysler's new Forward Look cars might be extremely popular and thus Ford needed to consider and use some of these styling ideas. Oros put Jim Darden, one of the most experienced designers at Ford, in charge of the project that became the *Quicksilver.* Oros gave a sketch to Darden that illustrated the basic design he wanted. His design included sloping front end, horizontal fins, and oval taillights. Interestingly, the wrap-around front windshield, a styling fad from the 1950s, was not included in the design.

Once Darden's design team completed its proposal, a full-scale clay model was created with one side shaped as a two-door and the other as a four-door. When the mockup was unveiled to George Walker, head of the Ford Design Department, he immediately approved it and ordered a show car be built from the design.

Ford soon learned that Chrysler's new car lineup was successful, and the styling was widely applauded. This, together with the knowledge of Chevy's 1959 styling, gave cause for deep concern among those responsible for the 1960 Fords. McNamara, now vice president of Ford, was approached with the idea of changing the already approved plans for these cars. McNamara and others went to the Product Planning Committee with the recommendation that a crash program be quickly approved for making major changes to the 1960 plan. Meanwhile, the *Quicksilver* mockup was set aside in the pre-production studio while the original 1960 Ford design got revised.

Quicksilver kept getting a lot of attention from the stylists, though. And finally, Henry Ford II made the decision to base the 1960 Ford on it. Various alterations were made to the *Quicksilver* design to get to the final layout for the 1960 Ford line. The oval taillights were changed to the half-moon type, with the lower half being made into a design in the bumper. The overall height of the car was also increased. Show cars have often served as the basis for future production features. In the case of *Quicksilver,* it went from show car to production car without even being a show car!

1961: THE CLASSIC LOOK AND MORE HORSEPOWER

The 1961 full-size Fords marked a return to a style Ford called the Classic Look. As a result, these models featured conservative fins, large round taillights, and new sheetmetal from the belt-line down to resemble the very popular 1957 and 1959 Fords.

The *Ford Dealer* magazine dated September/October 1960 explained the new look this way: "In a year when heavy emphasis is being placed on the loyalty of Ford owners—when every effort is being expended to build friends for Ford—the Classic Look, so well accepted in the past, has been restored to the 1961 Ford. It's literally custom built to win friends and keep them." The wording almost seemed like an apology for the look of the 1960 models, which many considered too radically styled at the time.

Styling of the 1961 models won the approval of the internationally recognized fashion authority, Centro per L'Alta Moda Italiana, which gave the 1961 Fords their award for "functional expression of classic beauty."

Despite being "literally custom built to win friends" and the styling award, the 1961 full-size lineup did

A new jeweled-button grille was one of the distinctive styling updates for the big Fords for 1961. This Raven Black Starliner was one of 29,669 were built for the model year.

not sell any stronger, and production dropped further. Total production fell by more than 119,500 units, as an economic recession plagued the auto industry. The recession, however, does not fully account for the lower sales. Even though sales dropped by about 200,000 units, Chevy still managed to sell over 400,000 more full-size cars than Ford this model year.

The contemporary automotive publications of the day had many favorable comments about the big 1961 Fords. In their October 1960 issue, *CARS* magazine said the test drive of a Fairlane Town Sedan

showed "the Fairlane... to reflect a logical and comfortable concept of automobile design. A happy combination of good taste, comfort and safety, the car stands an excellent chance of leadership in a class that's a little above the compact idea, but considerably below that of the all-out luxury extremes."

The March 1961 issue of *Motor Life* gave this opinion in regard to the revised styling: "Many design features from 1960 have been retained, but with sufficient changes to make this Ford's most attractive car in two years." The road test went on to say, "Front and rear end treatment is distinctive and different, and gives the car more of a 'Ford look' than its predecessor. From the indented horizontal grille, massive wraparound bumper and dual headlights to the subdued rear fins and circular taillights, the car is clean, sleek, and crisp... the entire car is better proportioned."

Inches were trimmed from the overall length and width of the 1961 big Fords. Overall length decreased to 209.9 inches and overall width spanned 79.9 inches, but interior dimensions were unaffected. Overall height measurements for the models remained unchanged, as they did for the wheelbase, front tread, and rear tread. Along with the reduced dimensions went a small weight decrease of roughly 50 pounds per model.

Beyond the retro taillights and mildly canted conservative fins, the so-called classic look Fords received an updated concave grille with center horizontal bar, directional lights in the wraparound front bumper, and torpedo-like sheetmetal bulges running fore and aft to round out the headlight and taillight encasements. The deck lid was nearly 10 inches wider than the 1960, allowing for easier access to the trunk.

The interiors received a cosmetic facelift, too. While the overall shape of the dash appeared the same, the instrumentation did not. The horizontal speedometer was a dual-plane design with the numerals on one level and the needle moving within a recess. An arrowhead shape outlined the fuel gauge on the left, while the clock was housed in a mirror-image arrowhead form opening to the right. The temperature gauge, marked simply with C and H, sat within a rounded-corner, square recess between the speedometer and

This 1961 full-size Fords brochure featured a Galaxie Club Victoria on the front cover. The two-door hardtop Galaxie was last offered for the 1959 model year.

clock location. Knobs were labeled above rather than on their bezels. The lower instrument panel was basically the same as the one for 1960. Door panels and upholstery patterns were also revised.

Mechanical enhancements to the brakes included increased brake lining area (up from 191 to 212 square inches), improved brake pedal geometry for better mechanical advantage, and self-adjusting brakes (based on those of Lincoln-Mercury). New, tough plastic seals and liners in combination with a new type of grease with a molybdenum-disulfide base lengthened chassis lubrication service interval to every 30,000 miles. Grease fittings were deleted from the 1961s and small threaded plugs were substituted. For lubrication, Ford service technicians temporarily installed normal grease fittings. However, chassis lube was extended to every

The Starliner was equipped with pleated shimmer-patterned nylon cloth, bright Mylar border, and Morocco grain vinyl bolsters. Black and yellow was one of seven standard color combinations.

Interiors for 1961 received modest styling changes. Though the instrument panel was similar to that of 1960, the speedometer had a dual-plane design. Comfort-Height, Posture-Perfect seats on the Starliner were covered in a combination of cloth and vinyl.

30,000 miles, with oil changes being recommended every 4,000 miles.

Other updates included a lighter, more flexible frame with a stronger body, a closed-crankcase ventilation system (standard on the 300-hp 390-ci), tempered sheet glass in place of the laminated type, softer rear springs on four-door models, re-calibrated shock absorbers, a new flexible coupling in the steering shaft along with new needle type and nylon bearings, and insulation improvements, plus the aluminized mufflers were now double-wrapped "for triple the normal life." Manual

A total of 44,614 Sunliners were built for 1961. The Sunliner offered a white or black vinyl convertible top, vinyl upholstery, and two-speed electric windshield wipers as standard issue.

Standard external trim for the Galaxie series included front fender ornaments, horizontal stainless steel spear, ribbed aluminum stone shields behind the rear wheel openings, and a stamped anodized aluminum panel between the taillights. Fender skirts, dual rear-mounted antennas, wheel covers, and bumper guards were extra-cost items.

For 1961, you could get a Country Squire in six- or a nine-passenger configurations. Six station wagon variants were in the lineup this model year.

A 220-hp, 352-ci V-8 powers this Desert Gold and Corinthian White Starliner. The engine is coupled to a Cruise-O-Matic 3-speed automatic transmission. Other options on this restored car include air conditioning and power brakes.

steering was also claimed to require up to 25-percent-less effort thanks to an increased ratio. Power steering was also improved for this model year. With these and other refinements, plus the updated styling, Ford claimed the new 1961 Ford was "beautifully built to take care of itself."

Sixteen Models

The series lineup for big Fords for 1961 was unchanged from 1960 (Galaxie, Fairlane 500, Fairlane, and the station wagon line), but there were some changes affecting three of the four series of cars resulting in 16 models. Within the Galaxie series, again, were the Club Sedan, Town Sedan, Town Victoria, Sunliner, plus the Starliner.

However, there was an additional body style added for 1961—the two-door hardtop Club Victoria was back. The Victorias, with their Thunderbird-inspired square roof, were very popu-

lar, and Ford sold 105,779. Well over two-thirds of that figure were the revived two-door hardtop Club Victoria, which incidentally had a base price matching that of the Starliner: $2,599.

Most popular for this model year was the Galaxie Town Sedan, with 141,823 units built. Sales of the Business Coupe were so low that Ford dropped it from the Fairlane lineup. The Custom 300 option for the Fairlane did return despite its very low

The Starliner featured an action-styled roofline with a trio of three, four-point stars on the thin, arcing C-pillars. This Monte Carlo Red example is powered by the 401-hp 390.

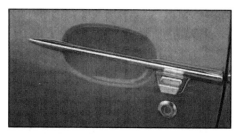

Flush-fitting, finial blade door handles flowed into the modest canted fins of the big Fords for 1961.

The thin-pillared, bubble-like, fastback roof with a trio of chrome ornaments decorating the thin C-pillars were exclusive features of the Starliner.

Ribbed-aluminum stone shields behind the rear wheel openings were standard issue on Galaxie models, including the Starliner.

sales; they were even lower this year with only 49 Club Sedans (body 64H) and 303 Town Sedans (body 58F) built—about 38 percent fewer than for 1960. This would be the final model year for that option. Starliner sales also plunged by more than 50 percent, with the total production reaching only 29,669 units.

The Country Squire gained a six-passenger version to go with the nine-passenger model. In addition to the six- and nine-passenger Country Squires, station wagon models were comprised of six- and nine-passenger Country Sedans, and the two- and four-door Ranch Wagons.

More Cubic Inches, More Power

The 390-ci joined the FE engine series, which began in 1958 in 332- and 352-ci displacements. The new 390-ci V-8 was created from the 352 block, but bore was increased .05 inch and stroke was lengthened .28 inch. The 390-ci was perhaps the most significant mechanical advent of the year, but we'll get back to it in a moment.

As before, pedestrian but economical powerplants were also offered. These included the Mileage-Maker 223-ci 1-barrel, the aging Thunderbird 292-ci 2-barrel Y-block, and the Thunderbird Special 352-ci 2-barrel. All three engines received lowered horsepower ratings this year: both the six and the Y-block lost 10 hp, while the 352-ci dropped 15 hp. The 300- and 360-hp 352s were deleted from the engine lineup, as the 390-ci took over high-performance duties.

The new 390-ci was available in 300-, 330-, 375-, and 401-hp variations, and all but the 330-hp engine were designated with the code Z in the serial number. The 300-hp version, also dubbed the Thunderbird Special, was equipped with a single 4-barrel carburetor, had 9.6:1 compression ratio, and hydraulic lifters. The next step up, the 330-hp engine code P, was ostensibly available solely to law enforcement agencies. It had solid lifters, high-lift camshaft, and header-type exhaust manifolds.

The top two performers in the group (375 and 401 hp), labeled Thunderbird Super V-8, were developed with factory-backed racing in mind. Both benefitted from a stronger block, enlarged oil passages, 10.6:1 compression, solid lifters, a high-lift cam (same as the 360-hp 352-ci), stronger push rods, heavier valvesprings, cast-iron headers, high-performance oil pump, and large port aluminum intake manifolds. An aluminum timing chain cover was also used to reduce the weight a bit on all 390s.

The 401-hp engine received its air/fuel mixture from a trio of Holley 2-barrel carbs with progressive linkage. This setup was dubbed the 6V Package and was sold over the parts

This 1961 Starliner is equipped with a 401-hp, 390-ci V-8. A trio of Holley 2-barrel carburetors sits under that oval air cleaner. A high-performance 375-hp 390-ci with a single 4-barrel carb was also offered. A manual 3-speed, column-shifted transmission, with or without overdrive, was required with the high-performance engines.

A trio of Holley 2-barrel carburetors with progressive linkage atop an aluminum intake feeds the air/fuel mixture to the combustion chambers. This setup was delivered in the trunk for dealer installation.

counter for $206.71. The 375-hp 390 was equipped with a single Holley 4-barrel. Both engines could handle revving to 6,500 rpm. Multiple carburetors were still not legal for the speedway races, but were allowed in drag racing. In fact, the 6V setup became available in late 1960, just in time to qualify for the NHRA Winternationals.

The available transmissions consisted of the Borg-Warner T-85 3-speed manual with overdrive optional and two automatics. The 2-speed Ford-O-Matic and the 3-speed Cruise-O-Matic were not offered with the high-performance engines.

A Borg-Warner T-10 4-speed manual transmission became available as a dealer-installed option in time to qualify for use in the NHRA Nationals held on Labor Day. It was a very welcomed addition among performance-oriented Ford fans. However, not everyone was pleased with it. The unit was very similar to the one Borg-Warner sold for use in Chevys, Pontiacs, and Studebaker Hawks—and General Motors' engineers designed

it! Understandably, GM was not pleased that Ford would be using it. The ratios in the Ford unit were not the same, though, which may have helped mitigate the delicate matter between the companies.

The Cruise-O-Matic also got its share of refinements, including a system of vacuum-throttle valve controls for smoother, more precise shifting without the need for periodic adjustment. A vacuum line connection eliminated the mechanical shift linkage completely. The weight of this transmission also decreased by about 25 pounds.

Racing

As previously stated, the higher performing 390s were part of Ford's involvement in racing. Ford got more serious about its racing efforts thanks in part to then General Manager Lee Iacocca. Iacocca knew the value of winning and believed Ford had lost its performance-car image, and the right image mattered greatly to the growing youth market.

Fred Lorenzen drove this Starliner for the factory-backed Holman-Moody racing team. He won three races in 1961, had six top-five and six top-ten finishes.

The 1961 season opened with Speedweeks and the third Daytona 500, but Ford wasn't officially backing anyone. At the Daytona Speedweeks, a 375-hp Starliner set a flying-mile class record of 159.320 mph. Ford was well represented with 21 of the 58 cars on the Daytona 500 Speedway. Fred Lorenzen, driving a Starliner owned by another driver, put the first Ford across the finish line taking fourth place in the process. Pontiacs took the first three places. Fireball Roberts in his Smokey Yunick-prepared 1961 Pontiac sat on the poll position by qualifying at a record 155.709 mph.

Curtis Turner, driving a Wood Brothers Starliner, qualified at 153.4 mph. The fastest Fords to date were still a few miles per hour slower than the lighter and well-prepared Pontiacs.

After Daytona, Ford backed Holman-Moody and the Wood Brothers. Ford managed seven wins in Grand National competition in 1961; three of these were super-speedway events, including the Rebel 300 convertible race at Darlington.

In USAC competition, Ford backed Zecol-Lubaid and the former Zecol driver, Norm Nelson, who had gone independent. Ford took seven wins in 22 events against Chevy's singular win in USAC. In the USAC-sanctioned Pike's Peak Hill Climb, Fords finished second, fourth, and fifth; Louis Unser drove a 409-powered 1961 Bel Air driven to first place. At the time, though, Pontiac was still the king of the racing circuit, with 30 Grand National and 14 USAC wins, but Ford was a rising star.

Pontiac, however, was not nearly as competitive on the drag strip. Chevys and Fords outdid all other competition at Pomona Raceway in Los Angeles. In the end, however, a 409-powered Chevy won the Super Stock class. It was a battle that probably could have gone either way, as the winning run was 13.63 seconds at 105.26 mph—an early run in a 401-hp Starliner ended in 13.33 seconds at 105.50 mph.

Even the 300-hp 390-ci offered some decent performance on the street. *Motor Life* reported a 0-60 mph time of 9.9 seconds in their test car, a Galaxie Club Victoria with the Cruise-O-Matic and a 2.91:1 rear axle. For comparison, they ran the same test on a 292-powered car, and came up with 16.4 seconds. Fuel mileage, by the way, was up to 15.5

mpg in highway driving conditions and as low as 9.3 mpg in heavy city traffic, while the 292-ci provided 17 mpg on the highway.

Standard and Optional Equipment

Standard equipment for the Galaxie series again included: front fender ornaments, stainless A-pillar and window moldings, hood lip molding, horizontal stainless steel spear blending into ribbed aluminum stone shields behind the rear wheel openings, a stamped anodized aluminum panel between the taillights, and back-up lights.

The interior featured an electric clock, nylon and vinyl upholstery, front and rear armrests, color-keyed rayon carpeting. The drivetrain package was a 223-ci Mileage-Maker 6-cylinder and 3-speed manual transmission.

Similar standard equipment was included on the Country Squire, though it lacked the stone shields on the quarters and woodgrain filled the area between the tail lamps rather than aluminum décor.

The Starliner remained distinctive due to its thin-pillared, bubble-like, fastback roof with a trio of chrome ornaments decorating the thin C-pillars. According to the 1961 *Ford Buyer's Digest*, the "Distinctive fastback roof line and silhouette evolved from extensive wind tunnel tests for efficient aerodynamic shape."

The Sunliner offered a white or black vinyl convertible top and vinyl upholstery and two-speed electric windshield wipers as standard issue.

Fairlane 500s came standard with the Mileage-Maker Six and 3-speed manual transmission. Exte-

rior styling consisted of a hood lip molding, bright A-pillar and window moldings, horizontal stainless steel spear molding, and Ford crest on the fuel-filler door. Nylon and vinyl upholstery, front armrests, and a color-keyed, two-toned, vinyl-rubber floor covering graced the interior.

The Fairlane series used the same standard powertrain as all other big Fords. Bright moldings for the front and rear windshields were standard, as was a stainless front fender molding and a Ford crest on the fuel-filler door. Standard wheel size was the same as on the Galaxie and Fairlane 500 series: 14-inch with 5.5-inch rims. The floor covering was a carpet-textured black rubber mat. Ford was never reserved about promoting its products, and said of the Fairlane 500: "Ford's great value leader gives you more standard extra values at no extra cost!"

Standard equipment for the woody-look Country Squires, as mentioned, was similar to that of the upscale Galaxies. Both versions of this model, as well as the nine-passenger Country Sedan, came standard with a power-operated tailgate window. The feature was optional on all other wagons. Otherwise, both Country Sedans were equipped similarly to the Fairlane 500 line, but also had front fender ornaments and carpet-textured black rubber floor coverings, while the floors of the Ranch Wagons were covered with black Saf-Tred rubber. Load-space floor coverings for all wagons were the same color-keyed ribbed vinyl.

A wide variety of options and accessories were available to the 1961 Ford buyer, such as:

- Master-Guide power steering
- Swift Sure power brakes
- power windows

- four-way Finger Touch power front seat
- padded dash
- seat belts
- SelectAire or Polar Aire air conditioner (except with the 375- and 401-hp engines).
- I-Rest tinted glass
- two-speed electric wipers (standard on the Sunliner)
- a push-button AM-radio transistor radio
- back-up lights (standard on Galaxies and Country Squires)
- bumper guards
- rocker panel trim
- remote trunk release
- compass
- vacuum-operated litter disposal
- two-tone paint (except Country Squires and Sunliner)
- wheel covers
- rear fender shields
- choice of wide whitewall tires or narrow-band white-walls
- Sport Spare Wheel Carrier
- hood ornament
- fender skirts

This was the final year for wide whites and the Sport Spare Wheel Carrier.

Paint and Interior

Once again, Ford offered a wide spectrum of color codes for its full-size models. Paint colors in Diamond Lustre Enamel totaled 13, one more than the prior year:
- Corinthian White
- Raven Black
- Montecarlo Red
- Aquamarine
- Garden Turquoise

- Cambridge Blue
- Chesapeake Blue
- Starlight Blue
- Algiers Bronze
- Desert Gold
- Silver Gray
- Laurel Green
- Mint Green

Two-tones were offered, such as Mint Green/Laurel Green, Aquamarine/Garden Turquoise, and Starlight Blue/Cambridge Blue, etc. Buyers could choose a Corinthian White roof with any other available color for the lower body. Incidentally, Ford claimed the paint never needed waxing.

Upholstery choices for the Comfort-Height, Posture-Perfect seats were numerous, and as per the past routine, they varied by model. Galaxies, including the Starliner, were equipped with pleated shimmer-patterned nylon cloth, bright Mylar border, and Morocco grain vinyl bolsters in the following color schemes: black/white pearl, black/yellow, brown, blue, green, red/white pearl, and turquoise.

The Sunliner differed with Morocco grain vinyl bolsters and pleated vinyl inserts with bright Mylar border in color choices of black/white pearl, black/yellow, two-tone blue, red/white pearl, and two-tone turquoise.

Fairlane 500s were upholstered in slat-patterned nylon cloth with Morocco grain vinyl bolsters; colors were blue, brown, gray, green, and turquoise. The low-cost Fairlanes had chain-striped-pattern nylon cloth with Morocco grain vinyl bolsters in just blue, gray, and green.

Upholstery for the Country Squire was similar to that of the Galaxie series, but did not include black/yellow and black/pearl white two-tones. The model also added

another pattern choice: Morocco grain vinyl bolsters and pleated vinyl inserts with a bright Mylar border in brown or red/white pearl. The mid-level Country Sedans also offered two upholstery patterns: block-patterned nylon cloth and Morocco grain vinyl bolsters or tweed-patterned vinyl and Morocco grain vinyl bolsters. The former came in blue, green, or turquoise, while the latter was offered in brown or two-tone red/white (not pearl).

Ranch wagons had fewer color selections, but like their higher priced counterparts, offered a choice of two upholstery patterns. These were stripe-patterned woven plastic with Morocco grain vinyl bolsters or a straw-patterned Morocco grain vinyl insert with Morocco grain vinyl bolsters. Blue and green were the only two color offerings for the former pattern, while the latter was limited to brown.

Interiors on all models were equipped with the so-called Lifeguard features: deep-dish steering wheel, safety-contoured dash, cushioned armrests, double-grip door locks, shatter-resistant double-swivel rearview mirror, and padded sun visors.

Looking Ahead

Sales during the 1961 model year were not as good as desired, nor were the race results. However, the 1962 models had already been designed—even before the 1961s went on sale. The 1962s would bring more excitement to the Ford lineup due to more cubic inches, more horsepower, and Lee Iacocca's mid-year introduction of some "Extra Lively" cars. There was even a bit of controversy thrown in as well!

1962 -1963:

THE EXTRA LIVELY ONES

Once again, the full-size Fords introduced to the public on September 29, 1961, appeared completely different with new sheetmetal, grille, taillights, trim, and bumpers. They were slightly shorter, narrower, lower, and even quieter than the 1961 models. The interior was not exempt from fresh styling either, and there was more horsepower. Such model year updates were the norm, but changes for 1962 went beyond fresh sheetmetal, dimensional differences, and mechanical tweaks.

One of the several notable changes was the elimination of the Starliner, and with its departure, the sleek roofline. All closed non-wagon models had the T-Bird-inspired box-top roof, which soon created a problem for those who were racing Fords on the super-speedways. An unusual solution to the drag-inducing boxy roofline was developed for the race car drivers, but it lasted for only a very brief time during the model year (more on this later in this chapter).

Also lost this year was the two-door wagon. The Fairlane and Fairlane 500 nameplates went to a newly created mid-size or "senior compact"

This Corinthian White 1962 Galaxie 500/XL Sunliner is one of 13,183 built for the model year. The pictured example is equipped with the optional Thunderbird 352-ci Special. Other extra-cost items include the stainless steel fender skirts, wire wheel covers, and outside rearview mirrors.

line to fill the void between the big Fords and the compact Falcon. Galaxie (or Galaxie 100 in some literature) became the low-priced series, while the Galaxie 500 series became the upper level of big Fords. The new Galaxie 500/XL was introduced mid-year. It was aimed at the emerging youth market composed of those who were seeking sporty attributes in their cars—a market niche clearly revealed with the success of Chevy's Corvair Monza equipped

with bucket seats. Additional horsepower was made available in the form of the M-series 390 ci and a pair of 406-ci V-8s.

The 1962 Lineup

The model year began with 12 models divided among the Galaxie, Galaxie 500, and station wagon lines. In the low-priced series, Galaxie, were two body styles: the two-door and four-door sedan.

Galaxie (or Galaxie 100 in some literature) became the low-priced series, while the Galaxie 500 series became the upper level of big Fords. The Fairlane nameplate went to a new intermediate-size Ford.

This grille was another feature of the Galaxie 500/XL. It housed the optional rear radio speaker when ordered. The dip in the seat back of the rear bench seat gave the look of bucket seats.

Ford strongly promoted its mid-year introduction of the 405-hp 406-ci and Galaxie 500/XL. The new model was aimed at the emerging youth market composed of those who were seeking sporty attributes.

All-vinyl upholstery with Mylar trim, bucket seats, console, "wall-to-wall" carpeting, and door panel mounted lamps were part of the Galaxie 500/XL's standard equipment. A Cruise-O-Matic was also included. This car has the optional air conditioner.

Galaxie 500 models were initially composed of the Club Victoria two-door hardtop, Town Victoria four-door hardtop, two-door Club Sedan, four-door Town Sedan, and Sunliner.

Introduced in February were the two bucket seat versions of the Galaxie 500, carrying the addendum, XL, which apparently was derived from *The Lively Ones*, a television show sponsored by Ford. The XL simply meant extra lively. As to the 500 appellation attached to Galaxie, its purpose reportedly was to more closely connect the cars to the 500-mile races such as the Daytona 500. Ford was now heavily promoting a performance image; even the smaller Fairlane 500 series received a bucket seat model this year, as had the Falcon one year earlier.

Station wagons were now available as a Fordor Ranch Wagon, six- and nine-passenger Country Sedans, and six-and nine-passenger Country Squires.

Standard equipment for the Galaxie two- and four-door sedans included bright-metal body trim on the belt-line, hood lip, body sides, lower C-pillars, windshield, side and back windows, and rear edge of the trunk lid. The model name appeared in script on the front fenders and in block-style letters on the lower trunk lid.

Other standard features were:

- cigarette lighter
- glove box lock
- front and rear armrests
- rear coat hooks
- dome light
- rayon-nylon carpeting
- front seat belt anchors
- two sun visors
- combination cloth and vinyl upholstery
- dot-pattern cloth headliner (replaced with the 500 style vinyl later in the year)
- fiber mat trunk floor covering
- single-speed electric windshield wipers
- 7.50x14 black sidewall tires
- 3.56:1 rear axle ratio
- 3-speed manual transmission
- Mileage-Maker 6-cylinder engine

The Galaxie 500 came with all the standard Galaxie equipment, as well as back-up lights, an electric clock, four-ply tires, and bright-metal trim to the roof drip rails, lower quarter panels, rocker panel, wheel lips, and the cove between the taillights. The body side molding was wider and featured a color insert stripe. "Galaxie 500" script was mounted at the rear of the quarter panels and a "500" plaque was attached to the fuel filler door in back. The Galaxie 500 Sunliners had Sunliner script instead of the Galazie 500 ID. In addition, ornaments were added to the grille center and front fenders.

The 500/XL versions had bucket seats, a console with gearshift lever and a glove box trimmed with a ribbed bright-metal plate and bright metal around the perimeter of its base, all-vinyl upholstery with soft Mylar accents, special door panels also decorated with Mylar trim, bright-metal trimmed pedal pads,

Round taillights returned for the 1962 model year. Galaxies did not have a bright-metal panel installed between them like the upper level Galaxie 500s.

Galaxies and Galaxie 500s had a bright-metal ribbed molding at the base of the C-pillars.

The Galaxie series' combination of cloth and vinyl upholstery practically rivaled that of the upscale Galaxie 500 models.

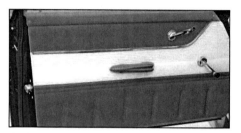

Galaxies had this design applied to the panels, which was similar to that used for the Galaxie 500s.

color-keyed heater housing, special horn ring, the 292-ci V-8, Cruise-O-Matic transmission, plus special identification on the quarters, C-pillars, and fuel filler door.

All-vinyl upholstery was also standard on the Sunliner regardless of whether it had a bench or bucket seats. Painted side seat shields were also standard equipment for the Victorias, while bright-metal shields

were included on the Sunliner and both 500/XL models. White sun visors and headliner were installed on Victoria models while color-keyed sun visors equipped the Sunliner.

The Ranch Wagon's standard equipment list nearly mirrored that of the Galaxie, but had painted window frames instead of bright trim and appropriate "Ranch Wagon" identification script on the tailgate.

The rare M-code 390-ci, rated at 401 hp, powers this Chestnut 1962 Galaxie 500 Club Victoria. The paint color was restricted to Galaxie 500 and Galaxie 500/XL models.

The anodized gold ornament on the grille was standard issue for 1962 Galaxie 500s. Galaxies had no such ornament.

The instrument panel was mildly redesigned for 1962. White numerals over an engine-turned metal background made for an impressive speedometer.

The M-code 390-ci had three Holley 2-barrel carburetors. Peak horsepower was rated at 401 at 6,000 rpm. This engine option was discontinued about mid-year and replaced with a 405-hp 406-ci.

A self-regulating electric clock was standard equipment on Galaxie 500s.

Wheel covers were optional on the Galaxie 500s. When no wheel cover option was ordered, the wheels were painted body color as seen here. The engine emblem was silver for 390-powered cars.

This 1962 Galaxie 500 was fitted with all-vinyl upholstery, a $25 option. Note the column-shifter indicating this car has a 3-speed manual transmission.

Country Sedans were equipped essentially the same as the Galaxie 500 line, but had model identification on the rear fenders. A circular ring with the Ford crest was added to the Ranch Wagon and Country Sedans when the optional power-operated windows were installed.

Country Squires were also similar to the Galaxie 500 in standard features, but had simulated walnut paneling with limed-oak-finish rails. Bright-metal-trimmed rocker, quarter panel, wheel lip, and rear cove moldings were deleted from the Country Squire. The nine-passenger version had a color-keyed vinyl/rubber mat on the third seat floor. Model identification appeared in script form on the doors and tailgate.

All big Fords benefited from engineers' efforts to quiet the ride. Such things as improved glove box hinges, weld-in door frames, and improved insulation were employed to reduce riding noise. A retuned frame with more flexible first and second crossmembers along with larger rubber for the rear spring front-hanger improved ride quality. Seat belt anchors were now also standard.

Extra-Cost Equipment

A plethora of options and accessories were offered so buyers could custom-tailor their car for their wants and needs. SelectAire with the combination air conditioning and heater/defroster remained on the list of options, as did the lower cost PolarAire, a recirculating-type air conditioner with a 3-speed blower. The latter was only available factory-installed with a V-8, or dealer-installed with the 6-cylinder or V-8.

Other options and accessories included:

- chrome engine dress-up kit
- power brakes
- power steering
- power windows
- heater delete (with credit)
- bumper guards
- heavy-duty battery
- outside rearview mirrors
- luggage rack for wagons

A Rangoon Red 1962 Galaxie 500 Sunliner was among the Fords displayed at the fall 1961 Texas State Fair in Dallas. (Texas State Fair Archives)

The six-passenger Country Sedan brought 47,635 sales for the 1962 model year. This one was painted Sandshell Beige and has the optional wheel covers. (Photo courtesy of Chuck Smith)

- load-adjusting shock absorbers
- heavy-duty suspension
- heavy-duty rear axle
- Equa-Lock differential
- two styles of stainless steel wheel covers
- rear fender shields (skirts)
- tinted glass
- two-speed electric windshield wipers
- remote trunk lid release
- AM-radio
- rear-mounted antenna
- two-tone paint
- tissue dispenser

A rarely seen dealer-installed accessory, or gadget, was the vacuum litter disposal. The unit (which first appeared on the Ford accessory list for 1960) was a vacuum-operated drawer-type litter tray that automatically pulled litter into a special glass jar concealed beneath the instrument panel. This accessory was not offered on cars with PolarAire (or on T-Birds).

One very unusual and short-lived option was the Starlift detachable fiberglass roof for the Sunliner. The roof was shaped basically the same as that of the steel-topped Starliner of the preceding two model years. It really was not seriously intended for typical owners of the Sunliner, but in order to qualify for use in NASCAR competition it had to be available to the general public. The idea behind it was simple—aerodynamics. Airflow over the boxy Galaxies became turbulent on the super-speedways, and thus top speed was reduced.

To solve the problem, Ford created the Starlift as an option for the Sunliner. It worked well for those who were racing Galaxies, but it was not a great item for the general public, as the rear side windows did not fill the opening and there was evidently no filler panel included with the top. NASCAR officials allowed it for just one race and then banned it. Ford had a special brochure printed detailing the option and, reportedly, showrooms of dealerships near major racetracks had Starlift-equipped Galaxies. Whether or not any were actually sold to customers is unknown, as is whether or not any survived, though some years ago one Sunliner was rumored to exist with the Starlift top.

Paint and Upholstery Choices

A total of 13 Diamond Lustre Enamels was offered for single-tone paint schemes, while the two-tone option (not offered on Country Squires) provided the buyer with 21 standard choices. Single-tone colors for 1962 were:
- Raven Black
- Corinthian White
- Rangoon Red
- Baffin Blue
- Viking Blue
- Peacock Blue
- Oxford Blue
- Castilian Gold
- Silver Moss
- Ming Green
- Sandshell Beige
- Heritage Burgundy
- Chestnut (limited to the Galaxie 500 and 500/XL series)

Color-keyed upholstery selections numbered 47. The low-level Galaxie came with basket-weave-pattern

This is one of the few publicity photos showing the Starlift top attached to a Sunliner. Reportedly, the option had a price of $660 and its part number was C2AZ-6350L-02A. Note that Thunderbird wheel covers were installed.

A white vinyl headliner was applied to Galaxie 500s. The all-vinyl upholstery seen here was an option; cloth-and-vinyl was standard.

Upholstery for the Country Sedans came in five standard choices of woven plastic (insert) and leather-grained vinyl combinations. This car has medium beige and light pearl beige upholstery. Seat belts were optional. (Photo courtesy of Chuck Smith)

nylon cloth inserts sewn to bolsters of leather-grained vinyl with chrome Mylar highlights. Front seat side shields were leather-grained plastic. Color choices were (insert/bolsters):

- medium blue/light blue metallic
- medium green/light green metallic
- medium turquoise/light turquoise metallic
- medium beige/light pearl beige
- medium gray/light gray metallic
- red/white

Galaxie 500 sedans, Victorias, and Country Squires were available with even more color choices:

- medium blue/light blue metallic
- medium green/light green metallic
- medium turquoise/light turquoise metallic
- medium beige/light beige metallic
- black/black
- red/red

- medium chestnut/medium chestnut metallic
- medium blue metallic/light blue metallic
- medium chestnut metallic/light chestnut metallic
- light beige metallic/light pearl beige

The pattern used for this series was an insert of pleated venice-pattern nylon-plastic cloth edged with chrome Mylar with bolsters of leather-grained vinyl. The headlining differed between the Galaxie 500s and the Country Squire; the former used a white lodestar-pattern vinyl, and the latter was equipped with a white perforated hardboard with chrome cross bows. An all-vinyl choice was also offered for the Country Squire, but was an extra-cost option for the sedan and Victoria models. Inserts remained pleated in this case. Vinyl color combinations for the Country Squire were: light beige metallic/light pearl beige, red/red, and medium blue metallic/light blue metallic.

The Sunliner had leather-grained vinyl upholstery as standard issue

again, with the inserts being pleated. Insert/bolster colors were:

- medium blue metallic/light blue metallic
- medium turquoise metallic/light turquoise metallic
- medium chestnut metallic/light chestnut metallic
- light beige metallic/light pearl beige
- black/black
- red/red

The Ranch Wagon had three choices: medium blue/light blue metallic, red/red, and medium beige/light pearl beige. Inserts were of woven plastic (except vinyl for the beige combination) and leather-grained vinyl was used for the bolsters.

Country Sedans had five woven plastic (insert) and leather-grained vinyl combinations:

- medium blue/light blue metallic
- medium green/light green metallic
- medium turquoise/light turquoise metallic

The high-performance 390s were replaced with the new Thunderbird 406-ci High-Performance V-8 and the Thunderbird 406-ci Super High-Performance V-8. Despite what the marketing lingo implied, the engine was not offered for the Thunderbird. The High-Performance version was equipped with a 4-barrel carb, while the Super High-Performance 406-ci had a 3x2-barrel setup.

An extra-cost chrome dress-up kit enhances the engine compartment of this 1962 Galaxie 500/XL Sunliner powered by a 220-hp 352-ci. Other options on this car include air conditioning and power brakes.

- medium beige/light pearl beige
- red/white

One all-vinyl type was also available in red/white.

There is evidence that some cars built late in the model year may have been fitted with 1963-style upholstery because the supply of some 1962 patterns became depleted.

Engines and Transmissions

The Mileage-Maker 223, Thunderbird 292, Thunderbird 352 Special, Thunderbird 390 Special, and Thunderbird 390 Police Interceptor remained available; performance figures for these engines were unchanged. Added to the engine choices for the full-size Fords (except wagons) were the Q-code and M-code 390s. Both were discontinued for the big Fords by about January. The M-code 390-ci in detuned form became a Thunderbird option. Both

engines were similar to the 1961 high-performance 390s, but had a half-point-higher compression ratio—11.1:1. As in 1961, the 401-hp V-8 featured a tri-carb intake with three Holley 2-barrels. Peak horsepower arrived at 6,000 rpm and the torque rating was advertised as 430 ft-lbs at 3,500 rpm.

The departure of the high-performance 390s was not a major loss for enthusiasts; these engines were replaced with the new Thunderbird 406-ci High-Performance V-8 (code B) and the Thunderbird 406-ci Super High-Performance V-8 (code G). Neither was ever officially listed as being available for station wagon models. Also, despite what the marketing lingo implied the engine was not offered for the Thunderbird, either. The High-Performance version was equipped with a 4-barrel carb, while the Super High-Performance 406-ci had a 3x2-barrel setup. They were rated at 385 and 405 hp, respectively, with both fig-

ures reached at 5,800 rpm.

The 16 cubic inches that brought the 390 to 406 ci was the result of an .08-inch increase in bore diameter. The 406s had thicker cylinder walls, new flat-top pistons, stronger connecting rods, and larger exhaust valves (1.625 inches vs. 1.560). Compression was 10.9:1 in both 406s. (When brought to specified tolerances through machining, compression could go up as much as a half-point and remain legal in NHRA racing.)

Other 406-ci features included cast-aluminum intake, header-type exhaust, and solid lifters. Unfortunately, cross-bolted mains were not included originally. With the two-bolt arrangement, main bearing and crankshaft failures were common after running for 300 to 400 miles on the race track. By spring, blocks with four-bolt mains (the center three) and higher strength main bearing webs were in production.

Cars equipped with a 406

included 15-inch wheels and nylon tires. Obviously, the two stainless steel wheel cover designs offered for 14-inch wheels did not fit, so Ford went retro, offering covers from the 1956 Mercury, slightly modified with the addition of a three-bar spinner. At mid-year, Ford began offering the 1956 Victoria and Thunderbird wheel cover, another reach into the past.

The 406-ci, was of course, the subject of much interest among those writing for the various automotive publications. Roger Huntington, writing for *Motor Trend*, stated the 406-powered car "puts Ford at the front of the Super/Stock competition."

Car Life reported in its March 1962 edition, "There's a new formula around FoMoCo these days and the magic word is performance. The formula goes like this: Take one Galaxie, add the '500' trim details, drop in a 405-bhp powerplant, and bolt on a 4-speed all-synchro transmission. The net result of this concoction is bound to be startling…" Their test car "would romp up to 6000 rpm in each of the 4 gears so fast that it would literally make our head swim… The 'full-race' engine is a little more noticeable than a 'stocker'—a slight bit of extra noise and rumble, a little rough on idle—but the average person getting innocently into the car for the first time wouldn't notice anything different… Of course the engine at wide-open throttle turns from a lamb into a tiger. There is a power roar that becomes nearly a scream as the revolutions approach 6000." The writer of the report estimated top speed to be over 150 mph "under favorable circumstances and with proper gears."

A quicker steering ratio of 22:1 was an available option for 406-powered cars, replacing the standard 30:1. Steering wheel turns lock-to-lock dropped from five to four with the faster ratio. Power steering was not available with either version of this high-performance engine.

Transmissions available with the 406-ci were the heavy-duty 3-speed column shift (standard issue), with overdrive being an option, and a 4-speed. Another option with the 3-speed was a floor-mounted shifter. *Car Life* judged the $188 charge for the 4-speed as "absolutely ridiculous" because "it just doesn't cost that much more to manufacture," and said the 3-speed "has good close ratios (2.37 in low, 1.51 in second gear)." An automatic was not offered for either 406. Beyond the high-horsepower engine and the Borg-Warner T-10 transmission, the buyer of a 406-ci Galaxie, Galaxie 500, or Galaxie 500/XL received heavy-duty shocks and springs.

The *Car Life* road test report showed some impressive acceleration times. Their 4,210-pound test car reached 0–40 mph in 4.1 seconds; 0–60 in 7 seconds flat; 0–100 in 18.6 seconds. Standing quarter-mile result was 15.3 seconds at 93 mph. (For comparison, *Car Life*'s earlier test of a Galaxie with the 300-hp 390-ci and Cruise-O-Matic produced a 0-60 mph time of about 10 seconds and an 80-mph end speed in the quarter-mile.) *Hot Rod* magazine's drivers did even better. Their 0–60 time was a full half-second faster with a quarter-mile time of 15 seconds at 95 mph. Clearly, the 406-ci offered tremendous performance.

The Cruise-O-Matic remained as an option for the 292-ci, 352-ci, and the 300-hp 390-ci while the Fordo-matic could be had with the 223-ci, 292-ci, and the 352-ci. All engines could get the 3-speed with overdrive optional, though according to factory literature, the XL could not be equipped with the 3-speed. Therefore, overdrive was not available for this model. The 4-speed was offered with all of the FE-block engines.

Racing Challenges

Ford's factory-backed racing efforts encountered many problems in 1962. Ford factory drivers experienced engine failures during the early part of the race season, while formal-roofed Pontiacs were getting 465 hp from their 421-ci and setting record speeds. In addition, Plymouths were downsized and powered with the 413-ci, while Chevrolet grafted the 1961 bubble top roof to the Bel Air for 1962 and ran with the 409-ci. Ford's new 406's additional horsepower was not enough to overcome the drag of the T-Bird roofline, which Ford estimated resulted in a 3-mph loss in top speed with the box-top Galaxies. This was a serious disadvantage for Holman-Moody drivers Fred Lorenzen and Nelson Stacy, Wood Brothers' driver Marvin Panch, as well as independent Larry Frank.

When the three-time, weather-delayed Atlanta 500 race finally took place in June, Ford had a solution to that problem: the aforementioned Starlift top. Officials with NASCAR, however, had great difficulty making a decision on whether or not to allow the Starlift-equipped cars to run. As explained in the September 1962 issue of *Motor Trend*, "…NASCAR Chief Inspector Norris Friel ruled that the slopeback-topped Fords campaigned by Lorenzen and Stacy were ineligible for further competition the day before the race, but allowed them to run the Atlanta event 'because they had no other cars to drive.'

Thus, Lorenzen's steed became what probably is the only 'illegal' champion in all of auto racing."

This weird turn of events actually began in May, when the Holman-Moody team built two true convertibles for Stacy and Lorenzen to drive in the Rebel 300. Instead of cutting the tops off regular sedans, as is the custom at the Darlington convertible race, Ford offered a sloping top that could be bolted onto Ford convertibles. At the Daytona 500 in February, the boxy-topped 1962 Galaxie proved to be very difficult to handle at high speed. In fact, the top was not aerodynamically efficient and it created excess drag at 150 mph or more in traffic. The plan, then, was to run the true convertibles in the Rebel 300 and bolt on the new slopeback tops for the following late-model sedan events.

Ford planned to unveil the setup at the next event scheduled, the World 600, but it couldn't because the required 45-day period between the announcement and competition use of a new component had not been met. Instead, Lorenzen and Stacy ran with sedans built for the USAC dirt track; Stacy won and Lorenzen finished third. The sedans were sent back to the USAC circuit and the convertibles with their Starlift tops in place were rushed to the Atlanta 500.

Friel declared the cars illegal until convertible-type X-members, which had been removed from the frames, were put back in place. The ruling was complicated by the fact that no other bolt-together automobile had been run on the Grand National circuit. Without such a precedent in place, the ruling, according to the writer at *Motor Trend*, became "hazy." In Friel's judg-ment, the convertibles raced at Darlington were permissible without X-members, but as sedans they had to have them. So the X-members were welded back in place.

Then Friel consulted NASCAR's Bill France about the issue. A decision was made the day before the race. The cars would be allowed to run in the Atlanta 500 race, but until NASCAR was satisfied that the bolt-on tops were "sufficiently available" and proper notice was given of a "new model" Ford, they would be ineligible for future races. Perhaps the rule-makers would have taken the Starlift top more seriously as an option if the quarter windows of the convertible actually filled the opening. Virtually no one would have wanted the top for their personal car. Those running in the Atlanta 500 had the openings filled with plastic side windows.

Obviously the top was really intended for racing purposes rather than as an option for everyday Sunliners. Even if the roof had been allowed beyond the one race, it would have been for only the remainder of the 1962 race season, as this was the final year in which convertibles would be raced.

In all, Ford took just six super-speedway wins—the fewest of any other make. At least in USAC competition, where the speeds were lower, Ford scored ten wins, which tied Pontiac's total. Curtis Turner drove a Ford to victory in the Pike's Peak Hill Climb.

Ford did not have any greater success on the drag racing circuit. Pontiacs and Chevys had big wins in NHRA competition. Dave Strickler, driving a 409-powered Bel Air "bubbletop," eliminated the remaining Fords to reach the finals. This included an unfortunate run for Les Ritchey driving a Galaxie; Strickler beat Ritchey off the line, but Ritchey missed the shift into second gear anyway. Had these misfortunes not occurred, a Galaxie might have made it into the finals competition.

Ford went so far as to have Dearborn Steel Tubing build 10 lightweight Galaxie two-door sedans. Modifications included fiberglass front fenders, hood, and deck lid, plus aluminum inner fenders and bumpers. Engines were equipped with aluminum intakes with 2x4-barrel carbs. These cars were readied in time for the 1962 NHRA Nationals and were raced in the A/FX (Factory Experimental, up to 8.99 pounds per cubic inch) class, but they had to race against the lighter Pontiac Tempests, which were consistently faster than the Fords.

Ford offered a lightweight kit through the parts department for the two-door sedan and convertible. The kit included the same parts as used on the factory experimental Galaxies with the exception of fiberglass doors. The doors of the two kits differed because these components were not interchangeable between the two body styles. The part numbers were C2AZ-6200012-A for the sedan and C2AZ-7600012-A for the convertible.

Before the 1962 racing season ended, NASCAR announced a 7-liter limit (about 427 ci) on engine size to be effective for 1963. This announcement terminated rumors of future engines of up to 500 ci.

Ford developed an experimental 483-ci monster from the FE block, but the new rule outlawed it from competition. Instead, Holman-Moody installed one in a Starlift Sunliner and took it to the Bonneville Salt Flats where it could race in the USAC-sanctioned Class B (upper limit of 8 liters or 488 ci) competition. Drivers Fred Lorenzen, Ralph

This Ming Green box top 1963 Galaxie 500/XL was one of 29,713 built. The tri-bar spinner wheel covers came as standard equipment on the 500/XLs. (Photo courtesy of Martin Siemion, Ford Galaxie Club of America)

The turquoise all-vinyl upholstery was one of seven standard colors offered. Mylar trim was again used on the Galaxie 500/XLs. (Photo courtesy of Martin Siemion, Ford Galaxie Club of America)

Moody, and Don White took their turns at the wheel and in the process broke 46 national and international records—some of which had stood since 1935.

Among the new records set was an average speed of 163.85 mph from a standing start to the end of 500 miles. The highest speed attained by the Ford was 176.978 mph (though a 182-mph top speed had been achieved at the Ford's proving grounds). The engine finally let go from the torturous driving, but it had proven itself. Basic specifications of the engine were: 12:1 compression ratio, 4.23-inch bore, 4.30-inch stroke, two Holley 4-barrel carburetors, and estimated 500 hp.

Production Numbers

A total of 704,775 full-size Fords were built for the 1962 model year, and 404,600 of them were Galaxie 500s. Of those, 41,595 were Galaxie 500/XLs, of which, 13,183 were convertibles. Production of the Galaxie 500 Sunliner totaled 42,646. After 1962, the name Sunliner was discontinued.

The overall production of big Fords was nearly 87,000 units lower than the prior model year. However, sales of the new mid-size Fairlane

and the compact Falcon resulted in more Fords being built than for 1961. The drop in full-size car production would be reversed for 1963.

1963: The Start of Something Big

Ford replaced the sheetmetal below the belt-line to freshen the styling of the big Fords for 1963. The result was an .8-inch gain in overall width and more than an increase of .6 inch in overall length. Model year updates included a new grille, trim, taillights, and bumpers. A concave grille was fashioned for the front; its lower border contoured to fit the stepped front bumper. Larger taillights were found in back though these were still round in shape.

Dashboards were altered, too, though the 1963 versions were similar to the previous design. The 1963 speedometer featured white numerals over a black background, which was an improvement over the previous year's speedometer. In fact, the 1962 speedometer used white numerals over an engine-turned metal background. It looked great, but the low contrast could make reading it a bit difficult. Enlarged, painted pods housed the deeply recessed gauges for 1963, rather than the shallow, bright-

metal pods of 1962. The lower dash was flattened, thus it was flush all the way across for the first time since 1959. Crank-operated vent windows replaced the lever-release type.

The revised convertible top was slightly lower and also 6.6 inches shorter. Both the windshield and rear window angles were changed to provide a more rakish top silhouette.

Revised Lineup

At the start of the model year, Ford offered 14 choices of big Fords in the revised 1963 lineup. The Ford 300 two- and four-door sedans were quickly added to what were billed as "America's liveliest, most carefree cars." They marked the low-end of the price range in the hierarchy. The Galaxie series was the next step up, and it was offered in the same two body styles. Galaxie 500s were again offered in the same body styles as the previous model year.

The Galaxie 500/XL gained a four-door hardtop body style. The Ranch Wagon was dropped leaving the Country Sedan and Country Squire as the choices in wagons. Both were obtainable in six- and nine-passenger versions. Later in the model year, Ford added a fastback, or Sports Hardtop, as Ford dubbed it. It could be had as a Galaxie 500 and 500/XL. (These 1963½ models will be detailed in Chapter 7).

Standard and Optional Features

Ford 300 sedans had standard features, which were similar to those of the 1961 Fairlane, including bright-metal front and rear windshield moldings, two sun visors, and armrests on all doors. A horn ring rather than a horn button was standard, however. There was no carpeting; instead, a color-keyed rubber mat served as the floor covering. Rear passengers did not have armrests. Galaxie sedans, Galaxie 500s and 500/XLs, and station wagons were equipped essentially the same as those of the prior model year.

Trim differences among the series were the major distinguishing characteristics. The 300, of course, had the least, with no body side moldings and simple bright-metal moldings around the windshield and rear window, plus "Ford 300" identification on the front fenders. Galaxies had a molding along the lower body side with a black stripe, drip rail moldings, "Galaxie" script on the front fenders, two chrome windsplit fender ornaments, trunk lip molding, horizontal-bar textured appliqué between the taillights, and a crest on the C-pillars.

Galaxie 500s added bright-metal moldings to the gravel deflector, window frames, and A-pillar moldings, an upper body side molding joined to the lower one in back, simulated louvers at the rear of the quar-

The Galaxie 500 four-door hardtop listed for $2,739 in base form. This factory promotional photograph shows a car equipped with the optional wheel covers and whitewall tires. Since no engine emblem is present, one can only state that a 6-cylinder, 260-ci (early cars), 289-ci (later cars), or a 352-ci is under the hood.

This factory promotional photograph shows a nine-passenger Country Squire. A total of 19,567 were built, starting at a base price of $3,088.

This Heritage Burgundy 1963 Galaxie two-door sedan is powered with the 425-hp, 427-ci V-8. (Photo courtesy of Mark Reynolds, Ford Galaxie Club of America)

ters, rear appliqué between the taillights textured to resemble the grille, "500" on the fuel filler, taillight inserts that created a starburst effect, and an anodized gold "500" medallion overlaid with the "Galaxie" script. The 500/XL externally wore special identification badges in place of the 500 ID, plus wheel covers with three-bar spinners and red/

The 220-hp 352-ci returned for the 1963 model year. Standard issue for the Galaxie 500/XL was a 164-hp, 260-ci small-block V-8 at the start of the model year. It was later replaced by a 195-hp 289-ci. (Photo courtesy of Martin Siemion, Ford Galaxie Club of America)

the big Fords equipped with a high-performance engine option; the modified 1956 Mercury wheel cover, however, remained available.

Colors and Upholstery

Eleven shades of Diamond Lustre Enamel were offered for 1963:

- Raven Black
- Corinthian White
- Rangoon Red
- Champagne
- Oxford Blue
- Viking Blue
- Glacier Blue
- Silver Moss
- Ming Green
- Sandshell Beige
- Heritage Burgundy

Two of these colors, Sandshell Beige and Ming Green, were not offered for the Ford 300.

Ten two-tone combinations were offered for the 300, 12 for the Galaxie and Country Sedan, 21 for the Galaxie 500, and a total of 22 for the Galaxie 500/XL. Two-tone schemes were not offered for the Country Squire.

Upholstery choices for the Ford 300 were minimal, including

white/blue inserts. All series cars were decorated with a chrome-plated ribbed molding at the base of the C-pillars.

Optional equipment was mostly unchanged, though a few new items should be noted. The venerable Y-block was replaced with the new small-block 164-hp, 260-ci V-8. It could be had with any transmission except the 4-speed. It was the standard engine for the 500/XLs for the first part of the model year.

As with the 4-speed, the 3-speed was now fully synchronized. Furthermore, the 4-speed was offered as an option for the Country Squire when equipped with the optional 390-ci.

Inside, a Swing-Away steering wheel, standard on the T-Bird, was now an option, but it required a V-8, an automatic transmission, and power steering. A rear speaker with a reverberator, which placed a delay between the front and rear speaker to create a stereo effect, was also added to the list of extra-cost

equipment. PolarAire was discontinued and replaced with the Ford Air Conditioner.

A new option for the Country Squires was bucket seats and console; it added $141.60 to the base price. Only 321 nine-passenger Squires and 437 of the six-passenger Squires were ordered with this option.

The 1956 Ford wheel cover was evidently dropped as an option for

This Chestnut 1963 Galaxie 500 convertible is a well-preserved original with just 25,000 miles on the odometer. The convertible top was lowered slightly and also 6.6 inches shorter for 1963. Both the windshield and rear window angles were changed, too, to provide a more rakish top silhouette.

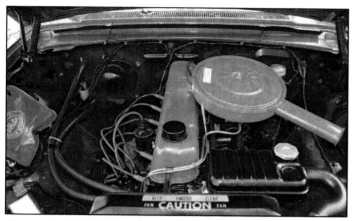

The standard engine for all Galaxie 500s was the 223-ci 6-cylinder, though most buyers opted for one of the V-8s. This is one of just 1,512 Galaxie 500 convertibles built with the 6-cylinder, according to the Standard Catalog of Ford.

The Galaxie 500 convertible was offered only with pleated all-vinyl upholstery in five standard selections. This example was fitted with chestnut vinyl.

cloth/vinyl combinations in blue, gold, or red. Evidently Ford's literature did not specify the specific style of upholstery installed. The Galaxie had two additional choices of beige or turquoise; the style was puff stripe cloth with vinyl.

Galaxie 500 sedans and hardtops offered seven gleam cloth/vinyl arrangements in black, blue, gold, turquoise, beige, red, and chestnut plus five optional all-vinyl selections: black, blue, gold, red, and chestnut. The Galaxie 500 convertible was offered only with pleated all-vinyl in these same colors, while the Galaxie 500/XL hardtops and convertible added turquoise and rose-beige to the list of available colors; pleated all-vinyl upholstery was also used for the 500/XLs. Country Squires featured gleam cloth with vinyl, while Country Sedans came with puff stripe cloth and vinyl.

Ford's ad writers made the Galaxie 500/XL seem like the most desirable car in the world when describing its interior: "Entrance to the Galaxie 500/XL is an experience in modern living accommodation—the wide-opening doors reveal the ultimate in beauty combined with quality work-

manship on the finest available materials known to the industry. The Mylar-trimmed vinyl door upper panels... extra-comfortable arm rests... paddle-type door handles... door lower panel carpeting to match the nylon-rayon floor covering... and the dual-lens courtesy-warning light in the center of the lower portion of the door. With the door open, the lights are each at the proper angle—one with the white lens to illuminate the entrance area and the other with a red lens directed rearward as a warning light to approaching motorists. Galaxie 500/XL's elegant sports-type interior belongs to the XL alone—unique and luxurious, with roominess and comfort, unobtainable in conventional cars."

Impressive Machine

"A fast, impressive machine that automates the functions which can benefit from it, and provides high performance motoring without removing the silence one tends to expect from a North American automobile," said the opening line of the July 1963 issue of *Canada Track & Traffic*. The writer added, "The car

performs extremely well in its design area—the big, wide, fast super highways of North America." The test car used for the evaluation was powered with the 300-hp 390 ci coupled to a 4-speed manual transmission.

There were few complaints made in the article. A couple of them were in regard to the simulated knock-off hubs on the wheel covers and the lack of a tachometer as standard equipment. Evidently, the writer found the hubs to be aesthetically lacking.

The test driver also found the car almost too quiet! "Both engine noise and exhaust noise are so completely muffled in this Ford that it is almost impossible to judge shift points for either high performance or economy." Tachometers in 6,000 and 8,000 rpm form in Ford's Rotunda brand were, however, offered through the Ford dealers' parts department as an extra-cost accessory.

The 1963 model year was off to a fine beginning. Furthermore, more mid-year surprises were in store including the addition of a fastback Sports Hardtop and more horsepower. Ford had just been warming up—it was about to unleash Total Performance!

1963½–1964: The Fastback and Total Performance

The half model-year introduction struck again for the 1963 model year. In January, the Sports Hardtop made its debut in Monaco at the Monte Carlo Road Rally along with other mid-year Fords. The Sports Hardtop, offered as a Galaxie 500 and a Galaxie 500/XL, was 1 inch lower in overall height and featured a semi-fastback roofline that provided greatly improved airflow at high speeds.

The "box top" body style remained in production, but a Sports Hardtops was introduced, which included a new and exclusive option to the "slantback," a black or white vinyl-covered roof. It simulated the look of a convertible top in the up position. To enhance the illusion, a narrow molding spanned the crease just ahead of the rear window.

Also new was a replacement for the 406 ci—the 427 ci—available with a single 4-barrel Holley carb and with a dual-quad Holley setup. Horsepower was rated at 410 and 425, respectively. A few who ordered their car with the 406-ci near the time of its replacement received it so equipped; even a very few 1963½ Sports Hardtops were built with the

Ralph Earnhardt drove this 1963½ Galaxie 500 in the 1964 Daytona 500. **(Photo courtesy of JDC collection)**

engine. However, most had their order filled with the 427-ci.

The 427-ci was bored .10 inch over compared the 406-ci (stroke was not altered). In reality, the displacement computed to 425.511 ci. Chrysler introduced its 426-ci Max-Wedge Stage II to their engine lineup, so perhaps for marketing purposes Ford rounded up just a bit. Ford's advertised displacement was very near the NASCAR rule limit of 7 liters.

Additional alterations to the latest FE engine included impact-extruded aluminum pistons (lighter and stronger than the previous cast aluminum type), redesigned valvesprings, a special cup-shaped washer (which provided a spring seat to keep the spring accurately centered), and heavier spring retainers. Exhaust valve stems were given a special electrolyzing surface treatment to reduce wear, and rocker arm shafts were located on iron pedestals (instead of aluminum) to reduce flexing. The larger exhaust valves and new connecting rods adopted late in 1962 were carried forward for the 427-ci.

In addition to these two 427s, a race version was also created. It featured 12:1 compression, 300-degree duration camshaft, and two 600-cfm Holley carbs. This engine went into a lightweight version of the Galaxie 500 Sports Hardtop (which will be detailed later in this chapter).

The Thunderbird 427-ci High-Performance V-8 came with some mandatory equipment, including heavy-duty suspension and battery, 6.70x15 four-ply nylon tires, and fade-resistant brakes. Power steering, power brakes, and air conditioning were not available with the 427-ci option.

The 427-ci was not the only updated engine to be introduced for 1963½; the 289-ci 2-barrel replaced the 260-ci. A .20-inch increase in bore size to 4.00 inches resulted in the increased displacement. Horsepower was rated at 195. The 289-ci became the standard engine for the Galaxie 500/XLs and Country Squires, but was an option for the other big Fords.

Along with the new 1963½-model Fords came a couple of new ad slogans—"The Super Torque Fords" and "Total Performance." Ford even printed a brochure with the latter slogan as its title. In it was an explanation of Total Performance:

"Ford Motor Company is in the business of providing 'Total Performance' for a safe, comfortable, convenient, and durable means of transportation for all to enjoy.

"Total Performance, as interpreted here at Ford, has many facets—roadability which provides built-in

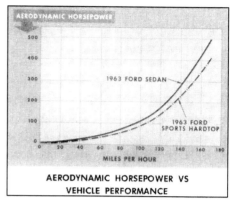

AERODYNAMIC HORSEPOWER VS VEHICLE PERFORMANCE

Ford published this chart to show the aerodynamic advantage of the semi-fastback roofline. For the typical driver, the semi-fastback roofline had an aesthetic advantage, but for the driver on the super-speedways, the sleek roofline meant an aerodynamic advantage.

features to help resist skidding and to hold the road... braking power that permits smooth, straight-line stops... steering, for effortless directional control... instruments and controls that are easy to read and to operate... visibility that reduces blind spots... suspension that provides a smooth ride without wheel-bounce... riding comfort in scientifically-contoured seats that reduce travel fatigue... and finally, Total Performance includes acceleration and speed."

Evidently, the ad campaign worked well. Ford sold more full-size cars and in excess of 100,000 additional cars overall than in 1962. Furthermore, Ford's success on the tracks surely gave substance to the slogan, "Total Performance."

The June 1963 issue of *Car Life* reported the results of their testing of a 1963½ Galaxie 500/XL. It was equipped with the standard 289-ci and Cruise-O-Matic. In their opinion, "The Cruise-O-Matic works very well with the 289, as our test data show. Acceleration, fuel economy, and

The half-model-year introduction struck again for 1963. The Sports Hardtop made its debut in Monaco at the Monte Carlo Road Rally along with other mid-year Fords. With the advent of the Sports Hardtops, a new and exclusive option to the slantback became available—a black or white vinyl-covered roof.

pulling power all fall into what we consider to be an adequate range."

As for the styling, the article stated, "Although not a true fast-back (where the roofline arcs from the windshield header to the bumper bar), its sharply raked roof supposedly promotes better airflow characteristics—according to Ford publicists—although anyone who looks at the plan view will doubt it. Somewhat reminiscent of the Starliner series (1960-1961), which had a more curving line, the flat-back 'scatbacks' have at least two values: they provoke interest and promote conversation, two things essential to increased showroom traffic. In other words, the slant back is an eye-catcher and the reflected glory of the three straight NASCAR victories which similar models have posted (Riverside, Daytona, Atlanta) enhances its ego-pleasing qualities."

Also noted was the "use of mastic deadener, glass fiber mats and felt, amberlite and jute pads," making the Galaxie "into one of the quietest, smoothest cars on four wheels." One complaint was in regard to the instrument panel: "Although nicely shielded and padded, it is nonetheless difficult to read and poorly designed."

The test driver judged handling to be "surprisingly well for a big sedan." The 289-powered 500/XL ran from 0–60 mph in 12.3 seconds and covered the quarter-mile in 19.0 seconds with a speed at the end of 73 mph.

As for the expressed belief that the slantback was more for styling than function, Ford claimed their testing revealed that the difference between the Galaxie sedan and the Sports Hardtop began to show itself by 60 mph though only slightly. However, the standard sedan would need roughly 65 more horsepower

than the Sports Hardtop to reach 140 mph. For the typical driver the semi-fastback roofline had an aesthetic advantage; for the driver on the super-speedways, the sleek roofline meant an aerodynamic advantage.

Car Life magazine's February 1964 issue provided a road test report on the NASCAR Ford Galaxie Sports Hardtop prepared by Holman-Moody. Acceleration tests showed 0-60 mph to take 6.3 seconds; 0–140 mph required 22.3 seconds; the quarter-mile took 14.2 seconds with an end speed of 105 mph. Total drag at 60 mph was 150 pounds.

Big Victories and Lightweight Galaxie 500s

For 1963, Fords would race with a 427-ci High Riser featuring a high-rise intake manifold. The improved aerodynamics of the 1963 Sports Hardtop combined with the up-graded 427-ci V-8 undoubtedly led Ford to its 23 NASCAR victories, including wins in every race of 500 miles or more. This year Mercury entered the competition; the Sports Hardtop body style was shared with this division.

Dan Gurney notched Ford's first win of the season at the Motor Trend 500 held at Riverside International Raceway on January 20. Just after this race, General Motors' division general managers demanded Chevrolet and Pontiac exit their racing activities. For many years, GM was alert to the possibility the federal government would break up the company under antitrust laws and they just did not need any extra attention; they had about half of the auto market anyway.

This action did not come before the 427-ci Mark IV Mystery Motor made it to the NASCAR tracks. Junior

The setting of this photograph was inside the original Holman-Moody shop just before the 1963 Motor Trend 500. The car in the background was driven by Dan Gurney, who won the race. Note the stock interior panels. Number 28 was Fred Lorenzen's ride. (Photo courtesy of JDC collection)

This 1963½ Galaxie 500 was driven by Nelson Stacy. Holman-Moody built nearly 15 Galaxie 500s in 1963. All of them were regular production 427-powered cars built on the Atlanta assembly line.

Johnson, driving a 1963 Impala with this engine, broke the record of the fastest 1962 Chevy by 10 mph with a 163.681-mph average speed, qualifying him for the pole position for the Daytona 500. Even though the engine was not available to the public, NASCAR officials allowed the Mark IV powered Chevys to race. Fortunately for Ford, these fast Chevrolets dropped out due to mechanical problems.

Instead, Ford scored an upset victory. DeWayne "Tiny" Lund driving a Wood Brothers' Ford took the checkered flag for the first Grand National victory of his career. His victory at the Daytona 500 came together like a Hollywood movie with a feel-good ending. In a practice session for the American Challenge Cup, a support race for the Daytona 500, Marvin Panch was injured when he barrel-rolled a Maserati GT. Lund was among those who pulled Panch from the flaming wreck. Panch was supposed to be the driver of the Wood Brothers' Ford Galaxie stockcar in the 500; after the crash, he asked the Wood Brothers to let Lund drive in his place.

With Pontiac out of factory-backed racing, "Fireball" Roberts switched to Ford and Holman-Moody. He won the Firecracker 400 and the Southern 500.

Fred Lorenzen took the checkered flag in his number-28 Galaxie 500 on six occasions, including the wins at the Atlanta 500 and World 600.

In USAC competition, Ford took five victories, while Plymouth managed six. Don White, driving a Zecol-Lubaid Galaxie 500, took one win for Ford.

While Ford was having great success on the race track, it was not doing so well on the drag strip. The new, lightweight Galaxie 500s were just unable to beat the Dodges and Plymouths. They got close and they were fast, but not fast enough. The factory lightweight Fords were capable of quarter-mile runs of just a bit over 12 seconds at speeds of 117 to 118 mph, while the Dodges and Plymouths would run sub 12-second quarter-mile times.

To shed hundreds of pounds from the standard Galaxie 500, fiberglass

Dearborn Steel Tubing built this 1963½ Galaxie 500 as one of a reported 212 lightweight cars built for Ford. Hundreds of pounds were shaved from the standard Galaxie 500 through the use of fiberglass panels, the lighter Ford 300 frame, aluminum bumpers, and other modifications.

The new lightweight Galaxie 500s just were not quite sufficient to beat the Dodges, Plymouths, Pontiacs, and Chevrolets. They got close and they were fast, but not fast enough. The lightweight Fords were capable of quarter-mile runs of just a bit over 12 seconds at speeds of 117 to 118 mph.

This is the race version of the 427-ci V-8. It featured 12:1 compression, a 300-degree duration camshaft, and 600-cfm Holley carbs.

A transistorized ignition was included on the lightweight Galaxie 500s. It was an option on other 427-powered Fords.

fenders, inner fenders, hood, doors, deck lid, thin rubber floor covering, plus lightweight bucket seats from the Econoline van were installed. (The earliest cars, however, did not have the fiberglass inner fenders and doors.) In addition, the underpinnings were lightened, cars were fitted with the lighter Ford 300 frame, aluminum bumpers and bumper brackets, and an aluminum case 4-speed.

Other items deleted from the standard Galaxie 500 for the light-

weight versions included: heater, armrests, sound deadener, seam sealer, as well as the spare tire, spare tire mount, and jack. Backing plates on the brakes were drilled full of holes

Full-sized Fords equipped with one of the 427s had this gold emblem on the front fenders.

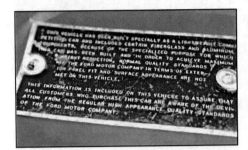

This plaque on the inside of the glove box door was affixed to all lightweight Galaxie 500s. It said, "This vehicle has been built specifically as a lightweight competitive car . . . Because of the specialized purpose for which this car has been built . . . normal quality standards . . . in terms of exterior panel fit and surface appearance are not met on this vehicle."

A thin rubber floor covering and lightweight bucket seats from the Econoline van helped reduce the normal weight of the Galaxie 500.

Other items found on the standard Galaxie 500 that were deleted for the lightweight versions included the heater, armrests, sound deadener, and even the seam sealer.

Fifteen-inch wheels came along with the 427. The lightweights came equipped with hub caps like any other Galaxie 500.

This teardrop shaped bubble was necessary to clear the top of the 427-ci High Riser. The hood was fiberglass.

to assist in brake cooling. Dearborn Steel Tubing built an initial run of 50 cars, and in all, a reported 212 lightweight Galaxie 500s were assembled.

Great Year in Sales

Ford's sales for the model year were about 20 percent higher than the total for 1962. The Sports Hardtops accounted for a sizable portion of the big gain with a combined total of 134,370 units; 100,500 of these were the Galaxie 500 and of course the remaining balance consisted of the Galaxie 500/XL. The other 500/XL models accounted for 60,860 sales; the least popular was the four-door hardtop version, with only 12,596 built.

1964: Car of the Year

September 23, 1963, was the start of another great model year for Ford. Sheetmetal and detail upgrades below the belt-line resulted in some of the best styling in Ford's history. Furthermore, the box top roofline was dropped. The semi-fastback was so popular the previous year that even the two- and four-door sedan models had a similar roofline. Model names were altered again; the name "Custom" returned to the lineup.

Unlike in the prior years, there would not be a bigger engine issued because the racing rule remained the same on the matter of displacement. The 427-ci would remain the high-performance engine for Ford. However, the 410-hp version was dropped as an option during March.

Motor Trend magazine gave its annual Car of the Year award to the entire line of 1964 Ford cars. The editor for *Motor Trend*, Charles Nerpel, wrote, "Basis of this year's award is engineering advancement in the

Large, round taillights were employed on the 1963 Fords. Galaxie 500 and 500/XL models now had backup lights as standard equipment.

Lightweight Galaxie 500s lacked a spare, spare mount, and jack. Carpeting was also deleted.

concept of Total Performance, based on high-performance testing in open competition. The editors... believe the 1964 Fords offer a better product to the public because of engineering improvements evolved from testing under the most rugged and demanding conditions ever conceived—open competition."

The magazine's road test report on two 1964 Fords: a Galaxie 500/XL four-door hardtop with the 390-ci and an automatic, and a Galaxie 500 two-door hardtop powered with the 427-ci 2x4-barrel and a 4-speed. Their 500/XL test car was also equipped with a 3.00:1 axle ratio, power steering, power brakes, tinted glass, and heater; the Galaxie 500 was equipped with a few extras as well, including radio, heater, seat belts, and tinted glass.

Choosing two cars to evaluate was done to "give our readers some idea of the variety offered by Ford." The magazine's assistant technical

Potential new car buyers were challenged to "Try Total Performance." The entire 1964 Ford line received Motor Trend magazine's Car of the Year award, as noted in this advertisement.

The fresh styling of the 1964 full-size Fords included a new grille composed of horizontal bars with three vertical peaks. (Photo by Dick Rozum, *Legendary Ford Magazine*)

This Phoenician Yellow and Raven Black 1964 Galaxie 500 two-door hardtop is an unrestored example with only 28,000 actual miles. It is equipped with the optional wheel covers, whitewall tires, and outside rearview mirror. (Photo by Dick Rozum, *Legendary Ford Magazine*)

editor, Bob McVay, wrote, "Both test cars showed results of Ford's Total Performance program—each in its own way. The top-of-the-line 500-XL Galaxie impressed us as a big, solid, comfortable family car, yet still slanted toward the sporty set. It had plenty of room for five people and enough trunk space for the longest trip. We could find only two faults: the car had considerable nose dive on quick stops, and the power brakes were a bit touchy."

The 427-ci test car "gave super Total Performance." It was said to "be as docile as a kitten or as tiger-like as we asked it to be. No power options here... standard 5.5 turns lock-to-lock steering, and manual brakes and clutch action required more work from the driver, but then it was a lot more fun to drive, too. Operating on one of its two 4-barrel carbs, the '427' was happy burbling along as slowly as 30 mph in fourth gear. It refused to overheat in traffic, and stalling at traffic lights wasn't a problem." Also noted was, "Performance, in every respect, was far better than our sedan's, most noticeably in acceleration and braking. Our factory-fresh '427,' with only 700 miles on it, turned the quarter-mile in 15.4 sec-

onds, hitting 95 mph on the nose—that with two *MT* staffers aboard and all our test equipment." The *Motor Trend* report concluded, "Although it can be docile, the '427' comes on with a roar and smack-in-the-back acceleration that can only be termed fierce at any speed. It isn't for the faint of heart... Our test cars showed the results of Ford's Total Performance program. They're big, solid cars, and they do what they were built to do—and very well indeed."

The New Look and Lineup

A convex tapered spear dominated the side view of the 1964 full-size Fords; it ran from the headlights to just beyond the midpoint of the front doors and set within a wide body-length concave section. In front was a new grille composed of horizontal bars with three vertical peaks. The front bumper was not as flat this year; it had a subtle point. Round taillights, though revised, returned for the fourth consecutive model year. The rear bumper dipped underneath the taillights. The convertible top was now equipped with an all-glass rear window. Made of pliant, lightweight safety glass with

The semi-fastback roofline was a well-liked styling trait of the 1964 Galaxie 500 and 500/XL two-door hardtops. (Photo by Dick Rozum, *Legendary Ford Magazine*)

low-sag properties, the new window was rubber-bonded to the satin-finish, three-ply vinyl top material. Unlike the clear vinyl used previously, the glass window was resistant to scratching and discoloration.

The instrument panel and dash remained largely the same as that of the prior model year. Black numerals on a dull silver background for the speedometer represented the most notable update there. Prior Ford owners had to adjust to the ignition switch being relocated to the right of the steering column.

Upholstery and door panel patterns were substantially altered. The Mylar trim was deleted from the

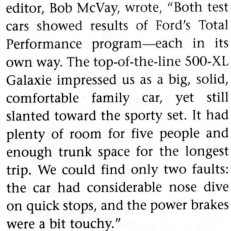

A 250-hp, 352-ci V-8 with 4-barrel carburetor was a new option for the 1964 full-size Fords. The 220-hp version was discontinued. (Photo by Dick Rozum, *Legendary Ford Magazine*)

This Rangoon Red and Wimbledon White 1964 Galaxie 500 four-door sedan is completely original with the exceptions of the battery and belts. In addition to the optional two-tone paint, the 920-actual-mile specimen is equipped with the extra-cost 195-hp, 289-ci V-8.

Galaxie 500/XL seats and door panels. Brushed aluminum panels brightened the latter on the bucket seat model. Furthermore, new thin-shell, pedestal-mounted bucket seats for the 500/XLs were said to provide increased comfort and an easier seat adjustment through newly designed seat rollers and slides. Both the bench and bucket seat adjustments could be adjusted 1 inch rearward thanks to holes provided in the seat track lower member, allowing for additional front leg loom for taller drivers. The adjustment could be made on request at the dealership.

The Galaxie 500s and 500/XLs represented the top tier in the lineup again in 1964. Body style offerings in these two series were unchanged. Standard equipment for the Galaxie 500/XLs remained the same as in mid-1963 (when the 289-ci took the place of the 260-ci).

Galaxie 500/XLs and Galaxie 500s shared the same side trim with the exception of a tri-color oval XL emblem on the quarter panel on the 500/XLs. These cars had a bright-metal cap fitting over the side spear; it tapered into a narrow

A 289-ci with 2-barrel carburetor was the smallest V-8 offered for the 1964 Fords. It was a $109 option on Galaxie 500s, Customs, and Custom 500s. Galaxie 500/XLs had this engine as standard equipment.

molding that ran to the rear. The model name appeared in a recessed area on the trim just behind the headlights. This recess was painted argent silver. Fender-top ornaments were also included; these were die cast pieces sleekly styled with a small fin.

In back, another bright-metal molding with blacked-out horizontal recesses fit the area between the taillights. The 500/XLs got a tri-color

oval emblem here as well. A three-piece molding was fitted to the deck lid lip and quarters with the breaks at the gaps. Taillights were fitted with back-up lights and chrome-plated die cast moldings in a sunburst pattern. Four-door models in these two series had a Ford crest added to the C-pillars. All windows were trimmed with bright metal as was the belt-line and drip rails. Dashes for both series had a brushed

Taillights on Galaxie 500s and 500/XLs were fitted with backup lights and chrome-plated die-cast moldings in a sunburst pattern.

Galaxie 500/XL convertibles accounted for 15,169 sales for the 1964 model year. This period illustration shows the optional wire wheel covers.

Other options on this pristine 1964 Galaxie 500 include the four-way power seat, AM-radio, all-vinyl upholstery, and power steering. (Photo by Dick Rozum, *Legendary Ford Magazine*)

The Galaxie 500/XL four-door hardtop returned for one more year in 1964 and 14,661 were built, which was about 2,000 more than for 1963.

satin appliqué behind the control knobs and across the full width.

The Galaxie no longer occupied the lower echelon of the big Ford line. Instead, the Custom 500 and Custom now represented the lower-priced models, and both were offered as two- and four-door sedans. The Custom 500 lacked the spear molding found on the Galaxie 500 and 500/XLs, but instead had a narrow side molding running the length of the front fenders with an ending point at the tip of the convex spear pressed into the sheet-metal. Integrated with it was an enamel-accented vertical bar appliqué conforming to the sculpturing at the forward portion of the fender. The model identification appeared on the quarters. In back

was a bright, enamel-accented molding between the taillights; the fuel filler door wore a Ford crest.

Customs had the rear panel trim deleted; instead "FORD" was spelled out in block letters here. Also deleted was the trim for the belt-line and body sides. Three vertical bright-metal chevrons were mounted on the forward part of the fenders in the convex spear. Customs and Custom 500s both had nylon-rayon carpeting front and rear.

The wagon lineup remained as in 1963 with the Country Squire and the Country Sedan both in six- and nine-passenger variants. The Country Squire's standard features included a power tailgate window, electric clock, and back-up lights. Both models came with the Mileage Maker Six and

3-speed manual transmission as standard equipment. The power tailgate window was also standard for the nine-passenger Country Sedan.

Paint and Upholstery

Paint selections numbered 13 in single tones and 14 in two-tone combinations. Color names this model year were:

- Wimbledon White
- Raven Black
- Silver Smoke Gray
- Rangoon Red
- Vintage Burgundy
- Skylight Blue
- Guardsman Blue
- Pagoda Green
- Dynasty Green
- Phoenician Yellow
- Prairie Tan
- Navaho Beige
- Chantilly Beige

Vinyl tops were again offered for the two-door hardtops in black or white. Phoenician Yellow, Prairie Tan, and Navaho Beige were discontinued during the model year, however.

Galaxie 500/XLs were offered with red, light blue/medium blue, turquoise/medium turquoise, beige, light silver-blue/medium silver-blue, white, and black crush vinyl interiors or with medium palomino crinkle vinyl. Convertibles were the same with the exceptions of light silver-blue, white, and palomino. Galaxie 500 hardtops and sedans had standard upholstery of blue, green, black, beige, and light turquoise/turquoise in chain weave cloth and crush vinyl combinations. Light blue/blue, light turquoise/turquoise, red, and pale beige/beige louver fabric and crush vinyl were the choices for the Custom 500 series. These same colors except turquoise were offered for the Custom sedans, except that bar-dot fabric with crush vinyl was used.

Country Squires had standard crush-vinyl upholstery selections of light blue/medium blue, light silver-blue/medium silver-blue, turquoise/medium turquoise, red, black, and palomino. Beige was available as a no-cost option in chain weave fabric and crush vinyl.

Country Sedan standard combination mosaic and crush-vinyl interiors were available in light blue/medium blue, light turquoise metallic/medium turquoise metallic, red, and medium beige metallic/ beige.

Options and Accessories

Many options and accessories were carried over to the 1964 Fords. However, the bucket seats with console and the 4-speed manual for the Country Squire were dropped. The Cruise-O-Matic (the aluminum-cased C4 for the small-block and the cast-iron version for the 352- and 390-ci) became the only automatic transmission option. The two-speed Ford-O-Matic, available since 1959, was discontinued.

A total of 58,306 1964 Galaxie 500/XL two-door hardtops were built for the model year. The pictured Rangoon Red example was ordered with a white vinyl top, rocker molding, and a 410-hp, 427-ci V-8. The wheels are an aftermarket type.

Bucket seats with all-vinyl upholstery, console, bucket-styled rear bench seat, and door panels with bright trim were all standard features of the 1964 Galaxie 500/XL.

Other items available were:
- Swing-Away steering wheel
- rocker molding
- remote-control outside mirror
- AM/FM radio
- simulated wire wheel covers
- SelectAire
- power seat

- power windows
- lake pipes
- transistorized ignition (427-ci)
- vinyl top in black or white (two-door hardtops)
- fender skirts
- bumper guards
- hood ornament

Additional options on this time capsule Galaxie 500 are the all-vinyl upholstery, AM-radio, and seat belts.

Wheel covers were optional on the Galaxie 500s, as well as the Customs and Custom 500s. A similar type with a different center was standard issue on the Galaxie 500/XLs. (Photo by Dick Rozum, Legendary Ford Magazine)

Win, Win, Win

Dan Gurney, at the wheel of the Wood Brothers' Galaxie 500, again won the opening NASCAR race of the 1964 racing season—the Motor Trend 500. Gurney's teammate Marvin Panch came in second. At Daytona, Ford was not so fortunate. Plymouths finished 1-2-3 thanks to their new 426-ci Hemi engines, while the closest Ford finished fourth, two laps behind. The Hemi was not even available as an option, nor was it easy to obtain through the parts department. Technically, it was not legal for NASCAR, but officials allowed the teams to use the engine because NASCAR needed Chrysler factory participation. In fact, Chevrolet and Pontiac were sitting out the race; Ford would not have had any factory-backed competition, except from Mercury.

With the Mopars running about 10 mph faster than the Galaxie 500s, Ford tried to get NASCAR to allow its 427-ci single overhead cam (SOHC, or "Cammer") to counter Hemi challenge, but the request was rejected,

ironically, because the engine was not a production item. Instead, Ford improved its 427-ci through a 7,000-rpm kit. Horsepower for the racing engine was boosted to 550 at 6,800 rpm versus a bit over 500 at 6,200 rpm. The setup consisted of a lighter valvetrain and hollow-stem valves. Also upgraded was the carburetion, via a 780-cfm Holley unit, and the crank was cross-drilled for better oiling. Ford's parts department sold the 7,000-rpm kit to the public, making it legal for NASCAR.

The high-rev kits helped Ford regain a competitive footing. Galaxie drivers won the Atlanta 500 and several of the next races on the schedule. At the end of the season, Ford won 30 Grand National races against 14 for Dodge and 12 for Plymouth. However, Fireball Roberts was severely injured in a crash at the World 600 in his Holman-Moody Galaxie 500, marring an otherwise successful season. Tragically, this legendary driver died six weeks after the accident.

Ford only won two USAC races, though Mercury managed seven wins along with the Pike's Peak Hill

Climb. Dodge won four and Plymouth tied Ford with two.

More lightweight Galaxie 500s were built for drag racing. These were equipped with the 427 Mk. II engine with a new camshaft, redesigned heads with larger ports along with 2.19-inch intake and 1.73-inch exhaust valves. Domed pistons and a redesigned combustion chamber gave a 14:1 compression ratio, plus a pair of 780-cfm Holleys on a high-rise intake manifold were also included. The engine was officially rated at 425 hp, but dyno testing revealed an output in excess of 500 hp. The carbs drew air through ducting that began at the open inboard headlight locations. A teardrop bubble hood was required to clear the high-rise/dual-quad setup.

The body of the lightweight Galaxie 500 was acid dipped to reduce weight, which made the skin very thin and, thus, as light as possible. A Ford 300 frame was again used underneath, as well as fiberglass panels. Bucket seat mounts were even drilled full of holes to reduce weight.

All of the weight reduction techniques were not enough, and the big Fords were still too heavy to compete in the Super Stock (S/S) class competition. However, they did qualify for the new AA/Stock class (7.00 to 8.69 full-size per advertised horsepower), where they dominated. Ford did not simply quit trying to win in the S/S category; a Fairlane Thunderbolt with the 427-ci Mk. II was created for this class and it dominated there.

Sales Figures Jump

Ford sold over 923,000 full-size cars for the 1964 model year, and the Galaxie 500 two-door hardtop was the most popular, at 206,998 units. This was an unusual result, as the four-door sedan typically accounted for the highest production total. In this case, the four-door sedan came in second, with 198,805 being built.

The Galaxie 500/XL four-door hardtop was the second lowest-production car, with 14,661 being purchased; the 500/XL convertible exceeded this figure by just over 500 units. Lowest in sales was the Galaxie 500 two-door sedan, with 13,041 being produced.

Overall 500/XL production reached its zenith in this model year at 88,136; 58,306 were two-door hardtops. Sales of the bucket seat model declined until the 1968 model year, when the bucket seats and console became an option resulting in a base price decrease. Furthermore, sales of full-size Fords with the 427 ci would decline dramatically starting in 1965.

Caravan of Stars, 1963–1964

In 1963 model car manufacturer AMT, TV car builder and customizer George Barris, and Ford Motor

Skip Hudson, a West Coast sports car racer, drove this Holman-Moody 1964 Galaxie 500 at at Riverside's Motor Trend 500 in January 1964. It was Holman-Moody's 1964 house car—an extra race ready vehicle kept for visiting drivers. (Photo courtesy of JDC collection)

FORD HARDTOP SIZZLER

(OPTIONAL 425 hp THUNDERBIRD V-8 SMOOTHS AND SHORTENS OUR LONG TEXAS ROADS!)

Texas Ford Dealers' hardtop sales are sizzling! And this Ford Galaxie 500 2-Door Fastback Hardtop is one powerful reason why. Hundreds of pounds heftier, it's stronger, smoother, steadier than any car in its field. It features total performance —tempered, honed and polished in open competition. Get acquainted with Ford's winning ways. Test-drive this Ford hardtop sizzler at your Texas Ford Dealer's.

This newspaper advertisement emphasized the high-performance and smooth riding qualities of the 1964 Galaxie 500 fastback.

Company joined forces to produce several custom cars to be shown around the country. Ford executives believed this program, which came to be known as the "Caravan of Stars," would bring even more attention to the company's cars. Others soon joined the effort—Bill Cushenberry, Gene Winfield, as well as Vince Gardener of Dearborn Steel Tubing.

Several Ford customs were built for 1963 and 1964, two of which were based on Galaxie 500s, while the others were the Falcon and Thunderbird models. The 1963 *Astro* featured a landau half-top covered with white vinyl. A filler panel could be put in place to create a full hardtop or the entire top could be removed to have a convertible. Stacked Lucas headlights set within round pods and a blacked-out grille with a horizontal divider dramatically altered the look of the frontal view. The looping side molding was deleted, rear wheel wells were radiused, and a custom rocker panel molding was applied. Kelsey-Hayes wire wheels were also installed. In back, tunneled taillights similar in style to the frontal lighting replaced the stock units. The body was first painted Aqua Pearl with shading applied to the sheetmetal creases, but later it was repainted Sea Blue Metallic. This custom's interior with four bucket seats was upholstered in white Naugahyde.

Winfield created the *Constellation* from a 1964 Galaxie 500 convertible. The stock grille was

"Win on Sunday; sell on Monday" was the theme of the 1960s. Ford promoted its racing victories as shown by this magazine advertisement boasting of the win at the Atlanta 500. Winning races was seen as great advertising.

maintained, but the headlights were replaced with Lucas bullet tips. A silver spear ran from the headlights to the mid-point of the doors. In back, the rear panel was recessed and smoothed. Custom units replaced stock taillights. Four chrome-plated exhaust tips added another custom touch. Dayton wire wheels mounted with Firestone tires were also installed. Bucket seats, a full-length console, and a walnut-rimmed steering wheel replaced the stock components. Upholstery was dark blue; the carpet was a contrasting Sky Blue.

The Alexander Brothers created the custom, high-performance Alexa, built from a 427-powered Galaxie 500/XL. Custom features of the *Alexa* included an extended front end with rectangular headlights mounted behind frosted glass and a custom-built grille. The extended rear end was rounded with no rear bumper. A rich, candy-red paint was applied to the body. Four bucket seats and a full-length console upholstered in pleated white Naugahyde were inside.

Additional customized full-size Fords would be built through 1969.

FORD TOTAL PERFORMANCE
WINS ATLANTA "500"
FOR 3RD YEAR IN A ROW!

1965–1966: *Luxury and the* *NASCAR Dispute*

Sales of the Galaxie 500/XLs dropped drastically for the 1965 model year. This Vintage Burgundy convertible is one of just 9,849 built.

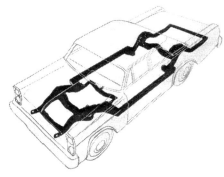

Frame design incorporated a front-end assembly, rear-end assembly, and straight box-section side rails. Torque boxes welded at each corner of these side rails joined the front and rear units. These torque boxes allowed a limited amount of flexing, plus dampened noise and vibration that would have otherwise been transmitted to the frame through the suspension system.

The 1965 full-size Fords were almost as different from their predecessors as the 1949 Ford was from the 1948, and were accurately described as "new from road to roof." About the only major components carried over were the V-8s. One ad went so far as to remark, "Even the keys are different," noting their new reversible feature. The ride quality, advertised as being "Quieter than a Rolls Royce" was another major selling point for the 1965 full-size Fords. One other important change for the model year was the addition to the line of the luxury oriented Galaxie 500/LTD.

The Road to Roof Changes

Ford Motor Company said of their new big cars, "Beginning, literally, with a clean sheet of paper, Ford engineers and stylists created an exciting and entirely new Ford car for 1965. A masterpiece in design, the 1965 Ford offers prospective buyers a level of comfort, luxury, riding qualities, performance—and most important, pride of ownership—heretofore believed obtainable only in America's higher priced cars."

Underneath the all-new body was an all-new perimeter frame. It was not simply a new frame, though. In the prior years, the frame was designed to provide complete beam and torsional strength. The 1965 full-size Ford frame was somewhat flexible, while the body was designed to be much stiffer than in the past. Plenty of sound-deadening insulation was

"Ford rides quieter than Rolls-Royce." "Oh come now, old boy!" Lots of people find it hard to believe. But it's a fact—in tests by a leading acoustical firm, 1965 Fords with 289 cu. in. V-8's proved quieter than a Rolls-Royce. This quiet does not mean a Ford is a $17,000 Rolls. It does mean Ford is strong, solidly built, designed with precision and great attention to detail. Underneath that trim, functional body, it's all muscle. **FORD**. If you doubt Ford is everything we say it is, take a test-drive and listen...listen hard!!

The 1965 Ford Galaxie 500/LTD was advertised as "quieter than a Rolls-Royce." In fact, though the claim was truthful as testing revealed, it was not so much more that the average person could notice the difference.

The velvet brute

The 1965 Galaxie 500/XL with a 425-hp 427-ci was advertised as "the velvet brute" due to its high-performance yet quiet, smooth ride.

installed, so the car provided a much quieter riding car.

Frame design incorporated a front-end assembly, rear-end assembly and straight box-section side rails. Torque boxes welded at each corner of these side rails joined the front and rear units. These torque boxes allowed a limited amount of flexing, plus dampened noise and vibration that would have otherwise been transmitted to the frame through the suspension system.

Three basic frames were used: one for sedans and hardtops, one for the convertibles, and the other for station wagons. The convertible frame did not have an X-member to reinforce the chassis as had been done in the past. The body was joined to the frame, though not directly, at only four points: just ahead of the cowl and immediately behind the rear passenger area. Rub-

ber biscuits were installed between the body and frame side rails.

Besides contributing to a quieter ride, the frame also had the virtue of

being much lighter than the 1964 version. Body construction was simplified, which also helped reduce overall weight. Approximately 200 pounds of weight was removed in the process.

The suspension, of course, was also new. A single arm replaced the lower A-arms of the independent-ball-joint front suspension. The upper A-arm was retained and was angled back to reduce nose diving while the brakes were applied. A diagonally mounted, rubber-bushed strut was employed to control fore-and-aft wheel movement, an anti-roll bar reduced body roll during cornering, and shocks were placed within the coil springs. This front suspension design was so superior it was used for NASCAR stock cars into the 1980s regardless of make.

A three-link, coil spring suspension was used in back. The longitudinal links controlled fore-and-aft motion of the rear axle assembly and absorbed acceleration and braking forces. Two of these links were positioned between the lower side of the

Few 1965 full-size Fords were equipped with the 427-ci V-8. This Custom 500 is one of those rare examples.

During mid-1964, Ford Motor Company dropped the 427-ci 4-barrel as an option, but it was not reinstated for 1965. Hence, all 1965 Fords with a 427 had the dual-quad setup as seen here.

axle housing and the frame torque box at either side. The third link was installed between the right-hand side of the differential at the top of the axle housing and the frame crossmember. A track bar was attached near the axle center and to a lateral point on the frame left rear rail. The rear suspension was fully isolated with rubber bushings and sleeves, which served to further reduce noise and vibration. Low-profile, 15-inch tires were an additional upgrade to improve ride qualities.

Manual and power steering systems were also redesigned. All Fords received a new parallelogram-type steering linkage with a cross link and idler arm for more positive vehicle control under all driving conditions. The overall steering ratio was increased to 30.9:1 to reduce steering effort. A valve-type power steering unit integral with the Magic-Circle steering gear and a new belt-driven power steering pump were additional advances for 1965. The optional power steering system's overall ratio was 21.9:1.

The engines from late 1964 were carried over to the 1965 model year, with the exception of the 223-ci 6-cylinder and the 427-ci with a single 4-barrel. A new 240-ci Big Six became the standard engine for all full-size Fords except the Galaxie 500/LTD, 500/XL, and Country Squire. It was the largest 6-cylinder engine in any American car for the 1965 model year.

Later in the model year, Ford released an upgraded 427-ci 2x4 barrel that was developed in racing. The improved design featured stronger connecting rods, revised combustion chambers for better flow, and a larger oil gallery for the main bearings. The larger oil gallery required more clearance in the block, so the block has a bulge in the lower left side, and the engine was dubbed as "the side-oiler."

Interiors got an entirely new look as well. A newly designed, swept-away instrument panel was 5 inches farther forward than in 1964. All instruments and controls, including the optional radio controls, were located directly ahead of the driver's position beneath a padded hood on all models.

Signal indicators, fuel gauge, speedometer, odometer, high-beam indicator, and the optional radio were on top of the instrument cluster. The speedometer featured white numerals against a satin-black background. A second row of instruments and controls was recessed in a horizontally styled housing along the bottom of the instrument cluster. To the right were the heater blower switch, heater controls, and the ignition switch. On the left were the switches for the headlights and windshield wipers. When so equipped, the electric clock was positioned directly over the steering column along the secondary row of instruments.

This Galaxie 500/XL is powered by the 300-hp, 390-ci 4-barrel. A 195-hp, 289-ci 2-barrel was standard for this model.

All 1965 Galaxie 500 series cars had hexagonal taillights. Unusually, the Custom series cars were equipped with round taillights mounted within a filler plate inside the hexagonal bezel.

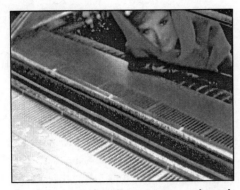

The four-door hardtops were equipped with Silent-Flo ventilation, as shown in this aged publicity photo. Outside vents in the sheetmetal behind the rear window were connected to passages in the body to another series of vents in the package tray behind the rear seat.

The luxurious Galaxie 500/LTD was available in two- and four-door hardtop varieties. This particular car was delivered to the selling dealer with imperfections in the paint and returned to the Louisville Assembly Plant after the customer refused to accept it. The VIN was stamped, "Salvage Unit—No Factory Warranty." (Photo by Ward Plauché)

When the optional SelectAire air conditioning was ordered, a different instrument panel was used on all models. The panel had four adjustable outlets to distribute cool air. SelectAire was completely integrated with the heater and fresh-air system, including the controls on the instrument panel.

Additional changes for 1965 included the use of curved side glass, a standard 42-amp alternator instead of a generator, a circuit breaker for the tail and brake lights was added to the headlight switch, ignition and trunk keys now had identical serrations on the key shank so the keys could be inserted with either side up, and luggage compartment space increased.

Joe Oros, Ford's chief stylist, was in charge of styling the big Fords, which featured a mix of horizontal and vertical attributes. In front, stacked headlights flanked a horizontal grille. Body sides had crisp lines; edges were sharp instead of rounded. The long-traditional round taillights were gone, except on the Custom 500 and Custom; hexagonal assemblies with "cross-hair" molding housing back-up lights were found on all other

full-size hardtops and sedans. Early during calendar year 1965, assembly plants began adding spear moldings on either side of the trunk ornament on all models. Although the sheetmetal and underlying structures were different, the rooflines were carried over from the previous year.

The New LTD

The model lineup changed as well. There was the new luxury-oriented Galaxie 500/LTD available in two- and four-door hardtop varieties. Various interpretations have been assigned to the LTD designation: Luxury Trim Décor, Lincoln Type Design, or simply Limited. However, according to a *Car Life* magazine review of the LTD, the designation was just three meaningless letters and went on to speculate that it could not stand for "Limited" because Chrysler was using the label and had the copyright to the name. Regardless of the intent of Ford Motor Company, Luxury Trim Décor and Lincoln Type Design fit the concept of the LTD very well.

This round medallion for the LTDs was mounted on the C-pillars. (Photo by Ward Plauché)

A center fold-down rear seat armrest was included as standard equipment on the LTDs. (Photo by Ward Plauché)

The Galaxie 500/LTD was an "executive" model, similar in concept to Pontiac's Bonneville Brougham, which debuted for 1964. Ford boasted that the LTDs "present a look of elegance and dignified taste inside and out. Designed for the discriminating, the LTD models will attract buyers who want hardtop styling with a classy flair, the ultimate in luxurious bench seat interiors, and smooth, lively power." It was definitely up-market—so much so that it almost seemed to be in direct competition with Mercury, or even to some degree, Lincoln. This true luxury vehicle was a bargain at a base price of $3,167 (for the two-door), which was the same as that of the Galaxie 500/XL two-door hardtop. The four-door hardtop version listed for $3,245.

Executives with Ford's ad agency, J. Walter Thompson, were impressed with how quiet the new Fords rode. Someone got curious about just how quiet they really were and went so far as to test a 1965 Galaxie 500/LTD four-door hardtop, a 500/XL, and a Galaxie 500 four-door sedan against a Rolls-Royce Silver Cloud III (two of them, in fact). Scientific testing revealed the Fords were technically quieter than a Rolls-Royce, though not to the point most people would actually notice. Even so, advertising made the most of the fact. One advertisement proclaimed, "Don't whisper in the back seat of a '65 Ford if you don't want to be heard in the front."

Standard equipment for the LTD included a 289-ci V-8, Cruise-O-Matic, full-length moldings on the rocker panels and lower edge of the quarters, wheel lip moldings, four-spoke wheel covers, hood ornament, horizontally styled "star" plaque on the quarter panels, circular LTD

From Ore Boat to Showboat

A Galaxie 500/LTD four-door hardtop sitting by the loading dock with an ore boat visible in the background appeared in one of the many magazine ads for the 1965 Fords. The eight sentences below the photo were quite revealing:

"When we began building it, this Ford Galaxie LTD was part of a mountain of ore in Minnesota. That's where our quality production begins—right with the raw iron ore.

We ship the ore in our own boats. We make almost 50% of our own steel. We make our own safety glass, vinyls, paint, Autolite batteries and spark plugs, too. We are the only manufacturer that builds a car from the ground up—controls quality every step of the way. This enables us to set and maintain unsurpassed quality standards. When it comes to quality, we move mountains."

emblem on the C-pillars, and for the four-door hardtop a thin bright-metal molding wrapping around the base of the C-pillars and underneath the rear window. Pedal pads also were trimmed in bright metal.

The biscuit and pleated Scotchguard-protected nylon upholstery was stretched over thick foam padding. A center fold-down armrest for the rear seat was also standard. The door trim panel design was exclusive to the LTD; the lower door area had color-keyed carpeting, while the upper area was vinyl with large pleats. Simulated walnut-grained paneling bordered with bright trim was laid over the pleated area. Simulated walnut appliqués also appeared on the lower edge of the instrument panel. Headlining and sun visors were of gabardine finish. An electric clock was included, too. In addition, the Galaxie 500 standard equipment carried over to the Galaxie 500/LTD.

Models and Features

Galaxie 500/XLs were available in only two versions; the four-door hardtop was discontinued. These models were still distinguished with bucket seats, console, 289-ci V-8, and an automatic as standard equipment. Other 500/XL features included bright moldings for the rockers, quarters, and wheel lips plus four-spoke wheel covers, hood ornament, and a horizontal star plaque on the quarter panels. Model identification in block-style lettering was mounted on the front fenders.

Inside, the seating was covered in all-vinyl upholstery. Shell-type front bucket seats with molded foam padding, and bright-metal shields was said to give "an expensive look of prestige." In between these seats was a painted vinyl-textured, bright-metal-trimmed console housing the transmission gear selector lever, and a glove box. Its back end also housed a courtesy lamp. Bright-metal trim was applied to the foot pedals. Door trim panels were unique to the 500/XL and featured a bright satin-finish appliqué surrounded by a bright-metal molding. The lower portion of the door panels was covered in color-keyed carpeting, while the upper area was covered in pleated vinyl. As before, a dual-lens courtesy-warning light was placed in the lower portion of the door panel. An extended armrest for the driver and passenger was also a standard item for the 500/XL. As on the 500/LTD, simulated walnut appliqués were on the lower instrument panel.

Galaxie 500s had a hood ornament plus bright-metal moldings on the rocker panels wheel lips, around the windows, and on the windshield posts, belt-line, and drip rails. Model identification appeared in chromed block letters on the front fenders. (Interestingly, the ID plaque was the same for the Galaxie 500/LTD. The circular medallion on each C-pillar gave away the LTD part of the model identification.)

The four-door hardtops (Galaxie 500 and 500/LTD) also had Silent-Flo ventilation. Outside vents in the sheetmetal behind the rear window connected passages in the body to another series of vents in the package tray behind the rear seat. A switch on the instrument panel opened and closed the vacuum-actuated ventilation system. When the car was moving, a low-pressure area formed around the outside vents, which assisted in drawing stale air out of the vehicle when the vents were opened. Silent-Flo ventilation was also helpful in defogging the rear window.

Cloth-and-vinyl upholstery was standard on all Galaxie 500s, except the convertible, which came with all-vinyl upholstery. Bright-metal front seat shields and a brushed-finish molding on the lower instrument panel were also standard. All two-door hardtops were equipped with rear interior roof pillar courtesy lamps; four-door hardtops, all sedans, and wagons had a dome light instead.

The Custom 500 and Custom series of Fords were offered in two- and four-door sedan styles. All versions had cloth upholstery, carpeting, white vinyl headliner, and a thin bright molding at the base of the C-pillar. Chromed block-type letters on the front fenders of the Custom provided model identification, while the Custom 500 ID was mounted on the quarter panels. The "500" moniker appeared as a plaque with a black background. The latter model also received a Ford crest on the C-pillars. Rocker and wheel lip moldings were not included, nor were glove box lights, side seat shields, and appliqués or bright trim on the lower instrument panel. All full-size Fords had a satin and black Ford crest on the deck lid or tailgate (except on the Country Squire).

Station wagon models totaled five, which included six- and

White pearl vinyl upholstery was one of eight standard colors offered for the Galaxie 500/XL convertible. Door trim panels for it and the hardtop version featured a bright satin-finish appliqué surrounded by a bright-metal molding. The lower portion of the door panels was covered in color-keyed carpeting, while the upper area was covered in pleated vinyl.

The Galaxie 500 four-door sedan sold in greater numbers than any other full-size Ford for the 1965 model year. A total of 181,183 were built.

The low-priced 1965 Custom 500 two-door sedan accounted for 19,603 sales. Somewhat surprisingly, about two-thirds of them were equipped with an optional V-8. The paint color was labeled Prairie Bronze.

An all-new dash was included in the new 1965 full-size Fords. The Custom and Custom 500 series had less décor than the higher series of cars. A plaque with model identification was mounted on the lower glove box door.

ten-passenger Country Squires and Country Sedans. Ten-passenger station wagons featured dual-facing seats in the rear compartment. Like the second seat, they could be folded down for additional cargo space. Standard trim on all Country Squires included dark-grained, simulated-wood paneling on the sides and tailgate surrounded by lighter grained, simulated-wood (actually fiberglass) rails decorated with simulated carriage bolts, back-up lights, clock, and hood ornament, plus most of the standard items on the Country Sedan.

The mid-priced wagon had bright-metal moldings around all windows, on windshield posts, rocker panels (not on Country Squire), and wheel openings. Both the Country Squire and Country Sedan had their respective model identifications on the front fenders; the Squire had an additional "horsehead with crossed riding crops" emblem on the front fenders, too.

Inside the Country Squire were Galaxie 500-type door panels with bright-trimmed "square saddle" design, bright-trimmed armrests, full-width instrument panel ornamentation, front seat side shields, and padded vinyl quarter trim pan-

els. Five all-vinyl upholstery choices or one combination cloth/vinyl arrangement came as standard issue.

Country Sedans had bright-trimmed armrests, four all-vinyl upholstery selections, and one cloth/vinyl choice. Door panels were similar to those of the Country Squire, but with reduced bright trim. As on the Country Squire, a locking rear storage compartment was provided.

The Ranch Wagon, the lowest-priced Ford station wagon, returned to the lineup. Standard items included bright-metal moldings around the windshield and tailgate window, plus bright quarter window moldings. Door panels were like those of the Custom, and quarter trim panels were of color-keyed textured steel.

Ford LTD Limousine Program

Ford Motor Company contracted Dearborn Steel Tubing to build 100 LTD and Mercury Parklane limousines for 1965 and 1966. According to Ford Vice President and General Manager Donald Frey, the LTD limousine was developed to test the market for such a vehicle. Ford intended to sell the cars through

authorized Ford and Mercury dealers. Reportedly, only ten of the LTD limousines were built for the two years combined. At least one was a 1966 model, and it appeared in one episode of the television series, *Mission Impossible*.

The stretched 1965 version measured 19 feet, 5 inches in overall length—nearly 2 feet more than a regular LTD. Price was approximately $9,000, or $2,300 less than a Cadillac limousine. The price included a 390-ci, air conditioning, padded vinyl top, seating room for eight (with two jump seats), TV, Princess phone, and for at least one example, Pyrex headlight covers. According to a *Time* magazine article (April 16, 1965), "The LTD already has 50 firm orders, will begin rolling off the assembly line by the end of the year."

The 1965 LTD limousines had metal added between the front and rear doors. For 1966, the rear doors were lengthened. In both cases, the chassis and suspension were strengthened to accommodate the increased weight of the limousine.

LTD Executive and Green Mist

The 1965 *LTD Executive* was a custom-built show car that was authorized by Ford, built by Gene Winfield, and shown at multiple venues across the country as part of the Caravan of Stars. It received a 1966-style grille, modified headlight bezels, recessed taillights, stainless steel panel from the windshield header to the midpoint of the roof, and padded vinyl covering from that point rearward. All emblems and name plaques were removed, and a special medallion was placed behind the front wheels. Upholstery was

The Country Squire was offered in six- and nine-passenger versions. Nine-passenger models outsold the six-passenger variant by roughly 6,000 units. Even though the 6-cylinder was standard for both, all but a few hundred had an extra-cost V-8.

fabric and leather. The car was photographed with stock wheel covers for early publicity photos, but these were later replaced with Kelsey-Hayes wire wheels. At some other point, it was fitted with Rader aluminum wheels.

Another show car, dubbed the *Green Mist*, was also a part of the Caravan of Stars. Like the *LTD Executive*, it was built from a Galaxie 500/LTD, but this was a two-door version. The *Green Mist* featured a custom-fabricated grille, NASCAR-type headlight panels, custom taillights, extruded aluminum rocker moldings, Rader Hot Wire wheels (fitted later), and a two-piece top. The rear component of the top was trimmed with fake landau iron (this section

could be left in place). With the whole top removed, a Thunderbird Sports Roadster style tonneau could be fitted behind the rear seat. As this car's name suggests, it was painted in a custom-mixed emerald green.

Paint and Upholstery Choices

Diamond Lustre Enamel paints for the full-size Fords were:
- Wimbledon White
- Raven Black
- Rangoon Red
- Vintage Burgundy
- Prairie Bronze
- Honey Gold
- Silver Smoke Gray
- Champagne Beige
- Phoenician Yellow

- Springtime Yellow
- Dynasty Green
- Ivy Green
- Tropical Turquoise
- Twilight Turquoise
- Silver Blue
- Arcadian Blue
- Caspian Blue

Again, extra-cost two-tones were offered for all models except the Country Squire. Four of these colors—Honey Gold, Dynasty Green, Twilight Turquoise, and Tropical Turquoise—were not officially offered for the Ranch Wagon.

Upholstery for the Galaxie 500/LTD was composed of shadow-striped cloth for the biscuit pattern in the cushion and lower seat back and pinseal cloth for the pleated areas and bolsters. Color availability was black, blue, palomino, ivy, gold, turquoise, and burgundy was exclusive for the 500/LTD.

Galaxie 500/XL models featured crush grain vinyl in blue, red, black, turquoise, ivy, gold, white pearl, or palomino. The 500/XL hardtop was given an additional selection of palomino cloth and vinyl.

Sedan versions of the Galaxie 500 were upholstered with Carthage cloth and crush grain vinyl; color offerings numbered seven: blue, red, black, turquoise, ivy, gold, and palomino. Four optional all-vinyl trims were available in blue, red, ivy, gold, and palomino. The hardtop added a black all-vinyl option to this list. Standard cloth/vinyl upholstery colors for the hardtops were the same as those of the sedans with the sole exception being black.

Custom 500s offered frost stripe cloth inserts with crush grain vinyl bolsters. Colors were blue, red, turquoise, and palomino. The color

Ford Motor Company contracted Dearborn Steel Tubing to build 100 LTD and Mercury Parklane limousines for 1965 and 1966. However, only ten of the LTD limousines were reportedly built for the two years combined. (Photo courtesy of Mitch Frumkin)

This 1965 show car, dubbed the Green Mist, was exhibited across the country. The emerald green show piece featured a number of custom features, including a unique grille, extruded aluminum rocker moldings, and a two-piece top. With the whole top removed, a Thunderbird Sports Roadster style tonneau could be fitted behind the rear seat.

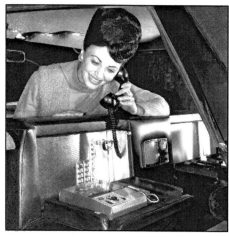

Upholstery for the LTD Executive was fabric and leather. Amenities, such as the telephone, were similar to those of the LTD Limousine. (Photo courtesy of Chicago Automobile Trade Association)

for the sole all-vinyl option was palomino.

Lowest in the full-size Ford hierarchy, the Custom, featured plaid-stripe cloth with crush grain vinyl bolsters in blue, red, or palomino. As with the Custom 500, palomino was the sole color choice for the all-vinyl option.

The 1965 LTD Executive was a show car exhibited at multiple venues across the country. It received a 1966-style grille, modified headlight bezels, recessed taillights, a stainless steel panel from the windshield header to the midpoint of the roof, and a padded vinyl covering from that point rearward. (Photo courtesy of Chicago Automobile Trade Association)

Country Squires offered all-vinyl upholstery in blue, red, black, ivy, gold, and palomino or the no-cost option of palomino cloth and vinyl. Country Sedan seating was all-vinyl in blue, red, turquoise, or palomino. The Ranch Wagon offered blue, red, or palomino all-vinyl upholstery.

Extra-Cost Hardware

Among the many options and accessories offered by Ford for 1965 were:

- SelectAire and dealer-installed Ford-Air air conditioning
- power steering
- power brakes
- power windows
- padded instrument panel
- lake pipes
- limited-slip differential
- AM/FM radio
- two-way CB radio
- Swing-Away steering wheel
- Safety-Convenience Control Panel
- automatic speed control
- body side molding

Frost stripe cloth inserts with crush grain vinyl bolsters were standard on the 1965 Custom 500s. However, this color scheme was an extra-cost option.

- deluxe rear-mounted antenna or dual rear-mounted antennas
- tinted glass
- tachometer
- reclining passenger bucket seat (500/XL)
- seat belts
- remote trunk release
- vinyl-covered roof (now offered for four-door hardtops)
- spotlight

A couple of the most interesting extras were Pyrex headlight covers (standard on the 427-powered cars) and High-Performance Engine Kit for the 352- and 390-ci. The headlight covers were glass units made for Ford by Corning and required a deeper headlight bezel to fit. The high-performance engine kit was comprised of triple 2-barrel carbs with a special intake manifold and air cleaner.

One more unusual option was the fold-down rear seat for sedan models. It was very similar to the second seat on station wagons. This option returned for 1966.

Racing Domination

The 1965 NASCAR racing season was a controversial one, to say the least. NASCAR banned the Hemi and the Ford High Riser in response to Chrysler Corporation's warning that it would build a double overhead cam Hemi if Ford were allowed to race with the 427 SOHC. NASCAR officials also set some new rules. Altogether, this was unacceptable to Chrysler, so they pulled out of NASCAR. USAC was asked to participate in the Hemi ban but did not, so Dodge and Plymouth race teams with factory backing continued to run in those events.

Ford responded by withdrawing their support for the Zecol-Lubaid team. The crowds started declining in the absence of the Chrysler-versus-Ford competition on the NASCAR circuit. By July, however, NASCAR, USAC, Ford, and Chrysler reached a compromise agreement; this agreement allowed the Hemis to continue to race and NASCAR would reconsider the Ford SOHC for 1966.

In the meantime, Ford won most of the NASCAR events—48 of 55, in fact. Ford won 32 consecutive races before Richard Petty, driving a Hemi-powered Plymouth, broke that streak at the Nashville 400. Ned Jarrett, dri-

ving a Bondy Long Ford, finished second. Earlier, Ford had a 1-2-3 finish at the Daytona 500 and a 1-2-3-4 finish at the Atlanta 500.

In USAC competition, Ford provided Holman-Moody Galaxies to A. J. Foyt and Parnelli Jones. Late in the season, Ford began supporting Zecol-Lubaid again. Still, Ford managed only one win, with independent Don White scoring another Ford win in a 1964 Galaxie 500.

Ford offered lightweight Galaxie 500s in two versions this year: a 289-ci with Weber carburetors and a 427-ci SOHC. The lightweight cars with the 427-ci were raced in B/FX class competition and the 289s in C/FX. Bill Hoefer drove a 289-ci lightweight to Junior Stock Eliminator honors in the 1965 NHRA Springnationals.

Production Numbers

Full-size cars accounted for 872,790 of Ford's 1965 sales. The top-selling model this time was the Galaxie 500 four-door sedan with the two-door hardtop taking second place in production totals, with 157,284 finding buyers. Demand for the new Galaxie 500/LTD was so strong that 105,729 orders were placed. The com-

petition took notice of the sales pace; Chevrolet and Plymouth released their luxurious Caprice and VIP, respectively, in mid 1965.

Galaxie 500/XL production declined significantly with a total run of 37,990. Only 9,849 were convertibles. Orders for big Fords with the 427-ci dropped greatly as well. The first couple of years' production had been well into the thousands. For 1965, 427-ci V-8 orders had dropped into the hundreds. If they were not the fastest full-size car in 1965, they were not far behind. *Car Life* testers drove a 427-ci 0-60 mph in 4.8 seconds and to a top speed of 136 mph. *Hot Rod* magazine's road testers ran the quarter-mile in 14.43 seconds with an end speed of 108.04 mph. Performance-minded buyers, though, were moving away from the heavier full-size cars to the lighter intermediates such as Pontiac's GTO.

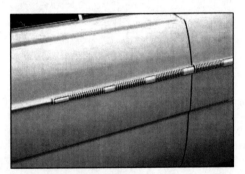

This body side molding was standard issue for the 1965 Custom 500s.

The Safety-Convenience Control Panel was new for 1965. The left button locked the doors, while the one to the far right actuated the emergency flashers. Warning lights in between indicated door(s) ajar, low fuel level, and reminded passengers to fasten seat belts. It added $51.50 to the price of a two-door and $64.40 to a four-door model.

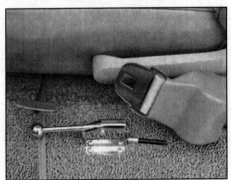

This remote trunk release was a dealer-installed accessory. The lever pulled a cable reaching to the trunk lid latch assembly.

Standard issue with 427-powered full-size Fords for 1965 was a set of Pyrex headlight covers. These were also available as an accessory for other non-427 cars. These are exceptionally rare items in either used or NOS form today.

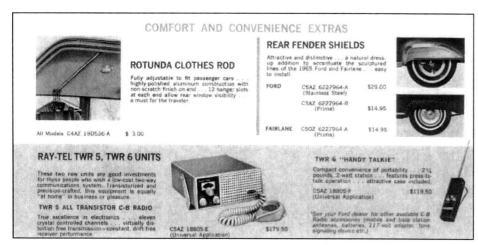

Other accessories offered for 1965 included a Rotunda brand clothes rod, fender skirts (in stainless or primer), two-way radio, and a Handy-Talkie radio.

1966: The Beat Goes On

The one-year-old full-size Fords received some new sheetmetal, yet they bore a strong resemblance to the 1965s. Up front, the stacked headlights and a horizontal grille remained, though the bezels and grille were redesigned. Actually two grilles were used: a chrome-plated diecast unit for the top-of-the-line models and an anodized aluminum one for the Galaxie 500s, Country Sedans, and on down the price ladder to the Customs and Ranch Wagon. The quarter panels received a subtle kick-up to create a coke-bottle profile, rear wheel openings were more open, and the roofline of the two-door hardtops swept back more. Square taillights were used for all big Fords this year, but the "cross hair" housings for the back-up lights, now standard in all models, survived in modified form. Seat belts and an outside rearview mirror for the driver's side became standard equipment as well.

The engine choices for 1966 significantly expanded. A 265-hp, 390-ci 2-barrel and a 315-hp, 390-ci 4-barrel were added, the 330-hp Police Interceptor was discontinued, and the

A rarely ordered option for 1965 Fords was this AM/FM radio. FM stations were not common at the time.

410-hp 427-ci returned. Two new 428-ci engines joined the lineup; one was a Police Interceptor. These were not super-high-performance types. Instead, the 428 produced impressive low-end torque to help move the cars, which were getting heavier. (Later this engine became the basis for the 428 Cobra Jet and Super Cobra Jet used in Mustangs, Torinos, and other FoMoCo cars.) The 1966 full-size Fords gained roughly 60 additional pounds, though the LTDs gained substantially more.

The 428-ci, which actually displaced closer to 427 ci, was rated at 345 or 360 hp in the Police Interceptor guise. Its size was the result of using the 406's 4.13-inch bore in combination with the 3.98-inch

Beginning in 1962, Ford offered a variety of tachometers including these appearing in this 1966 advertisement— 6,000- and 9,000-rpm Cobras and a 9,000-rpm Sun.

In 1965, Holman-Moody built 15 1965 Galaxie 500s. Those cars were the first "bodies in white" that Holman-Moody received from Ford, but were not serialized. As a result, those cars carried alloy Holman-Moody VIN tags. Fred Lorenzen drove this car to victory in the 1965 Daytona 500. (Photo courtesy of John Craft)

stroke of Mercury's 410-ci. Both versions had a compression ratio of 10.5:1 and were fed premium fuel via a single 4-barrel carb. The police engine was fitted with an aluminum intake and gained its extra horsepower with a different camshaft.

Ford's Cruise-O-Matic was updated with disc clutch plates in place of the old bands on low and reverse gears, improved valving in the hydraulic system, and a new combination of steel and composition plates in each of the clutch assemblies. It could handle up to 475 ft-lbs of torque. This transmission, dubbed Selectshift Cruise-O-Matic or simply the C6, could be shifted manually. It was offered on the 390- and 428-powered cars; the 352-ci came hooked to the old cast-iron unit when ordered.

An additional model was added featuring the 428 and C6 automatic as standard equipment. It was dubbed Galaxie 500 7-Litre and offered as a two-door hardtop and convertible. These two were the heaviest models in Ford's line, with the convertible weighing in at a hefty 4,059 pounds. The LTD was now separated from the Galaxie 500 line; it was now simply the Ford LTD.

Paint and Upholstery

Exterior colors offered were:
- Raven Black
- Wimbledon White
- Arcadian Blue
- Nightmist Blue
- Silver Blue
- Ivy Green
- Tahoe Turquoise
- Sahara Beige
- Springtime Yellow
- Silver Frost
- Sauterne Gold

Ford Motor Company's advertising for the 1966 Galaxie 500 7-Litre promoted both the luxury-oriented and sporty features of the new model.

The Galaxie 500s, Custom 500s, Customs, Country Sedans, and Ranch Wagons all received an aluminum grille. Other models had a distinctive die-cast unit.

- Candyapple Red
- Vintage Burgundy
- Antique Bronze
- Emberglo

Upholstery for the LTD was sewn in an exclusive diamond and pleated pattern. The diamond pattern was an insert on the seat back rests and the central portion of the door and quarter trim panels. Seating surfaces used shadow-stripe cloth; seat sides were of Cologne pattern vinyl. Standard colors numbered seven: blue, aqua, silver mink, burgundy, ivy gold, black, and parchment. A gabardine finish, color-keyed headliner and cut pile nylon-rayon carpeting were also LTD features.

Galaxie 500 7-Litres and 500/XLs came with crinkle and rosette vinyl upholstery; the latter was used as an insert on the seat cushions. Colors offered were blue, aqua, emberglo, red, ivy gold, black, and parchment.

The Galaxie 500 convertible offered crinkle vinyl upholstery in the same colors as the bucket seat models.

Standard upholstery for the bench seating of the Galaxie 500 hardtops and sedans was a combination of Olympia cloth inserts and crinkle-texture vinyl bolsters. The standard colors were blue, aqua, red, emberglo, black, and parchment.

Custom 500s used Eaton body cloth and crinkle-texture vinyl in four standard colors: blue, aqua, red, and parchment.

The Custom series came standard with Key body cloth and crinkle vinyl in blue, red, and parchment.

The six- and ten-passenger Country Squires had five pleated all-vinyl trims and a no-cost option of a single-cloth-and-vinyl combination. In all-vinyl applications crinkle and Venetian pattern vinyl combinations were used in blue, aqua, red, black,

Standard equipment for the Galaxie 500 7-Litre included a 345-hp, 428-ci 4-barrel V-8, Cruise-O-Matic transmission, special pin striping, styled steel wheel covers, and 7-Litre ornamentation. This model had its own body codes: 63D for the hardtop and 76D for the convertible.

A reclining passenger seat with headrest was an option for the Galaxie 500 7-Litre as well as the Galaxie 500/XL. Crinkle and rosette vinyl upholstery was standard for these models.

and parchment. Parchment Olympia cloth and crinkle vinyl was the sole no-cost option choice.

Country Sedans, whether six- or ten-passenger, came with crinkle and Venetian pattern vinyl in blue, red, aqua, and parchment. Steel load floor panels were color-keyed with vinyl paint.

The single Ranch Wagon model offered blue, red, and parchment in crinkle and match stick pattern vinyl. As with the Country Sedans, the steel load floor was coated with color-keyed vinyl paint.

Beginning in 1966 the luxurious big Ford was simply labeled, LTD. LTD sales totaled 101,096; the four-door hardtop counting for 69,400 (top). Upholstery for the LTD was sewn in an exclusive diamond and pleated pattern (bottom left). A unique trunk ornament was included on LTDs (bottom right).

All wagons this year received the Magic Doorgate that opened down as a standard tailgate or sideways like a door.

Galaxie 500 7-Litre

Ford said the new Galaxie 500 7-Litre models combined "the luxury of the 'XL' models, plus the spirit and performance of the 345-horsepower 428 V-8, a specially tuned dual exhaust system with a 'sound of power,' the smooth shifting capabilities and convenience of Cruise-O-Matic and the unexcelled stopping ability of power disc brakes on the front wheels."

Other standard features were the windsplit hood ornament (optional on other models), Lincoln differential with the 9¾-inch ring gear, low-restriction exhausts, wide oval tires, simulated woodgrain steering wheel, styled steel wheel covers, pin striping, additional sound deadener, and padded instrument panel. (By the way, the Lincoln differential was standard issue on any 427- or 428-equipped full-size Ford rather than an exclusive feature of the 7-Litre variant.) A 4-speed manual transmission was optional with the 428-ci, but mandatory with the 427-ci.

Martyn Schorr, writing for *CARS* magazine, said the 7-Litre was "A new top-of-the-line charger that's just the ticket for high speed hauling." He also wrote that the "7-Litre is a plusher, quieter riding and all around more impressive vehicle than Plymouth's VIP or Chevrolet's Caprice." Schorr was also impressed with "the obvious amount of quality control and sound engineering that

went into the design, construction and assembly of the car."

The best quarter-mile result attained by the *CARS* magazine driver in their 4-speed convertible was 15.8 seconds at 82 mph; in the automatic hardtop, it was 16.8 seconds at 84 mph. Braking was judged

This Galaxie 500 7-Litre convertible is just one of two examples ordered with the 425-hp 427-ci V-8. That is not the only factor making this car special. It is also painted special-order Sapphire Blue, a color used by Lincoln.

Martyn Schorr writing for CARS magazine said the 7-Litre was "A new top-of-the-line charger that's just the ticket for high speed hauling." He also wrote that the "7-Litre is a plusher, quieter riding and all around more impressive vehicle than Plymouth's VIP or Chevrolet's Caprice."

Special ornamentation for the Galaxie 500 7-Litre was attached to the grille (left), front fenders (middle), and deck lid (right).

Styled steel wheel covers were standard on the Galaxie 500 7-Litres and optional for other models. Note the 427-ci badge. 7-Litres equipped with the standard 428-ci did not have a similar 428-ci badge.

"sensational considering the weight distribution specifications and the overall weight." Handling, however, was not a particularly strong point: "The chassis, body, suspension have not been designed for maximum handling and cornering..." The optional heavy-duty suspension was strongly recommended.

Magic Cruiser and Black Pearl

Ford hired master customizer George Barris to build the 1966 *Magic Cruiser*, which could be transformed from a fastback to a station wagon and back via hydraulic and electric controls. Ford instructed Barris that the movable roof section needed to rise within seven seconds. A series of aircraft hydraulic systems, screw jacks, and a switch on the dash made that possible. Lowering the tailgate allowed for easy entry to a rear-facing third seat, and as on Ford's production station wagons, the second and third seats could be folded down for addition cargo storage.

Power windows cost extra. Controls were mounted on the console of the Galaxie 500 7-Litres and the 500/XLs.

In front, the two-door hardtop LTD-based *Magic Cruiser* had one-piece, tempered-glass headlights, shaved door handles, and a set of Western wire mag wheels. It was painted a custom-mixed Gold Sunset, and the interior was two-toned with pleated vinyl and lamb's wool carpeting. The new 428-ci was under the hood. This show car was probably re-skinned to become the *Magic Cruiser II* the following year.

The *Black Pearl* was built from another LTD two-door hardtop. It was a mild custom wearing Firefrost Black Metallic paint and a black vinyl top. Door handles, deck lid keyhole, and block lettering on the hood were removed. Taillights were deeply recessed. Stock wire wheel covers and with custom triple-stripe whitewall tires were fitted to the wheels. Pearl white seats with satin and leather bolsters covered the seats and a pearl white mouton carpet was applied to the floor.

Ford Withdraws from NASCAR

Again Ford tried to get its 427-ci SOHC legalized for NASCAR, but the organization said it was not a production engine. Ford argued it was available over-the-counter for $1,983. Meanwhile, Chrysler released a street Hemi for the Plymouth Satellite and the Dodge Charger and Coronet. The

The Galaxie 500/XL interior and a simulated walnut-grained steering wheel were included as standard equipment for the Galaxie 500 7-Litres. A 4-speed was an option for 428-powered cars, but mandatory with the extra-cost 427.

Only two Galaxie 500 7-Litre convertibles were ordered with the 425-hp 427-ci. Both still exist.

new Hemi option weakened Ford's claim.

While this dispute was ongoing, Dan Gurney won the opening race at Riverside in his 1966 Galaxie 500; the next Fords across the line finished fourth, fifth, and eighth. However, Richard Petty, in a Plymouth, took the checkered flag at the Daytona 500. Fords followed in second, fourth, and seventh. Some of the Fords used a specially contoured body that some termed "banana nosed." Despite the improved aerodynamics of the modified Fords, the Mopars were still faster.

NASCAR finally approved Ford's SOHC engine for competition, but at

---

FIRST LOOK AT YOUR CAR OF TOMORROW

MOTORCADE IND

JULY-AUGUST 1966 50c

NEW
STYLES
NEW POWER

FORECAST from DETROIT

ROAD TESTS
CAR ADVENTURES

FORD'S
CONVERTIBLE
FASTBACK/WAGON

The 1966 Magic Cruiser show car could be transformed from a fastback to a station wagon and back via hydraulic and electric controls. The two-door hardtop LTD-based Magic Cruiser had one-piece tempered glass headlights, shaved door handles, and a set of Western wire mag wheels. The new 428-ci was under the hood. (Photo courtesy of Tom Yanulaytis collection)

The most popular model for the 1966 model year was the Galaxie 500 two-door hardtop, which accounted for 198,532 sales. This one was ordered with two-tone paint in Ivy Green and Wimbledon White. The wheels are non-stock units. (Photo courtesy of Scott Wiley)

An LTD two-door hardtop was converted into the Black Pearl show car. It was a mild custom wearing Firefrost Black Metallic paint, and a black vinyl top. Door handles, deck lid keyhole, and block lettering on the hood were removed. Taillights were deeply recessed. (Photo courtesy of Chicago Automobile Trade Association)

The 427 Single Overhead Cam

Ford's Cammer was created to counter Chrysler Corporation's Hemi. Dodges and Plymouths were winning too many of the prestigious races, such as the 1964 Daytona 500, where Mopars scored a 1-2-3 finish. This was such an embarrassment to FoMoCo officials who had just launched the Total Performance campaign. Fords did well on the shorter tracks, but Mopars were winning on the longer ones and with an engine that really was not a production or stock item.

How could a non-stock car be legal in what was supposed to be stock car racing? Actually, NASCAR officials—particularly Bill France, the organization's founder and president—were not happy about the trend of ever-more-exotic engines powering stock cars. At the time, stock car racing was meant to be about racing cars the public could actually buy from a dealer. Anything else was considered to be a threat to attendance by fans who could easily identify with cars they owned—cars with engines that were readily available.

Ford was determined to beat the Hemi Mopars; it was as simple as that. The solution was to take an existing engine and modify it to do the job. The result of the engineers' work was the 427 Single Overhead Cam, or SOHC for short. It utilized the 427-ci cylinder block, single overhead camshafts with two rocker shafts per bank, roller follower-type rocker arms to eliminate complications of lubrication and metal compatibility, a lightweight chain-and-sprocket-type valvetrain drive mechanism, hemispherical combustion chambers, and a flexible induction system that could be adapted to multiple carburetors, supercharging, fuel injection, and exotic fuels. A nearly T-shaped valve

Ford's SOHC was created to beat the Chrysler Hemi. It utilized the 427-ci cylinder block, single overhead camshafts with two rocker shafts per bank, roller-follower-type rocker arms, lightweight chain-and-sprocket-type valvetrain drive mechanism, and hemispherical combustion chambers.

and a D-shaped profile for the exhaust port provided the best flow rate.

Large new head castings were required to accommodate the camshaft and pair of rocker arm shafts. Cast iron was used as a matter of practicality, as aluminum heads had a high scrap rate at the time. The cams were driven by a 6-foot-long chain tensioned by an adjustable idler accessible behind a removable plate in the engine's front cover. A stamped steel guide, lined with nylon, was mounted just above the top of the chain to keep it from thrashing across the long span between the cam gears. Two shorter sections were elsewhere in the route. A "dummy" cam was used to drive the distributor and oil pump. The ignition consisted of dual points operated by a transistorized amplifier fed the juice to wires with stainless steel cores and silicon jackets.

Dyno testing showed 616 hp at 7,000 rpm using a single 4-barrel carb. A dual-quad version boosted output to 657 hp, though only single carbs were allowed in NASCAR.

Then Bill France was approached with the request to allow the SOHC, which he contemplated for a couple of months. His choices seemed clear. He could allow the engine, only to find something even more exotic being proposed later. Or he could disallow the SOHC and anger FoMoCo, but at the same time send a message to the automakers that "factory" hot rods would not be allowed on NASCAR tracks. Fortunately, France found another path to follow. New rules were announced that would take effect on January 1, 1965, which not only disallowed the SOHC, but also disallowed the Hemi. Ford's race-only High Riser 427-ci was disqualified, too. Furthermore, roller cams and roller rockers would not be allowed.

The SOHC was not done, though. It was declared legal in NHRA A/FX class racing and later found its way into the Funny Car class. The Cammer engines were propelling supercharged and fuel-injected Funny Cars through the quarter-mile in 7.10–7.20 seconds by 1967.

a cost. The Fords would have to have a weight penalty of one pound per cubic inch, meaning the 4,000-pound Galaxies would have to gain over 400 pounds! Ford concluded this was unacceptable, so on April 15, Henry Ford II notified NASCAR it was withdrawing from NASCAR competition.

However, by July, Ford returned on a limited scale after watching Bud Moore's (now an independent) successes with his Mercury Comet, a near twin to the intermediate Ford Fairlane. Other independents were doing well with the Fairlane. They had proven the car was capable of running on the big tracks. With the exception of a few independents, this marked the end of the big Fords on the Grand National circuit.

In USAC racing, Ford failed to win even one race. On a more positive note, Mike Schmitt drove an SOHC-powered Galaxie 500/XL to Street Eliminator honors in B/FX competition at the 1966 NHRA Springnationals.

Production Numbers

Over one million full-size Fords were built for the 1966 model year. Ford sold 198,532 Galaxie 500 two-door hardtops, which far exceeded production from the previous year; the second most popular was the Galaxie 500 four-door sedan with 171,886 unit sales. Sales of the LTD totaled 101,096; the four-door hardtop was the most popular of the two body styles in this series with 69,400 finding buyers. Galaxie 500/XL production continued its decline, though the 7-Litre probably took some sales away from this series. Of the 32,075 Galaxie 500/XLs built, only 6,360 were convertibles. Only

11,174 Galaxie 500 7-Litres were built with just 2,368 being convertibles. The 7-Litre would be discontinued as a separate model and instead become an option package for 1967.

This Springtime Yellow 1966 Galaxie 500/XL two-door hardtop is one of 22,247 built, and it's equipped with a 390-ci 2-barrel and Cruise-O-Matic. The original owner installed the Torque Thrust wheels in 1967.

New audio technology was added to the option list. An under-dash 8-track stereo was available for the first time in 1966.

This stunning 1966 Galaxie 500/XL is painted special order Coventry Gray, a color used by Mercury that year. It is also equipped with the 425-hp 427-ci V-8, 4-speed (mandatory with the 427-ci), styled steel wheel covers, and dual rear-mounted antennas. Redline tires are a custom feature.

Crinkle and rosette (insert) vinyl upholstery was standard issue for the Galaxie 500/XL. Red was one of seven regular choices offered.

1967 –1968:

MORE EMPHASIS ON LUXURY

Ford released the new 1967 models on September 30, 1966. Major sheetmetal updates made the big Fords appear all-new, even though they were built on the 1965–1966 platform. Overall length grew 3 more inches as a result of the redo. Despite the increase in overall length, weight increased very little and in some cases there was a minor decrease, depending on the model.

Stacked headlights with redesigned bezels remained, and the grille got a major rework. As before, two grilles were used—a chrome-plated die-cast unit for the LTD, XL, and Country Squire; an anodized aluminum unit for Galaxie 500, Custom 500, Custom, Country Sedan, and Ranch Wagon. Both grilles came to a point, leaned forward, and were split horizontally.

The tops of the fenders were rounded, and the top side of the quarters was concave instead of flat. The fender-line crease flowed into the front door, arcing downward gently until fading at the door's mid-point. This crease resumed in an almost-mirror-image fashion just behind the front door on the quarter

This Vintage Burgundy 1967 XL convertible is also equipped with the 7-Litre Sports Package. According to Marti Auto Works, only 255 XL convertibles had this option.

panel of two-door hardtops and on the rear door of four-door models. Body sides had a full-length peak or character line; this is where the optional Body Side Accent Stripe or body side molding was applied when ordered. Farther down was another body side crease, though in LTD, XL, and Galaxie 500 form, the standard side moldings largely covered it. The quarter panels received a greater kick-up to emulate the styling coming out of GM.

Two-door hardtop rooflines swept back much more and two types were used. The LTD had a formal, wide C-pillar; the Galaxie 500 and XL shared a relatively narrow C-pillar. Taillight lenses and bezels on hardtops and sedans were drastically altered, though the cross-hair housings for the back-up lights continued in modified form. The rear bumper had U-shaped dips at each end to clear the vertically oriented, multifaceted, and crisply styled taillights.

Full-size Ford bodies were not simply restyled; they also got some additional strength. Stamped-in stiffeners, heavy-duty crossmembers

---

The center of the padded steering wheel hub on cars with the 7-Litre Sports Package had this special insert.

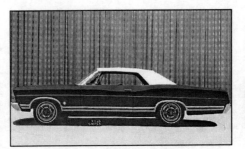

This photo of a mockup dated September 1, 1965, shows that Ford was planning for the continuance of the XL 7-Litre through 1967. If it had not been canceled, the model would have had twin non-functional hood scoops, styled steel wheel covers, and special round medallions on the front fenders. These medallions were patterned like the steering wheel hub insert included on cars equipped with the 7-Litre Sports Package. (Photo courtesy of Adrian Clements collection)

The LTD four-door hardtop was the most popular in the series, with 51,978 getting buyers, while the four-door sedan received only 12,491 orders. The base price for the hardtop was $3,363.49, and $3,298.12 for the sedan.

across the seat locations, double-panel rockers, and a U-channel section increased the rigidity of the floor pans. More strength came via box-section framing in the side rails of the roof, windshield, and rear window areas. Convertible bodies were stronger, as well, thanks to additional reinforcements in the body, frame, and floor pans.

The torque-box frame was improved, too, to further reduce road shock and noise transmitted to the body. A tubular crossmember was added near the rear axle location. The front suspension received re-calibrated shock absorbers, and larger bushings were employed on the strut rods. Larger bushings were used on the track bar and on the link arms supporting the coil springs and connecting the rear axle to the rear frame rails.

The interiors of all models were redesigned. All 1967 Fords now had a fully padded dash as standard equipment. The speedometer featured white numerals on a satin-black background; 70 to 120 mph was underlined in orange. It was flanked by the turn signal indicators and to the right by the position for the electric clock. (Even if the clock was not ordered, the clock face was still present.) Beneath the

speedometer was a plastic black, silver, and chrome instrumentation cover. It housed the fuel gauge, warning lamps, brights-on indicator, radio (when ordered), and switches for the headlights, two-speed electric wipers, power tailgate window or convertible top switch (as applicable), cigar lighter, and ignition.

The lower level contained the controls for the heater/defroster and optional SelectAire Conditioner as well as the pull-out controls for the fresh air vents located in each kick panel. A large slide-out ash tray was positioned between the instrument panel and the glove box.

As happened with the previous year's LTD, the XL was separated from the Galaxie 500 series this year; the bucket-seat and console-equipped hardtop and convertible were now simply Ford XLs. The Galaxie 500 7-Litre hardtop and convertible were dropped from the

lineup. However, a 7-Litre Sports Package, listing for $515.86, was offered for Ford XLs. It included the same features (minus the 7-Litre exterior badges) as the 1966 Galaxie 500 7-Litre.

The very popular LTD series gained a four-door sedan, thereby increasing the body styles to three in that series. However, this particular version was not very popular.

Engine choices dropped by one—the old 352-ci was gone. All others from 1966 were carried forward. For 1967, the 390-ci 2-barrel with a 9.5:1 compression and a single exhaust was offered in Y- or H-codes, depending on whether it was matched to a 3-speed manual or automatic transmission. The Y- and H-code 390s were originally advertised with 265 and 275 hp, respectively, but Ford officials later revised peak horsepower to 270 at 4,400 rpm for these two 390s. The other 390-ci V-8 (code Z) was topped with a 4-barrel, had a 10.5:1 compression ratio, and got dual exhausts, except in station wagon models, which came with a single exhaust.

Ford offered a wide variety of transmissions: 3-speed column-shift, overdrive, four-on-the-floor, plus the

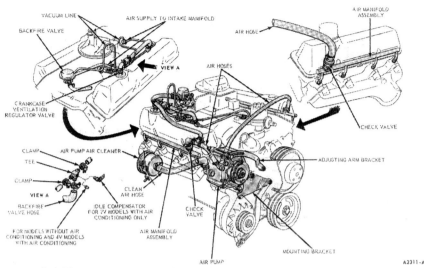

FIG. 20—Typical Thermactor Exhaust Emission System Installation

The Thermactor Exhaust Emission System was mandatory for cars built for California destinations. Its use began with the 1966 models.

C4, C6, FX, MX, and XPL Special automatics. The type installed depended on such factors as engine selection, whether a trailer-towing package was ordered, and when the cars were built (early versus later production).

Another major mechanical update was the replacement of the single-reservoir master cylinder with the dual-master cylinder, which became standard on all models. The front reservoir supported rear braking function, while the rear reservoir was for the front system. Failure in one system still left the driver with a functioning pair of brakes.

Additional new safety features were the Impact-Absorbing Steering Wheel with a deeply padded hub. Padded windshield pillars, thickly padded armrests, and paddle-type inside door handles were further safety enhancements offered on only for the LTD, Galaxie 500, and Country Squire. The Lifeguard marketing term, created in 1956, was still in use to encompass the 20 safety features of the 1967 Fords.

Ford upgraded the warranty on engines, transmissions, drivetrain, suspension, and steering from two years/24,000 miles to five years/50,000 miles, whichever came first. The two-year/24,000-mile warranty applied to the remainder of the vehicle, though.

Standard Features

Standard equipment for the LTD and XL series remained essentially the same as in the 1965–1966 model years, though the LTD four-door hardtop no longer had Silent-Flo ventilation. This feature was replaced with Comfort Stream Ventilation, with inlet vents located in the lower dash panel and exhaust vents located in the lower rear of the front door panel and the rear of the door shell above the latch. It was standard on all three LTD body styles and optional on the 15 other models when the optional air conditioning was not ordered.

Both models shared lower body side and wheel lip moldings. A series of recessed stripes was featured on the wide lower body molding. Prior to January 16, 1967, these were highlighted with black tape; afterward,

black paint in stamped recesses replaced the tape. Unlike the wheel lip moldings used for the Galaxie 500 and Country Sedan, there was no recess for a black stripe. Interestingly, photographs of what was evidently a prototype convertible with Galaxie 500/XL lettering on the quarters and Galaxie 500 side trim appeared in some publications of the time. The decision to reduce the name to XL and apply LTD side moldings to the bucket seat and console models may have been a relatively late one. The LTD and XL also shared a wide, anodized aluminum trunk molding patterned after the lower body side moldings.

Model identification appeared on the grille, C-pillars (LTD only), and deck lid ornaments as well as the standard wheel covers of the LTD, which were unique to the model. Full wheel covers were also standard on the XL (as well as the Country Squire), but had a turbine design with a metallic red-and-gold center insert. These were optional on other models except the LTD.

XL-only standard equipment included door panels with a brushed aluminum panel in place of the woodgrain insert used on Galaxie 500s. A rectangular trunk ornament with a horizontal bar emanating from each side provided XL identification in its center. A plaque almost identical to the LTD version appeared on the upper left side of the grille, but the chrome XL insert was set against a shimmering red background, rather than an LTD against a shimmering blue background. The Thunderbird-style bucket seats were trimmed around the edges with stainless steel moldings.

Galaxie 500 hardtop, convertible, and four-door sedan models

This Wimbledon White 1967 Ford XL two-door hardtop is one of 813 ordered with the optional 7-Litre Sports Package, according to Marti Auto Works. Ford XLs equipped with this option did not have an individual body code this time, since these cars were no longer separate models.

Ford XLs shared the anodized aluminum trunk molding with black stripes with LTDs. The trunk ornament was unique to the XLs. Bumper guards were offered only for the rear bumper this model year.

The Command Console for the XLs was color-keyed to the interior and included the gear selector, a glove box, and indentations to house the seat belt buckles when not in use. Note the optional Convenience Control Panel underneath the dash.

continued to have as standard equipment the inline 6-cylinder coupled to a 3-speed column-shifted manual transmission. Additional standard items included two-speed electric windshield wipers, heater, bright lower body and wheel well moldings with a single recessed black-painted stripe, and carpeting, plus lighting for the ash tray, glove box, and trunk compartment. A trunk molding similar to that of the LTD and XL was used; however, the stripe pattern was divided into five sections.

The LTD, XL, and the Galaxie 500 series of cars were each distinguished with a unique trunk ornament and all had "FORD" spelled out in chromed letters on the right side of the deck lid. Model identification for the Galaxie 500s appeared on the quarter panels as anodized block letters and numbers with black paint around their respective perimeters.

Custom 500 and Custom sedans had no lower body side or wheel lip moldings. Stainless steel window frames and drip rail moldings plus the body side molding (which was an option for the Custom, Galaxie 500, Ranch Wagon, and Country Sedan models) were included, however, on the Custom 500 line. Standard upholstery for each was a combination of cloth and vinyl and both lines included an automatic dome light. Bright-metal side seat shields were deleted from the Custom 500 and Custom models.

The deck lid of Custom 500 sedans had a unique, wide molding with widely spaced "FORD" lettering centered on it; no trunk ornament was applied. Custom sedans had no trunk molding or ornament, but had chrome lettering spelling "FORD," centered and widely spaced across the deck lid in place of the trunk molding. Model identification appeared on the front fenders of both the Custom and Custom 500. Stainless steel mold-

ings were applied to the windshield posts of all models in the big Ford lineup. Other standard equipment for all full-size Fords this year was comprised of two-speed electric wipers, fresh-air heater-defroster, colored-keyed carpeting, and color-keyed vinyl headliner.

Country Squires and Country Sedans were still offered in six-passenger and dual-facing rear seat versions. Power brakes became standard on the dual-facing rear seat models, and a power rear tailgate window was included on all Country Squires. The Squires offered a choice of six all-vinyl trims or a single no-cost cloth/vinyl option, while the Country Sedan brought the choices down to four all-vinyl interior trims.

The Ranch Wagon gave the buyer a choice of three all-vinyl upholstery selections. As on the Custom sedans, the Ranch Wagon was devoid of body side and wheel lip moldings.

All wagons continued to have the Big Six coupled to the Synchro-Smooth 3-speed manual transmission, lockable rear storage compartment, textured steel load floor color-keyed to the interior, and rear pillar air deflectors in standard form.

The Galaxie 500 two-door hardtop was the most popular model for 1967. A total of 197,388 were built in Ford's U.S. assembly plants, along with another 15,560 coming from the Oakville, Ontario, assembly plant.

On June 6, 1967, my car was built at Ford's assembly plant in Dallas, Texas. It was painted Candyapple Red and originally equipped with a black vinyl top, black all-vinyl interior, AM-radio, body side molding, wheel covers, tinted windshield, SelectAire Conditioner, 390-ci 2-barrel, Cruise-O-Matic, whitewall tires, and power steering.

Extra-Cost Items

Options and accessories for 1967 full-size Fords included:
- choice of the body side molding (except LTD, XL, and Country Squire) or body side accent stripe (except Country Squire)
- rear bumper guards
- SelectAire Conditioner
- AM/FM radio
- stereo multiplex unit for use with FM radio
- AM-radio/stereo tape player
- hang-on stereo tape player
- rear-mounted power antenna
- Philco television
- power steering
- power brakes (all drum or with front discs)
- Convenience Control Panel
- power windows
- electric clock
- tinted windshield or tinted glass
- two-tone paint (except convertible and Country Squire)
- Twin-Comfort Lounge Seats for LTDs (split front seat with individual armrests)
- Luxury Interior Trim for XLs
- headrests
- front seat shoulder harnesses
- litter basket
- fender-mounted turn signal indicators
- compass

Several special equipment groups comprised of various combinations of options were offered late in the model year, too.

Four wheel cover options were offered: a turbine-style type (except LTD), Styled Steel wheel covers, simulated mag wheel covers (dealer installed only), and wire wheel covers (dealer installed only). There were two types of 15-inch wire wheel covers used for 1967, though. A simulated tri-bar knock-off hub with a blue insert similar to that of 1966 was offered for only part of the 1967 model year. When supplies of the spinner type were exhausted, the wire wheel covers came with a round hub.

The Magic Doorgate could be opened like a door and folded down like a tailgate. Up to 103 cubic feet of load space was available with the seats folded down. Dual-facing rear seats gave a passenger capacity of up to four more people. Country Squires and Country Sedans with the feature were sometimes referenced as 6+4 passenger models.

The Custom (top) and Custom 500 models were the economy models in the 1967 lineup. Both cars are shown with optional wheel covers.

Bucket seats with a console continued to be standard issue on Ford XLs in 1967. This example has the 7-Litre Sports Package, which included the simulated woodgrain steering wheel. Also ordered for this car was the luxury interior trim.

LTD-style side panels were fitted to XLs ordered with the luxury trim interior.

Paint and Upholstery

Super Diamond Lustre Enamel colors offered for the full-size Fords for 1967 were:

- Raven Black
- Wimbledon White
- Brittany Blue
- Arcadian Blue
- Nightmist Blue
- Clearwater Aqua
- Frost Turquoise
- Dark Moss Green
- Silver Frost
- Lime Gold
- Sauterne Gold
- Candyapple Red
- Vintage Burgundy
- Springtime Yellow
- Pebble Beige
- Burnt Amber
- Beige Mist

Beige Mist was discontinued in late December 1966, and Lime Gold was first made available at about this same time.

Two-tone paint remained available for all models except the Country Squires and, of course, the convertibles. The optional pebble-grained vinyl top for two- and four-door hardtops and the LTD four-door sedan was available in black or white. Convertible tops came in a choice of black, white, or medium blue.

Standard upholstery for the LTD sedans and hardtops came in charcoal black, dark red, light parchment, light aqua, light silver, dark ivy gold, and dark blue Heath Tricot nylon protected with Scotchguard with crinkle vinyl bolsters. All-vinyl was offered in charcoal black and pastel parchment.

Buyers of the XL hardtop and convertible in standard trim were offered crinkle vinyl in charcoal black, pastel parchment, red, medium saddle, and light blue. The XL hardtop could also be had with pastel parchment crinkle vinyl and parchment Fremont cloth.

Standard issue upholstery for the Galaxie 500 convertible came in charcoal black, pastel parchment, red, light aqua, or medium blue crinkle vinyl. In the case of the closed versions of the Galaxie 500, Fremont cloth inserts with crinkle vinyl bolsters came in charcoal black, parchment, medium blue, medium aqua, and medium ivy gold.

Fender-mounted turn indicator lights are a rarely seen dealer-installed accessory.

Custom 500 sedans had just four standard color choices: medium blue, medium aqua, medium ivy gold, and parchment. The upholstery consisted of Ellipse cloth inserts sewn to crinkle vinyl bolsters.

Only three standard choices were provided for the Custom sedans: parchment, red, and medium blue. Upholstery was Lennox nylon cloth inserts and pleated vinyl.

Country Squires had six standard crinkle vinyl trims and one no-cost option of a parchment Fremont cloth and crinkle vinyl combination. All-vinyl colors were red, pastel parchment, light blue, light ivy gold, aqua, and medium saddle.

Country Sedans offered a choice of four all-vinyl trims consisting of light blue, light parchment, light aqua, and dark red. The Ranch Wagon could be had with light parchment, dark blue, or red vinyl.

Road Test Results

The March 1967 issue of *Motor Trend* provided interested readers with the results of a comparison test of the Galaxie 500, Impala Super Sport, and Plymouth Sport Fury (all two-door hardtops). In terms of handling and roadability, the Ford impressed the *Motor Trend* evaluators the most "due to its quietness more than its handling characteristics." They elaborated that, "With windows closed, the Galaxie interior is almost completely sealed from all road noises and those of passing cars. It didn't handle the best of the three, but we could learn to live with this a lot easier than leaking window seals and noises emanating from mechanical parts."

They also noted that the Galaxie 500 is "an equal performer to Chevy and Plymouth in all but the most severe cornering and rebound condi-tions—an area where most Galaxie owners won't research." The *Motor Trend* report indicated the three cars were very similar in all other areas.

The *Motor Trend* test car, equipped with the 315-hp 390-ci and Cruise-O-Matic, was capable of 0–60 mph in 9.2 seconds and covered the quarter-mile in 17.4 seconds with an end speed of 82 mph (figures which were reasonable though not excit-ing). Stopping with the optional front disc brakes required 183 feet from 60 mph.

Magic Cruiser II and *XL Interceptor*

FoMoCo used *Magic Cruiser II* and *XL Interceptor* to promote its new 1967 full-size cars. As done in previous years, Ford contracted with Barris to build the *Magic Cruiser II*. Ford described it as a "super fastback" that could be turned into a station wagon when the fastback section of the roof and two special window-side panels were electrically raised. It was possi-bly built from the original *Magic Cruiser* shown during 1966.

The *XL Interceptor* had numerous modifications, such as magnesium wheels, special tires, textured appliqués on the lower body sides, floating design taillights, reflector slots in the quarters, a modified grille, and plastic lens covers over the headlights. The light-blue murano pearl show vehicle featured a 428-ci under the hood. The two unique cars were shown nationally at various events that year such as the Chicago Auto Show.

Production Numbers

As in the previous year, the Galaxie 500 two-door hardtop was the most popular model in the line up, selling 197,388 units. One of those, a two-door hardtop, was Ford's 70-millionth car; it was built at the Norfolk, Virginia assembly plant. An additional 15,560 Galaxie 500 two-door hardtops rolled off the Oakville, Ontario assembly line. Predictably, the Galaxie 500 four-door sedan was the second most popular model, with 136,760 finding buyers, including production from the Oakville plant.

Sales of the LTD, after three model years, remained strong in the U.S and Canada. Altogether, 117,038 were built, including 13,117 of the new four-door sedan version. The four-door hardtop accounted for 55,118 units. Clearly, LTD buyers preferred a four-door over the two-door hardtop.

Sales of the Ford XL were the lowest in the history of the model. Only 23,335, including just 5,161 convertibles, were built in Ford's U.S. assembly plants. Another 3,047, including 168 convertibles, were built at the Oakville plant.

Magic Cruiser II built by George Barris was, as Ford described it, a "super fastback" that could be turned into a station wagon when the fastback section of the roof and two special window-side panels were electrically raised. It may have been built from the original Magic Cruiser *shown during 1966. (Photo courtesy of Adrian Clements collection)*

The XL Interceptor *show car had numerous modifications such as magnesium wheels, special tires, textured appliqués on the lower body sides, floating design taillights, reflector slots in the quarters, a modified grille, and plastic lens covers over the headlights. A 428-ci resided under the hood of the light blue murano pearl show vehicle. (Photo courtesy of Adrian Clements collection)*

Full-size Fords equipped with a 427 ci were built in low numbers, and according to Marti Auto Works, only 89 came so equipped.

Altogether, 952,553 full-size Fords were assembled, which includes 75,414 cars built at the Oakville plant.

1968: Quiet, Strong, Beautiful

An all-new skin gave the big Fords, said to be "quiet, strong, beautiful," a different look for 1968. The stacked headlight design was gone. The frontal design of the LTD and XL were now much more distinguishable from those of the lower-cost series, as hidden headlights were standard for these two top series.

A choice of rooflines was provided for the two-door hardtop Galaxie 500: a fastback and a formal or notchback type. The body side peak was no longer linear, but followed the sweeping curve of the quarter panels in back. In back, the openings for the taillights were very similar to those of 1967, but the lenses and back-up light assemblies were totally different. Federally mandated side marker lamps/reflectors made their first appearance for 1968.

Along with the new sheetmetal was a restyled interior. In another move toward improved safety, the steering wheel and column were better able to absorb forces in a crash. In place of the padded hub used in 1967 was a flat, wide crossbar. Instrumentation was arranged in a manner similar to the 1966 model layout.

The 427-ci returned to the list of optional engines for any full-size Ford except wagons, but it was not the same Total Performance V-8 of the past. Offered only with a single 4-barrel, the lower-output Cobra V-8

This set of photos dated October 11, 1965, shows a number of styling elements of the 1968 full-size Ford two-door hardtops that differed from the final design. Note the 1967 Galaxie 500 fastback roofline on this mockup.

had hydraulic lifters and a small decrease in compression to 10.9:1. Horsepower was advertised as 390 at 5,600 rpm. Furthermore, this 427-ci could be had only with a Selectshift C6 automatic.

Other standard equipment listed for a 427-powered full-size Ford were power disc brakes, 80 amp-hour battery, G70x15 wide-oval tires, heavy-duty suspension, and a heavy-duty 3.25:1 axle. The 427-ci option was dropped entirely by the end of the 1967 calendar year without a single full-size ford being so equipped. No record of even a prototype being built with this engine seems to exist.

Other engine changes for the 1968 full-size Fords included the departure of the 289-ci; it was replaced by the 210-hp 302-ci 2-bbl. The gain in cubic inches was the result of an increase in the stroke from 2.87 to 3.00 inches. Horsepower was lowered by 5 for the 390-ci 2-barrel and the 428-ci 4-barrel, though the 428-ci Police Interceptor remained at 360 hp.

Ford LTDs were watered-down a bit. An automatic transmission became an option, as did the previously standard leather-like vinyl top.

The Ford XL underwent some major changes in standard equipment and the 7-Litre option package offered the previous model year was dropped. It was replaced by another sporty option package.

A new station wagon model was added this year—the Custom 500 Ranch Wagon.

Standard Equipment

The LTDs came with:
- die-cast grille
- concealed headlights
- full wheel covers
- 302-ci V-8
- 3-speed manual transmission
- electric clock
- courtesy lighting
- loop pile carpeting
- Limousine-Luxury pleated cloth and vinyl upholstery

The 302-ci small-block came as the result of a .13-inch increase in the stroke of the 289-ci. It replaced the 289-ci option in big Fords for 1968. (Photo courtesy of Scott Wiley)

A 345-hp 428-ci coupled to a 4-speed transmission powers this rare 1968 XL convertible with the GT Equipment Group.

- woodgrain accents on the dash and door panels
- bright-metal trim around the accelerator, brake, and emergency brake pedals
- rocker, wheel lip, and lower quarter panel moldings.

Outside, series identification appeared on the hood, C-pillar, and deck lid.

The Ford XL, available as a fastback or convertible, had the traditional bucket seats and console as standard issue. However, for the first time it could be fitted with a bench seat as an option. By February, the reverse was true—bucket seats and console became optional. In addition, the small V-8 and automatic transmission became options; these had been standard for XLs since the beginning of the series in mid 1962. A base model Ford XL could be had with a 150-hp 6-cylinder, 3-speed manual transmission, and a bench seat! The reduction in standard equipment meant an approximately $200 base price decrease from the 1967 XL figures.

Other standard items included bright-metal accented foot pedals, all-vinyl upholstery, loop-pile carpeting, and hidden headlights. Series identification was mounted on the hood, C-pillars, and trunk lid.

Galaxie 500s came in five body styles (one more than in the past): fastback, two-door hardtop, four-door hardtop, four-door sedan, and a

The LTD was more popular than ever for 1968. A total of 54,163 two-door hardtops were built, along with 61,755 four-door hardtops and 22,834 four-door sedans.

The 7-Litre Sports Package was dropped at the end of the 1967 model year. In its place was the GT Equipment Group. It was offered for XLs ordered with either a 390-ci 4-barrel or the 428-ci. Only a few hundred convertibles were ordered with this option.

This XL was built in December 1967 when bucket seats with a console were still standard equipment. At this time, a bench seat was an option. The reverse was true within a couple of months after this car rolled off the Chicago assembly line.

The console was redesigned for 1968. Note the 4-speed shifter and the optional tachometer.

A total of 50,048 Ford XL hardtops were built for the 1968 model year. A 390-ci 4-barrel V-8 with a 4-speed manual transmission powers this Candyapple Red example.

Hidden headlights were a new feature for 1968. Only LTDs, XLs, and the Country Squire were so equipped.

This Ford XL was built after the bench seat became standard for the model. All-vinyl upholstery was also standard.

convertible. Included in the base price of a Galaxie 500 was the 240 Big Six, 3-speed manual transmission, rocker and wheel lip moldings, fashion-right fabric with vinyl upholstery (all-vinyl for the convertible), and loop carpeting. External series identification appeared on the quarter panel in script form.

LTDs, XLs, and Galaxie 500s were all equipped with a trunk molding with a pattern resembling the design of the hidden headlight grille.

The Custom 500 sedans came equipped with the 240-ci 6-cylinder, 3-speed manual transmission, loop-pile carpeting, courtesy lights, and three choices of cloth-and-vinyl upholstery. A unique trunk molding was applied to the trunk lid.

Custom sedans reduced the standard upholstery choices to two and deleted the trunk molding.

Country Squires came equipped essentially the same as the LTD, along with station wagon-only features. Six all-vinyl upholstery trims were included in the base price.

Heavy-duty suspension was newly added to the standard features of the Squire and the rest of the wagon line.

The six- and ten-passenger Country Sedans featured all-vinyl upholstery in five choices, one more than in 1967.

The Custom 500 Ranch Wagon was new to the wagon line. This four-door wagon featured a choice of four all-vinyl upholstery selections, courtesy lamps, and loop-pile carpeting. The unembellished Custom Ranch Wagon reduced the all-vinyl upholstery color options to just two.

Paint Colors

Ford offered 15 enamel paint colors for 1968:
- Raven Black
- Wimbledon White

- Diamond Blue
- Brittany Blue
- Presidential Blue
- Seafoam Green
- Highland Green
- Tahoe Turquoise
- Gulfstream Aqua
- Sunlit Gold
- Lime Gold
- Pebble Beige
- Phoenician Yellow
- Candyapple Red
- Vintage Burgundy

Twenty-three two-tone schemes were available.

Options and Accessories

A Brougham trim option consisting of Twin-Lounge Seats (split bench front seat with individual armrests)

This low-mileage original 1969 Galaxie 500 wears Candyapple Red enamel paint and is equipped with red all-vinyl upholstery, wheel covers, whitewall tires, power steering, 302-ci V-8, and an automatic transmission. (Photo courtesy Scott Wiley)

These mag-style wheel covers were standard issue with the GT Equipment Group. They actually date back to 1966 when they were dealer-installed accessories.

with knit-nylon upholstery and tufted backs with embroidered center panels was offered for the LTDs.

XLs with a big-block V-8 had an optional GT Equipment Group consisting of a heavy-duty suspension, power brakes with front discs, 3.25:1 axle, low restriction exhaust system, wide-oval tires, simulated mag-type wheel covers, special striping, and a GT emblem on the lower body. It also offered the choice of a 4-speed with the 390-ci 4-barrel, as well as the 428-ci.

Other goodies included:

- deluxe wheel covers
- styled steel wheel covers

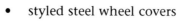

In the foreground is a 1968 Country Sedan with dual-facing rear seats. To the upper left is the Ranch Wagon, and to the upper right appears the Custom 500 Ranch Wagon, which was new to the wagon lineup this year.

- two-tone paint (except convertibles and Country Squires)
- Philco TV
- headrest kit
- tachometer
- floor mats
- cruise control
- child seat
- rear defroster
- AM/FM radio
- CB radio
- reverb
- tissue dispenser
- compass
- hand-held vacuum cleaner
- fire extinguisher

XL Road Test

The January 1968 issue of *Car Life* reported its evaluation of the 1968 XL fastback with a 340-hp 428-ci, automatic transmission, 2.80:1 rear end, and power disc brakes. According to the article, "The 1968 Ford XL is a large, comfortable luxury car worthy of comparison to prestigious U.S. land yachts... This is the largest, most highly styled car in the Ford lineup. It is ideally suited to long trips over freeways and turnpikes. Around town driving is hampered by the overall bulk of the car, but driven in a calm, unhurried fashion, the XL provides a quiet, smooth and comfortable ride. Straight-line performance is more than adequate..."

Acceleration from 0–60 mph for the 4,586-pound test car required 8.2 seconds and the standing quarter-mile took 16.68 seconds with an end speed of 87.3 mph. Handling, not surprisingly, was not considered "one of the XL's strong points" due to "very strong understeer... even with low-effort power steering...

Slow, small-radius turns were a struggle, with overloaded and over-stressed front tires howling and groaning. High-speed, large-radius turns were more acceptable, and the strong understeer characteristics of the XL were helpful in providing exceptional straight-line stability." As for stopping ability, brake testing revealed "this system to be very good."

Fiera

The 1968 XL-based *Fiera* show car featured several styling modifications. Among these was a lowered roofline that altered the angles of the front and rear windshields for a very sleek look. The mostly stock-looking grille was deeply recessed and had auxiliary rectangular driving lights positioned on either side of the stock grille divider. Under the louvered hood was a 428-ci. Vent windows, side moldings, front side

The 1968 XL-based Fiera show car featured several styling modifications. Among them was a lowered roofline, deeply recessed grille with auxiliary rectangular driving lights positioned on either side of the stock grille divider, and iridescent autumn copper paint shaded from light at the top to dark at the bottom. (Photo courtesy of Mitch Frumkin)

marker lamps, and rear side reflectors were deleted. Racing-style outside mirrors replaced the stock units. The rear wheel openings were enlarged a bit, and a pair of brake cooling vents was installed just ahead of the rear wheels. Wide-oval whitewall tires were fitted to a set of custom wheels. A wide trunk molding extended to the taillights; the extensions replaced the stock back-up lamp assemblies.

An iridescent autumn copper paint, shaded from light at the top to dark at the bottom, covered the exterior. Inside, gold-tone cloth-and-vinyl upholstery was fitted.

Production Numbers

Sales of the LTDs rose substantially for 1968; a total of 138,752 were built. The Galaxie 500 series continued to be the most popular with 339,262 finding buyers. Of those, 117,877 were the four-door sedan, making it the most purchased car in the Galaxie 500 lineup. The formal roof, two-door hardtop outsold the fastback by a sizable margin—84,322 versus 69,760.

Production of the XL fastback totaled 50,048 and the drop-top version (the least ordered full-size Ford for 1968) brought another 6,066 sales. This represented a huge percentage increase in XL orders and was due no doubt to the lower price tag for the series. Despite these higher numbers, overall full-size Ford production was down by about 10,000 units from the 1967 total. This was likely the result of a 57-day strike at the company near the start of the model year.

Incidentally, the 1968 model year introduced the long-running advertising campaign "Better Ideas," and the image of a light bulb replaced the "O" in Ford logo.

The GT Equipment Group consisted of a heavy-duty suspension, power brakes with front discs, 3.25:1 axle, low-restriction exhaust system, wide-oval tires, simulated mag-type wheel covers, special striping, and a GT emblem on the lower body.

1969 -1970:

WIDER, LONGER, QUIETER

The 1969 models made their public debut on September 27, 1968. Full-size models had undergone a major redesign from top to bottom— bodies and chassis were new. As a result of the redo, overall length and width grew a few inches. The front and rear tread width went up 1 inch in front and 2 inches in the rear, and the wheelbase spanned 121 inches. With the increase in size came another increase in weight by as much as about 200 pounds. The actual weight gained and the overall dimensions varied by model.

The two-grille practice for upper and lower level car lines continued. LTD and XL series cars featured a grille arrangement with hidden headlights; these cars had the center section divided by a nearly V-shaped stack of horizontal bars thrust forward from the center. A body-color strip divided the entire grille. Other models had exposed headlights and a relatively flat grille. It, too, was split horizontally, but with a bright-metal divider. Because of the differences in these grilles, the hood and front bumper of the LTD and XL series were not the same as those of the other models.

For 1969, the Ford XL came in two varieties: a convertible and as a Sportsroof as shown. The grille with hidden headlights was a standard feature of the XL series. This Candyapple Red example is equipped with the 360-hp, 429-ci 4-barrel, 4-speed transmission, black vinyl top, and bucket seats with console.

The C-stripe, as seen on this Candyapple Red 1969 Ford XL, was included among the features of the GT Performance Group.

Two-door hardtop rooflines again came in two forms for the XL and Galaxie 500. The formal type was shared with the LTD two-door hardtop; the other gave the appearance of a fastback in profile due to a sail panel grafted onto the C-pillars. Another term for the styling was "tunnel back." Ford dubbed the sail panel roofline SportsRoof.

The lower body sheetmetal tucked-in sharply, with the resulting

---

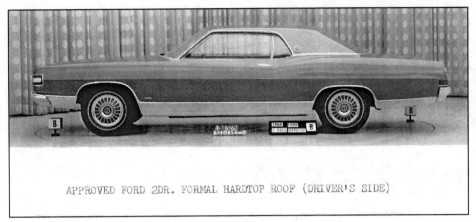

APPROVED FORD 2DR. FORMAL HARDTOP ROOF (DRIVER'S SIDE)

The basic shape of the 1969 LTD two-door hardtop had been determined by early 1967, but plenty of details remained to be settled.

Bucket seats with console became an option for the XLs starting in mid 1968. Note the front seat headrests, which were now standard for all models.

The Flight-Cockpit dash was new for 1969. It had instrumentation in three tiers and controls arranged in an arc. Some contemporary automotive journalists complained about the layout. The bench seat with knitted vinyl inserts was standard for the XLs. Note the optional Rim-Blow steering wheel.

crease leaving a place to apply bright trim or the simulated-wood lower border for the paneling on the Country Squires. The lack of a vent window also had an effect on the profile view of hardtops, as well as convertibles. The change was said to reduce wind noise.

The quarter panels received a greater kick-up, not unlike the 1967–1968 design. Taillight lenses

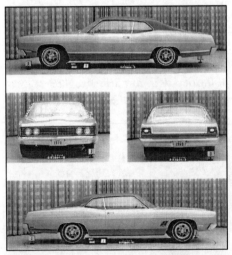

By early 1968, the major styling elements for the 1969 Galaxie 500 Sportsroof had been decided though a few details remained to be determined. Note the right side profile view at bottom; a set of either functional or non-functional vents was mounted on the front fender.

and bezels on all but wagons were now trapezoidal, though the concept of cross-hair housings for the back-up lights continued to be used.

The Magic Doorgate on station wagon models got a welcomed change this year. Since its introduction for 1966, the doorgate opened only when the rear window was lowered. With the 1969s, though, it could be opened from the side while the window remained up.

Models were altered a bit for 1969. Country Squires were now part of the LTD series, Country Sedans were in the Galaxie 500 line, the Custom 500 now had six- and eight-passenger Ranch Wagons, the Custom series had a six-passenger Ranch Wagon. In all, seven station wagon models were available, but none were ten-passenger versions as in the past. The dual-facing rear seats could now seat a total of two passengers instead of four. As a result of the new design, station wagons gained 5 cubic feet of cargo space.

A so-called S-type frame was underneath the new body. The terminology was derived from the S shape of the front frame rails. This feature provided additional protection in the event of a head-on collision. An outer

frame brace plus reinforcement to the front torque boxes were also added in the interest of greater safety.

Interiors on all models were redesigned as well. The Flight-Cockpit dash had the three-tiered instrumentation and controls arranged in an arc. On top, from left to right, was the location for the optional radio, speedometer/odometer, and the position for the electric clock. If the clock was not ordered, the clock face was still present. The speedometer design was essentially the same as that of the prior model year with white numerals on a satin-black

Transmission offerings were unchanged for 1969, but the 4-speed manual transmission was in its final year of availability and could be had only with the optional 360-hp 429-ci.

The Twin-Comfort Lounge Seats with a reclining passenger side and Brougham Trim was an option for the LTD Brougham.

Ford gave its full-size cars a dose of muscle for 1969. This XL is powered by the 360-hp 429-ci V-8 coupled to a 4-speed manual transmission.

background and an orange underline beneath 70 to 120 mph.

In the middle row from left to right were the radio controls (when applicable), fuel gauge, cigarette lighter, and fan control knob. The bottom row was the location of the controls for the windshield wipers, headlights, warning lamps, gear indicator (auto trans) or cover plate (4-speed trans), and the heater/defroster (as well as the A/C when ordered). The interior redesign and increased size of the 1969 models gave owners more leg, hip, and shoulder room than in the 1968s.

Built-in front seat headrests became standard this year on bench seat models. The bucket seats were of a high-back design, thus headrests were not needed.

Engine offerings changed for 1969. Two new V-8s became available for the big Fords this year: the 351-ci Windsor and the 429-ci Thunder Jet. The former was available with only a 2-barrel in the full-size models, while the 429-ci came in 2- and 4-barrel forms. The 429-ci was a new design, part of the 385 series first offered in the 1968 Thunderbird. The 351-ci, was created by increasing the 302's stroke by 1/2 inch.

The 351-ci 2-barrel cranked out 250 hp, while the Thunder Jets offered 320 hp with the 2-barrel carb and 360 hp with the 4-barrel. The 390-ci 4-barrel and the 340-hp, 428-ci V-8s were discontinued. However, the 360-hp, 428-ci Police Interceptor remained in the engine lineup, as

This 1969 LTD two-door hardtop is a very rare example in having the 360-hp 429-ci with a 4-speed manual transmission. Wheel covers were standard on LTDs, but this car has dog-dish hub caps per owner preference.

Ornamentation identifying this car as a Ford XL appeared on the hood (not shown), C-pillar, and trunk lid. Although each shared the same basic design, they were not identical.

Taillights were reshaped for 1969. A red reflector panel ran along the cove underneath the taillights and the edge of the deck lid on LTDs and XLs.

did the 302-ci 2-barrel (with a compression increase) and the 390-ci 2-barrel. The 360-hp engine was for law enforcement use only.

Transmission offerings were unchanged, but the 4-speed manual transmission was in its final year of availability and could be had only with the optional 360-hp 429-ci. The 3-speed manual transmission was not offered with either 429-ci.

Standard Features

LTDs came with a standard powertrain package of 302-ci 2-barrel and 3-speed manual transmission. The interior came in a choice of six cloth-and-vinyl trims and electric clock, plus lighted glove box, simulated woodgrain appliqués on the instrument panel and doors.

On the exterior, customers were treated to a die-cast grille with hidden headlights and luggage compartment. A red reflector panel ran along the cove underneath, the taillights, and the edge of the deck lid on LTDs and XLs.

The XL series had standard features nearly identical to an LTD, but had the 6-cylinder for the standard engine and six choices of all-vinyl upholstery.

Galaxie 500 convertibles were offered in six choices of all-vinyl trims, while closed versions had five standard cloth/vinyl combinations from which to choose. A power-operated top with a tempered-safety-glass rear window was also standard for convertibles. Buying a Galaxie 500 as well as the lower two series of Customs meant getting dog-dish hub caps and an aluminum grille with exposed headlights.

Custom 500 sedans offered a choice of four cloth/vinyl trims but no light for the glove box and trunk. Selecting a Custom reduced the buyer's standard upholstery choices to three all-vinyl trims.

Country Squires were equipped much like the LTD sedan and hardtops; Country Sedans were similar to the Galaxie 500 series, but with vinyl upholstery. Standard equipment for the Custom 500 Ranch Wagon and Ranch Wagon paralleled that of the Custom 500 and Custom, respectively. A power tailgate window was standard on Country Squires and eight-passenger wagons.

Options and Accessories

The Brougham option remained available for LTDs, as did the GT Performance Group for the XLs. A requirement for the latter, however, was the purchase of either the optional 390- or 429-ci. Comfortweave, a breathable knitted vinyl upholstery was standard on bucket-seat XLs. At the start of the model year, buckets seats with console were an available option for an XL. Shortly after the start of the model year bucket seats and console became an option for Galaxie 500 two-door hardtops and convertibles as well.

Other extra-cost equipment included:
- power front disc brakes
- Fingertip Speed Control
- AM/FM stereo radio
- Stereo-Sonic Tape/AM Radio System
- tilt steering wheel
- rear window defogger
- intermittent windshield wipers
- Convenience Group (warning lights for low fuel, door ajar, lights on, and seat belt reminder)
- Rim-Blow Steering Wheel
- reclining front passenger seat (Galaxie 500 four-door models)
- Country Sedan and Squire with Comfortweave knitted vinyl
- XLs with bench seat (LTDs only)
- tachometer
- radial tires
- limited-slip differential
- carpeted load floor for wagons

Exterior Colors

Again a wide range of exterior colors were offered:
- Raven Black
- Wimbledon White
- Brittany Blue

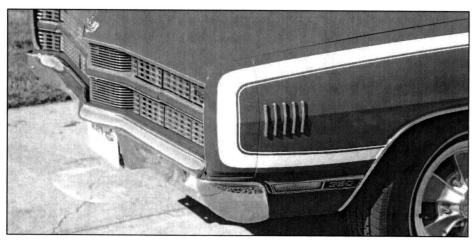

Chromed louvers and mag-style wheel covers were included with the GT Performance Group option. Engine displacement appeared within the molding behind the front side marker light.

- Dresden Blue
- Presidential Blue
- Aztec Aqua
- Gulfstream Aqua
- New Lime
- Meadowlark Yellow
- Champaign Gold
- Lime Gold
- Indian Fire
- Candyapple Red
- Royal Maroon

Road Test

The June 1969 issue of *Car Life* featured a road test report on a 360-hp 429-powered LTD four-door hardtop. It was highly critical of the dash layout. In fact, the first eight paragraphs were devoted to the perceived shortcomings of the arrangement! One such paragraph began, "...one tester would hop in and have to search for the ignition switch (it's buried up under the dash). Another search for the headlights (they're buried somewhere else under the dash and the steering wheel blocks the view). The seat belts defied efficient snapping. The whole dash panel seemed to be designed to frustrate the new driver (we found, after driving the car rather extensively, that it's not true that you can get used to anything)."

The *Car Life* article was not without some praise, though: "First, among its virtues, we felt was the quietness of the interior. Engine noise simply doesn't exist, and wind noise is deceptively low. Only a whisper of the road rumble creeps through all of the computer-calculated acoustics," began the ninth paragraph. Braking was the next area to be given approval—it was judged as "extremely good." Deceleration rates of 28 ft/sec/sec were consistently recorded "with no fade evident."

Acceleration was not a strong point of the test car. "Its 360 bhp, after being delivered through the Cruise-O-Matic and 2.80:1 rear axle, was not impressive..." was their contention. In comparison to three other so-called Power cars evaluated (383-powered Plymouth Fury, 440-powered Dodge Monaco, and a 427-powered Chevrolet Caprice), the Ford was the "second slowest" and handling was found to be "at the bottom of the group... It had the usual Ford Motor Co. han-dling characteristics—heavy front, large camber change in the curves, and lots of lean. The result is understeer, initial and final."

The end of the *Car Life* report was no more flattering than the beginning: "There's something strange about this new body by Ford. Side windows are tightly curved inward. The doors do not have a very wide opening and when there's a car parked alongside, it is nigh impossible to get into the back seat. The first impression is that the window is place there to catch the bottom of an unsuspecting chin. More than once we had to roll the back windows down just to get in or out of the car."

Aurora II

The pearlescent white-gold 1969 *Aurora II* show car was built from a production LTD Country Squire. It underwent some major modifications, mostly to the interior. However, the body did not escape a bit of reworking. The Aurora II had three side doors: one on the driver's side and two suicide doors on the other. The two-door side of the car had no center pillar between the doors; instead, they latched to the body sill.

The three-door arrangement was necessitated by the design of the interior featuring a curved lounge seat in place of the stock second seat. In front were bucket seats; the passenger side one swiveled 180 degrees to face the "sofa" seat. In the rear was another curved lounge, or sofa, seat accessible through the doorgate. Also here was an 8-inch Philco TV built into the interior side panel. Other gadgets inside the *Aurora II* were an AM/FM stereo and an 8-track tape recorder/player.

The 1969 Aurora II show car was built from a production LTD Country Squire. It had three side doors with the singular unit on the driver's side. The curved lounge seat in place of the stock second seat necessitated the three-door arrangement. In front were bucket seats; the passenger side one swiveled 180 degrees to face the sofa seat. (Photo courtesy of Mitch Frumkin)

In the rear of the Aurora II show car was another curved lounge, or sofa, seat accessible through the doorgate. Also here was an 8-inch Philco TV built into the interior side panel. Other gadgets inside the Aurora II were an AM/FM stereo and an 8-track tape recorder/player. (Photo courtesy of Mitch Frumkin)

Production Numbers

Total full-sized Ford production equaled 1,014,750 units. The LTD two- and four-door hardtops were the most popular with, 111,565 and 113,168, respectively, being built. Galaxie 500 four-door sedans accounted for 104,606 of the overall production. Formal-roof two-door hardtop Galaxie 500s outnumbered the Sports Roof variety 71,920 vs. 63,921. Production of the XLs increased; 61,959 were assembled, of which, 7,402 were convertibles, making it the least produced full-size Ford for 1969.

1970: "The Going Thing"

Mod art and the slogan "It's The Going Thing" appeared in some of Ford's advertising for the new model year. The full-size models received no major sheetmetal changes, only minor revisions.

Up front were revised grilles for the LTD/XL and the Galaxie 500/Custom 500/Custom series of cars. The LTD and XL continued to have hidden headlights, but the headlight doors and grille-work featured a fine-mesh pattern within rectangular segments. The horizontal divider that was painted the body color used in the prior model year was deleted.

Other full-size models were distinguished from LTDs and XLs with exposed quad headlights and a pattern of rectangles split horizontally with a pair of bright, thin, closely spaced parallel bars divided vertically in the center with a crest. A wide, bright molding along the hood lip and leading edge of the front fenders further decorated the Galaxie 500s and the pair of Custom series.

The side marker lamps were reshaped, as were the taillights. The latter no longer had the cross-hair-style backup lamps; these were relocated to the rear bumper. Endpoints of the rear bumper had a U-shaped dip to clear the rounded-corner rectangular taillights. Running between the taillights on LTDs (except Squires) and XLs was a panel with a pattern of blacked-out rectangles; the Galaxie 500 sedans and hardtops had a narrow, silver-and-black molding with FORD stamped across its width; no molding was applied here on the Custom 500 and Custom models.

Side trim also got revised, with LTDs (except the Country Squires) getting a rocker panel molding and a narrow fender-cap molding that continued all the way to the base of the C-pillar. Galaxie 500s lacked these moldings, but had a thin body side spear filled with a dent-resistant color-keyed vinyl insert.

The Brougham, which had been a trim option for the LTDs, was elevated to model status for 1970. This change created the LTD Brougham two- and four-door hardtops, as well as the LTD Brougham four-door sedan.

The Galaxie 500 convertible was dropped this year, leaving the XL convertible as the only drop-top in the full-size lineup. Also absent this year was the two-door sedan body style in both the Custom and Custom 500 series. Incidentally, a Custom 500 two-door hardtop was offered in Canada.

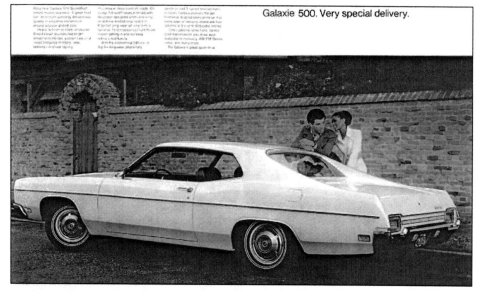

Galaxie 500. Very special delivery.

Two Galaxie 500 two-door hardtops were again available for 1970. This, of course, is the Sportsroof variant, which received 50,825 orders.

LTD.
The car that Ford
is keeping quiet.

Ford's heavily emphasized the quiet ride of the LTD in literature and advertising. Illustrated here is the LTD four-door hardtop, the most popular full-size Ford for 1969. It had a base price of $3,261 and accounted for 113,168 sales.

The ignition switch was relocated to the right side of the steering column. The steering wheel was locked without the ignition key inserted. Shoulder harnesses (for the front seat only) were now combined with the lap belt resulting in a Uni-lock single buckle per front seat passenger.

Standard Features

Power disc brakes became standard for 1970 on all LTD offerings, as well as on cars with the trailer towing package and wagons equipped with the 390-ci and SelectAire or with a 429-ci.

LTD Broughams were equipped with:

- die-cast grille with hidden headlights
- wheel covers
- electric clock
- special steering wheel
- wood-tone appliqués (steering wheel dash door panels)
- six choices of cloth and vinyl upholstery
- cut-pile carpeting
- heater/defroster
- five courtesy lights
- front seat center armrest
- bright seat side-shields
- special roof pillar ornamentation
- bright drip rail moldings
- wheel opening and rocker panel moldings
- 351-ci 2-bbl
- fully synchronized 3-speed manual transmission

LTDs were similarly equipped, but had one less upholstery choice and lacked the wheel covers, electric clock, bright seat side shields, special steering wheel, and courtesy light group.

The Ford XLs in standard trim came with:

- 351-ci 2-bbl
- fully synchronized 3-speed manual transmission
- die-cast grille with hidden headlights
- six all-vinyl upholstery selections
- wood-tone appliqués on the dash and door panels
- lighted glove box and trunk
- full wheel covers
- bright-metal molding on drip rails and wheel openings

- power-operated top with a glass rear window for convertibles

Galaxie 500s were equipped nearly the same as the XLs, but with the 240-ci 6-cylinder as standard issue. Standard upholstery was a combination of cloth and vinyl in five color options.

During the spring, a Maverick Introduction Special Galaxie 500 was released. (The Maverick was a new compact model.) It came equipped with several otherwise optional items: whitewall tires, wheel covers, and Rim-Blow steering wheel. Discounts for air conditioning, tinted glass, and V-8s were also included.

The Custom 500 offered four color choices of cloth and vinyl upholstery, while the Custom had vinyl in three alternative colors. A bright-metal body side molding was also standard issue for the Custom 500, but bright-metal moldings for the drip rails and wheel openings were deleted from both series of Custom models. Color-keyed nylon loop-carpeting was yet another standard feature of these low-priced models.

A power tailgate window was standard issue for Country Squires and wagons with dual-facing rear seats. Being a member of the LTD series meant it was similarly equipped to the hardtops and sedan versions.

Country Sedans and all Ranch Wagon models were powered with the 240-ci Big Six, though the array of V-8s could be had for extra dollars. Other standard features remained basically the same as for 1969.

Extra-Cost Equipment

Twin-Comfort Lounge Seats with a reclining passenger side was an

The Ford XL convertible got only 6,348 buyers for 1970. This was the final year for it and the XL hardtop. As seen in this period photograph, Ford did, however, offer a full-size convertible in the LTD line.

option for the LTD Brougham. As before, this front bench seat option featured individually adjustable driver and passenger sides and came with individual fold-down armrests.

High-back bucket seats with a console remained an option for the Galaxie 500 two-door hardtop. A vinyl top could now be had for LTD Country Squires and Galaxie 500 Country Sedans. Vinyl tops were offered in white, black, blue, green, and brown.

The GT Performance Group was discontinued for 1970. However, most of the features of the GT option were available as individual options. Furthermore, a Traction-Lok differential was offered.

Plaid was in fashion, therefore plaid trim was offered for the Country Squires and Country Sedans. Other wagon options included an adjustable luggage rack with rear window air deflector and power door locks including tailgate.

Other extra-cost "better appear-

ance ideas" included a vinyl covered roof (for all hardtops, LTD Brougham and LTD sedans as well as the Galaxie 500 sedan, Country Squires, and Country Sedans), dual color-keyed "Racing Mirrors" for two-door models, and simulated mag wheel covers.

So-called "better performance ideas" offered were Automatic Ride Control (self-leveling system), 55- or 65-amp alternator, heavy-duty battery, power steering, belted H70-15 Wide-Oval white sidewall tires, and trailer towing package.

"Better convenience ideas" were comprised of SelectShift transmission, left-hand remote-control outside mirror, power door locks, power windows, Convenience Check Group and warning lights, rear window defogger, intermittent wipers, and an automatic front seat back release for two-door models.

SelectAire, tinted glass, Comfortweave Vinyl Trim, and six-way power front seat were among the better comfort ideas offered for 1970.

Exterior Colors

Exterior colors offered were:
- Raven Black
- Wimbledon White
- Diamond Blue
- Acapulco Blue
- Dark Blue
- Medium Blue Metallic
- Dark Ivy Green Metallic
- Medium Ivy Green
- Light Ivy Yellow
- Yellow
- Bright Gold Metallic
- Champagne Gold
- Ginger
- Candyapple Red
- Dark Maroon

A total of 24 two-tone combinations were available, as were 15 Dual Tone two-tone paint schemes for the XL. This option placed flat black on the hood fender tops, door tops, and upper quarter panels just beneath the windows. The flat black area and the primary color were separated with an LTD-type molding running along the fender line to the base of the C-pillar. Additionally, any one of five extra-cost accent stripe colors could be had: black, white, red, gold, and silver.

Road Test

The March 1970 issue of *Motor Trend* magazine provided a comparison report on the similar Ford XL, AMC Ambassador, Chevy Impala, and the Dodge Polara. In the tester's judgment, the Impala emerged "slightly ahead of the other three." However, unlike the evaluation by *Car Life* from one year earlier, the *Motor Trend* evaluation did not indicate the same level of frustration shown by those in the earlier *Car Life* report. The dash arrangement, which was mostly unchanged from 1969, did receive some criticism (i.e., radio controls inaccessible to the passenger, glove box too small, with tilt steering the speedometer can be difficult to read, etc.), but they praised the controls for the cruise control, which were placed in the steering wheel crossbar.

Handling of the XL hardtop got a mixed review. "The XL goes through corners quite flat, with only a little lean or roll. There is some wheel hop noticeable and it is somewhat annoying. It also occurs during hard braking. Steering is fast and responsive, but with 3.9 wheel turns lock-to-lock it has the most play. Only a slight road feel comes through the power steering. Ford power steering usually has a solid feeling." Of the four cars in the test, the Ford came in second to the "impressive" Impala in regard to handling.

Acceleration tests revealed the XL equipped with a 390-ci 2-bbl, automatic transmission, and 2.75:1 axle ratio needed 12 seconds to reach 60 mph from rest. The heavier Polara with a 290-hp engine actually shaved 1/2 second from that result. The other cars had 4-barrel carbs and gearing more suitable for acceleration. Both were considerably faster in the 0–60 mph run and tied with a 9.5 second run. As for stopping ability, the XL proved superior, requiring just 127 feet to come to rest from 60 mpg.

Production Numbers

Total full-size Ford production equaled 852,992 units—a decrease of nearly 162,000 cars from the 1969 sales total. The Galaxie 500 four-door sedan claimed the top spot, with 101,784 built. Again, the formal roof Galaxie 500 two-door hardtop got more buyers (57,059) than the Sports Roof version (50,825). Taking second place was the LTD two-door hardtop with 96,324, though the four-door hardtop was not very far behind with 90,390. Production of the XL in its final year totaled 33,599, with only 6,348 of these being convertibles, making it the least-ordered full-size Ford in the United States.

Epilogue

Following the 1970 model year, full-size Fords continued to be offered in Custom, Custom 500, Galaxie 500, and LTD forms. However, the Custom was dropped for 1973, while the Galaxie 500 line was discontinued with the end of the 1974 model year. This was also the final year for the hardtop body style. With the demise of the XL at the end of the 1970 model year there would have been no convertible to offer, but the LTD gained a drop-top and was produced through 1972.

The LTD continued to be offered into 1991, undergoing various redesigns, and it even got split into a full-size (LTD) and mid-size (LTD II) lines for 1977. In 1983, the big version was renamed the LTD Crown Victoria, thus reviving a name from the mid 1950s. At this time, a smaller version, dubbed simply LTD, was built on the Fox platform. It lasted through 1986.

The full-size Ford has remained popular with police departments for many years and today the descendent of the LTD—the Crown Victoria Police Interceptor—is a mainstay of the police departments across the United States and some foreign countries.

1955 –1970: FLEET CARS

Fords were popular choices for entities needing a fleet of cars. Fleet service cars were those used by the police and fire departments, ambulance services, funeral homes, rental car agencies, taxi services, breweries, etc. Local, state, and federal agencies were also fleet buyers.

The low-cost models were typically ordered for obvious reasons, and in the case of Ford, that meant models such as the Mainline (1955–1956), Custom (1957–early 1958), Custom 300 (1958–1959), Fairlane (1960–1961), Galaxie (1962–1963), and Custom (1964–1970). Ambulance and funeral service cars were modified versions of the Courier Sedan Delivery and Country Sedan. Amblewagon of Birmingham, Michigan, was one company who performed the conversion work with the cars being sold through Ford.

Ford Police Cars

As more and more cars began filling the streets of America during the early part of the twentieth century, safety regulations had to be developed to maintain orderliness of traffic. As a result, states created department of public safety offices during the 1920s and 1930s to handle enforcement of the rules of the road.

This 1963 Ford 300 Police Sentinel was found in a Georgia salvage yard and restored to original condition. The Police Sentinel package consisted of a small-block V-8, five-blade cooling fan, 15-inch wheels, plus heavy-duty suspension, radiator, brakes, and battery. It is also equipped with ribbed-vinyl upholstery offered only on fleet vehicles. (Photo courtesy of Thomas Glatch)

The police car itself had been around as early as 1909. In the 1930s, the Ford V-8s were the car of choice by law enforcement (as well many criminals), due to their ability to sustain long-term high-speed pursuit. By the early 1950s, automobile manufacturers began offering police packages for fleet sales to law enforcement officials, but Ford still held the largest percentage of orders by a wide margin.

Ford's fleet division was the first to market a police package consisting of heavy-duty suspension, heavy-duty cooling system, and high-

performance engine. The police car also benefited from the horsepower race of the 1950s. For 1955, Ford was in its second year of offering the Y-block, and Ford police cars could be ordered with the 198-hp 292-ci. However, the following year, Ford offered a 210-hp, 312-ci Police Interceptor to law enforcement agencies.

Ford was fast becoming the most popular vehicle for law enforcement agencies. The front cover of their 1958 Ford Police Cars and Emergency Vehicles catalog stated that "more Ford police cars are sold than all other makes combined." This was

In the 1950s, Ford quickly became the most popular vehicle for law enforcement agencies. In 1956, Ford Motor Company offered a 210-hp 312-ci Police Interceptor to law enforcement agencies.

For 1958, Ford police vehicles were the Custom 300 two-door and four-door sedans, two-door and four-door Ranch Wagons, and four-door Country Sedan Wagons in both six- and nine-passenger varieties. Shown is an original Texas Highway Patrol car.

AMBULANCE CONVERSION

Ford Police Wagons--the Ranch Wagon, Country Sedan (6-passenger) and Country Sedan with dual-facing rear seats—are ideally suited for ambulance conversion. The Magic Doorgate, standard on all Ford wagons, adds outstanding versatility to these vehicles. It can be swung down in a conventional manner for loading emergency gear or opened to the side like a door to admit ambulatory cases or load stretchers. Only Ford wagons have it.

The ambulance and patrol wagon conversions have been thoroughly tested and proved in many police applications. Complete details and conversion options data are available from your Ford Dealer.

Ford advertised its Ranch Wagon, six-passenger Country Sedan, and Country Sedan with dual-facing rear seats as ideal vehicles for conversion to an ambulance. (Photo courtesy of Adrian Clements collection)

The 1964 Ford Custom served as a Nebraska Highway Patrol car. It is powered by a P-code 390-ci Interceptor coupled to a Cruise-O-Matic transmission.

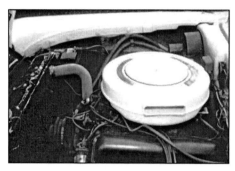

The 300-hp 352-ci Interceptor powers this ex-Texas Highway Patrol car. It is also equipped with a 3-speed manual transmission with overdrive.

a true statement, as more than 70 percent of the state police cars sold during the time wore the Ford name.

The inside of the catalog went on to note the "proven" aspects of the 1958 Ford—"rapid acceleration and top performance," "stamina and dependability," plus "safety and comfort." Any option offered to regular Ford customers could be ordered for police vehicles, including air suspension and air conditioning. Limited state budgets often precluded luxury items from making there way onto these cars.

Ford police vehicles for 1958 were offered as Custom 300 two-door and four-door sedans, two-door and four-door Ranch Wagons, and four-door Country Sedan Wagons in both six- and nine-passenger varieties.

Engine choices depended on the model. The 145-hp 223-ci Mileage-Maker Six, 265-hp 332-ci Interceptor, 300-hp 352-ci Police Interceptor, and the 303-hp Police Interceptor 361-ci Special could be had in all of these models; the 205-hp 292-ci was restricted to the Custom 300; the 240-hp 332-ci Interceptor was restricted to the station wagon models.

Dual exhausts were standard on the 352- and 361-ci Police Interceptors.

The latter engine, used by the new Edsel, was available exclusively for police use; therefore, the typical Ford customer could not order it, although it was standard issue for the Edsel Ranger, Pacer, and station wagon models.

Transmission availability depended on the engine and model chosen. A 3-speed manual with or without overdrive was offered for all. The top-performing 352- and 361-ci could be ordered with any transmission

This decal was applied to the rocker arm cover of the 390-ci Police Interceptor engine.

The speedometers for police vehicles were specially calibrated and marked in 2-mph increments, as shown on this 1964 Custom two-door sedan, which was originally a member of the fleet of the Nebraska Highway Patrol.

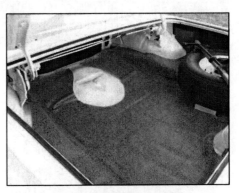

The relocated spare tire, which provided better weight distribution, was an interesting option for Ford police cars.

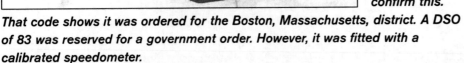

This alternator with dual-belt drive was among the equipment offered on police cars.

This 1966 Custom 500 is believed to have originally been part of the U.S. Government fleet, though its DSO code of 11 does not confirm this. That code shows it was ordered for the Boston, Massachusetts, district. A DSO of 83 was reserved for a government order. However, it was fitted with a calibrated speedometer.

The body side and trunk moldings distinguished the 1966 Custom 500s from the Customs.

For 1966, full-size Ford hardtops and sedans shared the same taillights, as opposed to the prior model year, where Custom and Custom 500s had round lenses while the rest of the non-wagon lineup had hexagonal lenses.

Full-size 1966 Fords used 15-inch wheels painted the main body color when a wheel cover option was not ordered. This hub cap style was introduced in 1965 and continued until mid-year 1967.

Light blue crinkle vinyl and blue Eaton pattern cloth combination was one of the four standard upholstery choices for 1966 Custom 500s. Note the 4-speed shifter and rubber floor mat. The latter was typical of fleet cars.

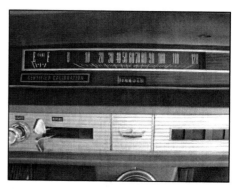

This Custom 500 is equipped with a calibrated speedometer marked in 2-mph increments. Note the block-off plate used when the electric clock was not ordered.

including the Ford-O-Matic or the new Cruise-O-Matic.

Cubic inches continued to be added to the FE engine. By 1961, Ford offered four 390s with one ostensibly restricted to law enforcement agencies. The P-code 390-ci offered 330 hp at 5,000 rpm. However, as in the past, any engine Ford produced could be ordered by these organizations. The P-code 390-ci stayed in production through the 1965 model year. Incidentally, despite being officially assigned to police use, the P-code 390-ci was legal in NHRA D-stock and D-stock automatic competition (at least in 1965).

For 1966 through 1970, Ford offered the 360-hp 428-ci, again designated with engine code P in the serial number. It was strictly for law enforcement departments.

In 1968, the 302-ci was added to the possible engine choices for police departments and other fleet buyers. It was part of the Police Sentinel Package.

A complete listing of all equipment packages for police versions of full-size Fords from 1955 to 1970 is beyond the scope of this book. How-

Listed in the catalogs for fleet buyers was this fold-down rear seat for four-door sedan models. However, it was not restricted to fleet sales. The equipment was nearly identical to that used for station wagons. (Photo courtesy of Tom Yanulaytis collection/1966 Full-Size Registry)

ever, a list from 1967 is reasonably representative. Police packages offered were broken down into Interceptor, Defender, Cruiser, Guardian, Sentinel, and Deputy.

The Interceptor was composed of:
- 360-hp, 428-ci Police Interceptor
- 80-amp heavy-duty battery
- 42-amp alternator with dual-belt drive
- maximum handling package (heavy-duty springs, extra-

control shocks, heavy-duty link-type stabilizer bar, heavy-duty front suspension arms)
- manual front disc brakes
- calibrated speedometer (2-mph increments)
- heavy-duty front seat
- Police Cooling Package with higher-capacity radiator
- seven-blade viscose drive fan
- heavy-duty front and rear rubber floor mats
- 15x6-inch rims
- lubricator-fitted universal joints

All other packages had a 70-amp battery.

The Defender was identical except of course for the 345-hp 428-ci. The Cruiser came with the 390-ci 4-bbl, while the Guardian came with a 390 2-bbl Police Sentinel and Deputy versions lacked the extra-cooling package and front disc brakes included in the other packages, and came with a 289-ci 2-bbl V-8 and 240-ci 6-cylinder, respectively.

Extra-cost equipment categories were RPO (Regular Production Options), LPO (Limited Production Options), and DSO (Domestic Sales Office).

Those in the RPO group included manual front disc brakes for 240- and 289-powered cars, plus:

- SelectShift Cruise-O-Matic
- 4-speed fully synchronized transmission
- overdrive with 240- and 289-ci engines
- radial ply tires (240- and 289-ci only)
- power brakes
- power seat
- Convenience Control Panel
- limited-slip differential
- various axle ratios
- power windows (with Convenience Control Panel)
- power doorgate window on wagons (standard on Country Sedan with dual-facing rear seats and Squire)
- AM-radio with front antenna
- AM/FM radio with front antenna
- right rear quarter mount antenna
- tinted glass

- two-tone paint
- roof rack (wagons only)
- MagicAire heater
- courtesy light group
- fold-down rear seat (sedans only)
- headlight covers
- special PRNDRL detent plate (blocks first and second on Cruise-O-Matic transmission)
- automatic speed control

LPO items were:

- pancake-type alternator with built-in silicon rectifier
- transistorized voltage regulator
- extra cooling package
- radio noise suppression equipment
- dual wiring for roof beacon
- single key locking system
- left-hand spotlight
- high-speed police tires (8.15 and 8.45x15 sizes)

Those under DSO equipment included:

- suppression spark plugs with non-suppressed wiring

- locking-type hand throttle
- oil pressure gauge
- flexible conduit for radio cable (sedans only)
- pace-type speedometer with needle stop
- right-hand spotlight
- charge indicator gauge (standard with 60-amp alternator)
- spare tire relocation (to right rear of luggage compartment sedans only)
- glove box and ash tray light

Dealer-installed items offered were bumper guards, electric clock, mud and stone deflectors (wagons only), rubber cargo deck mat (wagons only), Ford SelectAire, and bumper steps (six-passenger wagons only).

Ford Taxis

A highly detailed account of Ford taxis from 1955 to 1970 is likewise beyond the scope of this book. Still, a good representation can be given by taking a look at a few random model years.

The standard Taxi Package included the 3-speed manual transmission, lubricator-fitted universal joints, extra-heavy-duty 100,000-mile seats with formed foam rubber front and foam rubber rear seat cushions, beige vinyl upholstery, heavy-duty battery, cooling package with five-blade fan, and other equipment. (Photo courtesy of Adrian Clements collection)

The Courier Sedan Delivery was one of the vehicles of choice for use by emergency services. The Courier was a station wagon-based car, typically without side windows except, of course, for the doors. It was also well-suited for use by various businesses. Ford considered the Courier as part of its light-duty truck line.

Cost was always a major factor for taxi services in determining the right car to buy. For 1956, Ford claimed it offered the "most profitable" models due to its "low initial cost... style-leader attraction... low operating and maintenance costs... and traditionally high resale value." Ford's taxi brochure also emphasized Lifeguard Design safety and seating comfort.

For 1962, Ford offered the Galaxie Mainliner Taxicab. The company's special taxi brochure underscored its maintenance advantages —30,000 miles between major chassis lubrication and coolant changes, 6,000 miles between oil changes, and the self-adjusting brakes and mechanical valves (6-cylinder). The Galaxie Mainliner Taxicab was also touted as offering "luxury-car room, comfort and style at special fleet savings."

The standard interior of the Mainliner was offered in blue, gray, or green with stripe-patterned cloth with vinyl bolsters. Also available was a taxi-duty interior in beige, green, or red vinyl.

Other standard components of the taxi package were comprised of heavy-duty brakes, springs, clutch, seats, and steel speedometer gears (6-cylinder only).

The Expanded Taxi Package offered:

- rear seat armrests
- ash receptacle in front seat-back
- and heavy-duty front and rear floor mats.
  Auxiliary Taxi Package (40-amp, low cut-in generator or alternator)
- four-door operated dome light with red door ajar warning light
- roof light wiring
- assist straps
- right-hand rear door metal pull handle
- lubricator-fitted universal driveshaft

- glove compartment
- 170-hp, 292-ci V-8
- overdrive
- Ford-O-Matic Drive
- Cruise-O-Matic
- MagicAire heater
- SelectAire
- power steering
- padded instrument panel
- two-tone paint
- several generator and alternator choices
- back-up lights

Other Special-Duty Fords

Fleet sales were also aimed at other municipal emergency services such as fire departments. The Courier Sedan Delivery was one of the vehicles suited for such use. The Courier was a station wagon-based car typically without side windows except for the doors. Ford considered the Courier as part of its light-duty truck line. It was discontinued after the 1960 model year.

The Custom 300 was marketed toward taxi services. Comfort and ruggedness were emphasized in the taxi brochure.

Ford actually named their Ford taxi a Galaxie Mainliner for 1962.

1955 –1970:

FOREIGN FULL-SIZE FORDS

Ford built a number of models in foreign markets such as the Consul, Cortina, Taunus, and Zephyr—these were completely different models than the ones sold here. However, full-size versions of U.S. designs were also sold in foreign markets.

Australia

Ford Australia officially began on March 31, 1925, in Geelong, Victoria, producing Model Ts. The headquarters moved to Melbourne in 1961.

For 1955 and 1956, the right-hand-drive Customline was the top-of-the-line Ford in Australia. The 3-speed automatic became available for 1956. The 1955–1956 design stayed in production through late 1959. The 1958 versions were actually a mixture of components from the U.S. Ford and the Canadian Meteor.

In August of 1959, Ford Australia opened its Broadmeadows assembly plant in Victoria. The 1959 U.S. Fairlane replaced the 1955–1956 design, but the parts were sourced through Ford of Canada.

At first, the Australian 1959 Ford was offered as the Custom 300 sedan

A couple of minor external changes were made to the Australian 1967 Galaxie 500: The antenna was relocated from the right fender to the left and the stone shield behind the front bumper was painted body color rather than argent. **(Photo courtesy of Adrian Clements collection)**

and the Fairlane 500 sedan. In September 1960, the Ranch Wagon was added. These models were powered by the 332-ci V-8. The basic 1959 design stayed in production through 1962, with various trim changes (from Mercury and Meteor parts bin) being made along the way.

The early 1960s models, however, were available in extremely small numbers. These were fully imported models from Ford of Canada, which at the time was the worldwide supplier of U.S.-based Ford vehicles. With Australia a member of the British Common-

Discover how prestige and value go so beautifully together: Ford Galaxie 500

The Australian 1964 Ford Galaxie 500 was identical to the U.S. version on the outside. (Photo courtesy of Darren Will collection)

SOLID, SILENT LUXURY-POWERED BY FORD! Galaxie 500

Exterior trim for the 1966 Galaxie 500 sold in Australia was identical to that of its U.S. counterpart. (Photo courtesy of Darren Will collection)

The interior of the 1967 Galaxie 500 sold in Australia appears to be more luxurious than even the LTD sold in the United States. The seating appears to be similar to that of a contemporary Lincoln, while the dash design was based on a 1961–1963 Lincoln. (Photo courtesy of Adrian Clements collection)

wealth, favorable import duty concessions were obtained importing the cars from Canada rather than acquiring them directly from the United States.

The year 1963 brought an increase in the number of Galaxie 500s available to the Australian market. Even larger numbers became available for the 1964 model year through selected Ford dealers. The Ford Australia-imported 1964 Galaxie 500 four-door hardtops and sedans appeared identical to U.S. versions. Engine choices were limited to the standard 195-hp 289-ci or the optional 280-hp, 390-ci 4-bbl with 7.9:1 compression.

In late 1964, assembly of the 1965 Galaxie 500 sedan commenced at the Homebush assembly plant in Sydney's inner west. Assembly continued at Homebush through 1968. Ford Australia designated the 1965 model GE, then later dropped the two-letter model designation for the Galaxie 500. By the way, Galaxie 500s built at the Homebush assembly plant had the letter K in the VIN. Engine choices for 1965 were unchanged, though the 289-ci gained 5 extra horsepower. For 1966, a 280-hp, 390-ci 2-bbl was optional.

The 1965 Australian Fords were more luxuriously equipped than their American counterparts. Power steer-

ing, power brakes, front and rear center seat armrests, driver's side rearview mirror, single-speed wipers with intermittent control, padded dash, clock, and full wheel covers were standard issue. Additionally, when the 390-ci was ordered, an AM-radio was standard. The 1967–1970 models received front single-piston disc brakes as standard equipment.

The 1969 and 1970 Galaxie LTDs, as they were named for the Australian market, were fully imported from the United States and converted to right-hand drive at the Broadmeadows plant. The instrument panel for both model years was essentially a mirror image of the U.S. versions.

Whereas contemporary U.S. automotive publications complained about the dash layout of the 1969 and 1970 full-size Fords, at least one

For 1968, the Galaxie 500 and Galaxie LTD were offered in South Africa, as well as Australia. The modified wheel covers on the pictured LTD have 1967-style red-and-gold inserts. (Photo courtesy of Darren Will collection)

For 1969 and 1970, Galaxie LTD instrument panels were essentially a mirror image of the U.S. versions. (Photo courtesy of Darren Will collection)

Australian writer had a very different viewpoint: "Inside, the LTD is awe-inspiring. The driver's instrument console is reminiscent of a movie palace Wurlitzer as the dials, panels and switches are arranged in an all-encompassing, curved panel."

After 1964, the four-door hardtop could be had via special order (as could other body styles) through some dealers. Station wagons continued to be available after 1960, but were sold in miniscule quantities.

Brazil

With the completion of the 1966 model year, Ford shipped the tooling for their Galaxie 500 four-door sedans to Ford Brazil S.A. (South America).

The 1966 U.S. version of the Galaxie 500 four-door sedan was built there from February 1967 until 1975 with minimal changes. It received significant styling refinements the following year and was discontinued at the end of 1982 production. An LTD version was introduced for 1969, and was produced through 1983. These cars remained left-hand drive, but did have the speedometer marked in kilometers per hour. The Galaxie 500 and especially the LTD (and later the Landau) represented status symbols to the rich and powerful.

For the first few years, only one engine was available, the old Y-block 272-ci, which was coupled to a 3-speed manual transmission. Beginning in September 1968, air conditioning became an option.

This was at the same time the LTD four-door sedan debuted there. It was a more luxurious version of the Galaxie 500 and was powered with the 292-ci V-8s, rated at 173 hp. It featured black jersey and leather upholstery, woodgrain appliqués on the dash and door panels, vinyl-covered roof, die-cast grille (like the American counterpart), and LTD identification on the hood and C-pillars. An automatic transmission was optional.

For 1970, minor styling updates were implemented and the 292-ci was standard on all models.

Canada

The Ford Motor Company of Canada began operations in 1904 in Walkerville, Ontario, just outside Windsor. (Eventually the suburb became a part of downtown Windsor.) From 1904 through 1946, Fords built in the U.S. and Canada were nearly identical. However, in 1949, the Meteor was introduced. This model was essentially a Ford, but with a different grille and side trim. The Meteor, like the Ford, was subdivided into three series: the top-of-the-line version was dubbed Rideau, and was followed in the hierarchy by the mid-level Niagara and the Meteor. These cars were designed in Dearborn since the Canadian operation did not have a styling department.

In 1955 and 1956, the Meteor line followed the U.S. Ford line with one exception—there was no Crown Victoria Skyliner equivalent. Grilles and trim differed as before, but another minor variation was adopted when engine colors for the V-8s were changed for Canadian vehicles.

This was followed in 1958 by revised engine selections. The 292-ci was the smallest V-8 offered in the United States but the 272-ci continued to be available in Canada. The Edsel 361-ci was the largest V-8 offered in the Meteor this year.

For 1959, engine offerings in Canada included the 6-cylinder, 332-ci, and the Edsel 361-ci. However, this year, the Canadian Fords and their American counterparts became identical in appearance with the exception of some differences in exterior paint colors.

The new 1960 models in Canada paralleled the American lineup with three series, but resorted to a unique grille and trim. Engine choices for

Miles ahead value, in styling and in thrifty

In 1955 (and 1956), the Canadian Meteor line followed the U.S. Ford line with one exception: there was no Crown Victoria Skyliner equivalent. Grilles and trim on the Canadian cars differed from those of the U.S. Fords. The Meteor was the base model in the Canadian line. (Author's collection)

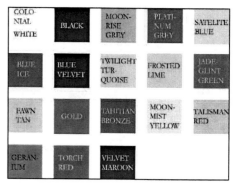

Choices of paint colors were tailored toward Canadian tastes. This shows samples of the colors offered for the 1959 models. (Illustration by author)

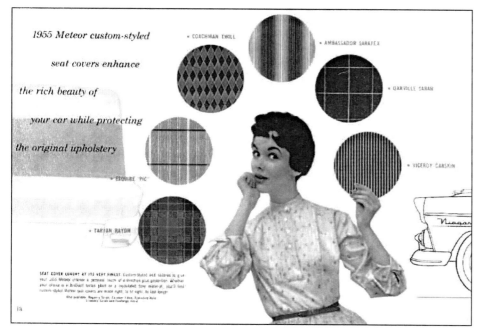

1955 Meteor custom-styled seat covers enhance the rich beauty of your car while protecting the original upholstery

Upholstery was also another way in which the Canadian Fords differed from the U.S.-built examples.

the Meteor were the 223-ci 6-cylinder, 332-ci, and 300-hp 352-ci; the 292-ci and the 360-hp 352-ci were not offered.

In 1961, the Meteor name made a (temporary) final appearance. Engine selection was nearly identical with the exception of the 300-hp 390-ci replacing the 300-hp 352-ci.

Starting in 1964, the Meteor name was reborn, but for an entirely different vehicle marketed in Canada. The full-size Canadian Fords after 1961 were nearly identical to the U.S.-built cars though there remained some variation in engine choices and even model offerings. For instance, in 1966, the 352-ci 4-barrel and the 390-ci 4-barrel were not available in Canada; the Galaxie 500 7-Litre was not offered either.

Prior to the Automotive Products Trade Agreement, also known as APTA, many cars sold in Canada were also built there due to trade barriers. Virtually all Fords before 1966 and many, if not most 1966 models, sold in Canada were built at the Oakville assembly plant, which opened in 1953.

The APTA was signed by Canadian Prime Minister Lester B. Pearson and U.S. President Lyndon B. Johnson on January 16, 1965. This agreement removed tariffs on cars, trucks, buses, tires, and automotive parts between the two countries, greatly benefiting the large American car makers. In exchange the Big Three car makers agreed that automobile production in Canada would not fall below 1964 levels and that for every five new cars sold in Canada, three new ones would be built there. Each vehicle built in Canada also had to have at least 60-percent Canadian content in both parts and labor.

Hardtop 2 portes Galaxie 500/XL

LA FORD À COUPLE SUPER ÉLEVÉ se vend comme jamais auparavant! Séduisante et luxueuse à un degré inconnu jusqu'à présent, elle jouit d'une popularité qui s'étend à tous les coins du pays. A l'extérieur, un style d'un brio étourdissant; à l'intérieur, une somptuosité nouvelle; au volant, une sensation inégalée de stabilité et de confort dans cette voiture *plus massive* et, par conséquent, *robuste et silencieuse* à souhait! Vaste choix de 16 modèles magnifiques, en 4 séries, comprenant la Custom, la Custom 500, la Galaxie 500 et la Galaxie 500/XL.

FORD

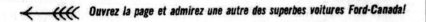
← ◄◄◄ *Ouvrez la page et admirez une autre des superbes voitures Ford-Canada!*

The full-size Canadian Fords after 1961 were nearly identical to the U.S.-built cars, but there remained some variation in engine choices and even model offerings. This advertisement for the 1964 Galaxie 500/XL is in French.

Mexico

Ford of Mexico opened its first assembly plant in Mexico City in 1932. In 1964, a new plant was opened in Cuautitlán, Izcalli, that produced the Galaxie 500 four-door sedan and later the LTD. These cars were left-hand drive, but had a metric speedometer and odometer.

South Africa

The full-size Fords with right-hand drive seemed to have entered into the South African market in 1959 with the Custom 300 Fordor, Fairlane 500 Town Sedan, Galaxie Town Sedan, and Galaxie Club Victoria. All but the Custom 300 were powered by the 332-ci V-8; it had a 6-cylinder. An interesting departure from the U.S. counterparts was the use of the 1956-style wheel cover.

The Galaxie 500 with an automatic transmission and a 390-ci 4-bbl arrived in 1965. It was imported from Canada, while the 1959–1964 models had been imported from the United States. Interestingly, the Fairlane 500 nameplate continued to be used here, but was applied to a lower-cost, full-size car. Unlike their American counterparts, the LTD was a Galaxie 500/LTD in South Africa.

Other unusual deviations from the U.S. versions included completely different dashboards. The earlier cars used a design based on the 1960–1961 Comet; the latter cars had a 1961–1963 Lincoln-type instrument panel. There were even local variations for that. Some used a simulated wood paneling around the instrumentation, while others had ribbed bright-metal surround. These big Fords continued to be marketed in South Africa through 1968.

Tariffs were applied if these conditions were not met.

In 1964, 7 percent of vehicles made in Canada were sent to the United States. Four years later, 60 percent of Canadian-built vehicles were sent to the United States, while 40 percent of the vehicles purchased in Canada were built in the United States. In 1970, Canada registered a small auto trade surplus with the United States for the first time.

Not all Canadian-built Fords were sold in Canada and the United States, though. Others went to countries such as Australia, Belgium, Britain, France, the Netherlands, and South Africa.

R.I.P.–RUSTING IN PIECES

Many millions of full-size Fords were built between 1955 and 1970. Finding parts for these cars is usually not too difficult as there are a number of salvage yards devoted to older cars. There are sometimes surprising finds in open fields, too!

A 1959 Galaxie Town Sedan quietly awaits a buyer or a parts hunter in Texarkana. (Photo courtesy of Charles D. Barnette)

This 1964 Galaxie 500 two-door hardtop was built for NASCAR competition. It was put out to pasture, literally, in 1967. Among its drivers were Bobby Marshmann (1964 Daytona 500), Augie Pabst (250 km support race to the 12 Hour at Sebring), and Larry Frank (Atlanta 500). (Photo courtesy of JDC collection)

Ford's 1966 six-passenger Country Sedan accounted for 55,616 sales, making it the most popular of the wagon series. (Photo courtesy of Charles D. Barnette)

This 1967 Custom 500 four-door sedan, now sitting in a Texarkana salvage yard, was one of 109,449 built in U.S. assembly plants. (Photo courtesy of Charles D. Barnette)

ENGINES AND ENGINE CODES
(U.S. ONLY)

Model Year	Code	Type	CID	hp @ rpm	Torque (ft-lb @ rpm)	Compression	Carburetion
1955	A	I-6	223	120 @ 3,900	195 @ 1,200	7.5:1	1-bbl
	U	V-8	272	162 @ 4,200	258 @ 2,200	7.6:1	2-bbl
	M	V-8	272	182 @ 4,400	268 @ 2,600	8.5:1	4-bbl
	P (M/T)	V-8	292	193 @ 4,400	280 @ 2,600	8.1:1	4-bbl
	P (A/T)	V-8	292	198 @ 4,400	286 @ 2,600	8.5:1	4-bbl
1956	A	I-6	223	137 @ 4,200	202 @ 1,600	8.0:1	1-bbl
	U (M/T)	V-8	272	173 @ 4,400	260 @ 2,400	8.0:1	2-bbl
	U (A/T)	V-8	272	176 @ 4,400	264 @ 2,400	8.4:1	4-bbl
	M (M/T)	V-8	292	200 @ 4,600	285 @ 2,600	8.0:1	4-bbl
	M (A/T)	V-8	292	202 @ 4,400	289 @ 2,600	8.4:1	4-bbl
	P (M/T)	V-8	312	215 @ 4,600	317 @ 2,600	8.4:1	4-bbl
	P (A/T)	V-8	312	225 @ 4,600	324 @ 2,600	9.0:1	4-bbl
1957	A	I-6	223	144 @ 4,200	212 @ 2,400	8.6:1	1-bbl
	B	V-8	272	190 @ 4,500	270 @ 2,700	8.6:1	2-bbl
	C	V-8	292	206 @ 4,500	297 @ 2,700	9.0:1	4-bbl
	D	V-8	312	245 @ 4,500	332 @ 3,200	9.7:1	4-bbl
	E	V-8	312	270 @ 4,800	336 @ 3,400	9.7:1	2x4-bbl
	E	V-8	312	285 @ 5,300	–	9.7:1	2x4-bbl
	F*	V-8	312	300 @ 4,800	–	8.6:1	4-bbl
	F*§	V-8	312	340 @ 5,300	–	8.6:1	4-bbl
1958	A	I-6	223	145 @ 4,000	206 @ 2,200	8.6:1	1-bbl
	C	V-8	292	200 @ 4,400	285 @ 2,400	8.8:1	2-bbl
	B§§§	V-8	332	240 @ 4,600	345 @ 2,200§§§	9.5:1	2-bbl
	G	V-8	332	265 @ 4,600	360 @ 2,800	9.5:1	4-bbl
	H	V-8	352	300 @ 4,600	395 @ 2,800	10.2:1	4-bbl
1959	A	I-6	223	145 @ 4,000	206 @ 2,200	8.4:1	1-bbl
	C	V-8	292	200 @ 4,400	285 @ 2,400	8.8:1	2-bbl
	B	V-8	332	225 @ 4,400	325 @ 2,200	8.9:1	2-bbl
	H	V-8	352	300 @ 4,600	380 @ 2,800	9.6:1	4-bbl
1960	V	I-6	223	145 @ 4,000	200 @ 2,000	8.4:1	1-bbl
	W	V-8	292	185 @ 4,200	292 @ 2,200	8.8:1	1-bbl
	X	V-8	352	235 @ 4,400	350 @ 2,400	8.9:1	2-bbl
	Y§	V-8	352	300 @ 4,600	381 @ 2,800	9.6:1	4-bbl
	Y§	V-8	352	360 @ 6,000	380 @ 3,400	10.6:1	4-bbl

Model Year	Code	Type	CID	hp @ rpm	Torque (ft-lb @ rpm)	Compression	Carburetion
1961	V	I-6	223	135 @ 4,000	200 @ 2,000	8.4:1	1-bbl
	W	V-8	292	175 @ 4,200	279 @ 2,200	8.8:1	2-bbl
	X	V-8	352	220 @ 4,400	336 @ 2,400	8.9:1	2-bbl
	Z§	V-8	390	300 @ 4,600	427 @ 2,800	9.6:1	4-bbl
	P	V-8	390	330 @ 5,000	427 @ 3,200	9.6:1	4-bbl
	Z§	V-8	390	375 @ 6,000	427 @ 3,400	10.6:1	4-bbl
	Z§	V-8	390	401 @ 6,000	430 @ 3,500	10.6:1	3x2-bbl
1962	V	I-6	223	138 @ 4,000	200 @ 2,000	8.4:1	1-bbl
	W	V-8	292	170 @ 4,200	279 @ 2,200	8.8:1	1-bbl
	X	V-8	352	220 @ 4,300	336 @ 2,600	8.9:1	2-bbl
	Z	V-8	390	300 @ 4,600	427 @ 2,800	9.6:1	4-bbl
	P**	V-8	390	330 @ 5,000	427 @ 3,200	9.6:1	4-bbl
	Q***	V-8	390	375 @ 6,000	430 @ 3,400	10.6:1	4-bbl
	M***	V-8	390	401 @ 6,000	430 @ 3,500	10.6:1	3x2-bbl
	B****	V-8	406	385 @ 5,800	444 @ 3,400	11.4:1	4-bbl
	G****	V-8	406	405 @ 5,800	448 @ 3,500	11.4:1	2x4-bbl
1963	V	I-6	223	138 @ 4,000	203 @ 2,000	8.4:1	1-bbl
	F***	V-8	260	164 @ 4,400	258 @ 2,200	8.7:1	2-bbl
	C****	V-8	289	195 @ 4,400	282 @ 2,400	8.7:1	2-bbl
	X	V-8	352	220 @ 4,300	336 @ 2,600	8.9:1	2-bbl
	Z	V-8	390	300 @ 4,600	427 @ 2,800	9.6:1	4-bbl
	P	V-8	390	330 @ 5,000	427 @ 3,200	9.6:1	4-bbl
	B***	V-8	406	385 @ 5,800	444 @ 3,400	11.4:1	4-bbl
	G***	V-8	406	405 @ 5,800	448 @ 3,500	11.4:1	2x4-bbl
	Q****	V-8	427	410 @ 5,600	476 @ 3,400	11.6:1	4-bbl
	R****	V-8	427	425 @ 6,000	480 @ 3,700	11.6:1	2x4-bbl
1964	V	I-6	223	138 @ 4,000	203 @ 2,000	8.4:1	1-bbl
	C	V-8	289	195 @ 4,400	282 @ 2,400	8.7:1	2-bbl
	X	V-8	352	220 @ 4,300	336 @ 2,600	8.9:1	2-bbl
	Z	V-8	390	300 @ 4,600	427 @ 2,800	9.6:1	4-bbl
	P	V-8	390	330 @ 5,000	427 @ 3,200	9.6:1	4-bbl
	Q***	V-8	427	410 @ 5,600	476 @ 3,400	11.6:1	4-bbl
	R	V-8	427	425 @ 6,000	480 @ 3,700	11.6:1	2x4-bbl
1965	V	I-6	240	150 @ 4,000	234 @ 2,200	9.2:1	1-bbl
	C	V-8	289	195 @ 4,400	282 @ 2,400	8.7:1	2-bbl
	X	V-8	352	250 @ 4,400	352 @ 2,800	9.3:1	4-bbl
	Z	V-8	390	300 @ 4,600	427 @ 2,800	9.6:1	4-bbl
	P**	V-8	390	330 @ 5,000	427 @ 3,200	9.6:1	4-bbl
	R	V-8	427	425 @ 6,000	480 @ 3,700	11.6:1	2x4-bbl
1966	V	I-6	240	155 @ 4,000	239 @ 2,200	9.2:1	1-bbl
	C	V-8	289	200 @ 4,400	282 @ 2,400	9.3:1	2-bbl
	X	V-8	352	250 @ 4,400	352 @ 2,800	9.3:1	4-bbl
	Y	V-8	390	265 @ 4,400	401 @ 2,600	9.5:1	2-bbl
	Z	V-8	390	315 @ 4,600	427 @ 2,800	10.5:1	4-bbl
	W	V-8	427	410 @ 5,600	476 @ 3,400	11.1:1	4-bbl
	R	V-8	427	425 @ 6,000	480 @ 3,700	11.1:1	2x4-bbl
	Q	V-8	428	345 @ 4,600	462 @ 2,800	10.5:1	4-bbl
	P**	V-8	428	360 @ 5,400	459 @ 3,200	10.5:1	4-bbl

Model Year	Code	Type	CID	hp @ rpm	Torque (ft-lb @ rpm)	Compression	Carburetion
1967	V	I-6	240	155 @ 4,000	239 @ 2,200	9.2:1	1-bbl
	C	V-8	289	200 @ 4,400	282 @ 2,400	9.3:1	2-bbl
	Y†	V-8	390	270 @ 4,400	403 @ 2,600	9.5:1	2-bbl
	H††	V-8	390	270 @ 4,400	403 @ 2,600	9.5:1	2-bbl
	Z	V-8	390	315 @ 4,600	427 @ 2,800	10.5:1	4-bbl
	W	V-8	427	410 @ 5,600	476 @ 3,400	11.1:1	4-bbl
	R	V-8	427	425 @ 6,000	480 @ 3,700	11.1:1	2x4-bbl
	Q	V-8	428	345 @ 4,600	462 @ 2,800	10.5:1	4-bbl
	P	V-8	428	360 @ 5,400	459 @ 3,200	10.5:1	4-bbl
1968	V	I-6	240	155 @ 4,000	239 @ 2,200	9.2:1	1-bbl
	F	V-8	302	210 @ 4,600	300 @ 2,600	9.0:1	2-bbl
	Y	V-8	390	265 @ 4,400	401 @ 2,600	9.5:1	2-bbl
	Z	V-8	390	315 @ 4,600	427 @ 2,800	10.5:1	4-bbl
	W***	V-8	427	390 @ 5,600	460 @ 3,200	10.9:1	4-bbl
	Q	V-8	428	345 @ 4,600	462 @ 2,800	10.5:1	4-bbl
	P**	V-8	428	360 @ 5,400	459 @ 3,200	10.5:1	4-bbl
1969	V	I-6	240	155 @ 4,000	239 @ 2,200	9.2:1	1-bbl
	F	V-8	302	220 @ 4,600	300 @ 2,600	9.5:1	2-bbl
	H****	V-8	351	250 @ 4,600	355 @ 2,600	9.5:1	2-bbl
	Y	V-8	390	265 @ 4,400	401 @ 2,600	9.5:1	2-bbl
	P**	V-8	428	360 @ 5,400	459 @ 3,200	10.5:1	4-bbl
	K	V-8	429	320 @ 4,400	460 @ 2,200	10.5:1	2-bbl
	N	V-8	429	360 @ 4,600	480 @ 2,800	10.5:1	4-bbl
1970	V	I-6	240	155 @ 4,000	239 @ 2,200	9.2:1	1-bbl
	F	V-8	302	220 @ 4,600	300 @ 2,600	9.5:1	2-bbl
	H	V-8	351	250 @ 4,600	355 @ 2,600	9.5:1	2-bbl
	Y	V-8	390	265 @ 4,400	401 @ 2,600	9.5:1	2-bbl
	P**	V-8	428	360 @ 5,400	459 @ 3,200	10.5:1	4-bbl
	K	V-8	429	320 @ 4,400	460 @ 2,200	10.5:1	2-bbl
	N	V-8	429	360 @ 4,600	480 @ 2,800	10.5:1	4-bbl

* Realistically 325 hp and 360 hp
** Police Option
*** Discontinued Mid-Year
**** Mid-Year Engine
§ Both 300- and 360-hp engines used the F code
§§ The 300-, 375-, and 401-hp engines used the Z code
§§§ Not widely published—estimated by author
† Manual Transmission
†† Automatic Transmission

PAINT COLOR CODES
(U.S. ONLY)

Year	Code	Color Name	Year	Code	Color Name	Year	Code	Color Name
1955	A	Raven Black	1956	A	Raven Black	1957	A	Raven Black
	B	Banner Blue Met.		B	Nocturne Blue Met.		C	Dresden Blue
	C	Aquatone Blue		C	Bermuda Blue		D	Silver Mocha Met
	D	Waterfall Blue		D	Diamond Blue		E	Colonial White
	E	Snowshoe White		E	Colonial White		F	Starmist Blue
	F	Pinetree Green Met.		F	Pine Ridge Green		G	Cumberland Green
	G	Sea Sprite Green		G	Meadowmist Green		H	Gunmetal Gray Met
	H	Neptune Green		H	Platinum Gray		K	Dark Silver Mocha Met
	K	Buckskin Brown		K	Fiesta Red		L	Doeskin Tan
	M	Regency Purple Met.		M	Goldenglow Yellow		N	Gunmetal Gray Met
	R	Torch Red		V	Mandarin Orange		T	Woodsmoke Gray
	T	Thunderbird Blue		W	Springmist Green		V	Berkshire Green
	V	Golden Rod Yellow		Y	Sunset Coral		W	Springmist Green
	W	Tropical Rose					Y	Sunset Coral
	X	Regatta Blue					Z	Coral Sand
	Y	Mountain Green						
	Z	Coral Mist						
1958	A	Raven Black	1959	A	Raven Black	1960	A	Raven Black
	C	Desert Beige		C	Wedgewood Blue		C	Aquamarine
	D	Palamino Tan		D	Indian Turquoise		F	Surf Foam Blue
	E	Colonial White		E	Colonial White		G	Yosemite Yellow
	F	Silvertone Green		F	Fawn Tan		H	Beechwood Brown Met
	G	Sun Gold		G	April Green		J	Monte Carlo Red
	H	Gunmetal Gray Met		H	Tahitian Bronze Met		K	Sultana Tan
	J	Bali Bronze Met		J	Surf Blue Met		M	Corinthian White
	L	Azure Blue		Q	Sherwood Green Met		Q	Orchid Gray Met
	M	Gulfstream Blue		R	Torch Red		T	Meadowvale Green Met
	N	Seaspray Green		T	Geranium		W	Adriatic Green
	R	Torch Red		Y	Inca Gold		Z	Platinum Met
	T	Silvertone Blue Met		Z	Gunsmoke Gray Met			
				1	Grenadier Red Met			

Year	Code	Color Name	Year	Code	Color Name	Year	Code	Color Name
1961	A	Raven Black	1962	A	Raven Black	1963	A	Raven Black
	C	Aquamarine		B	Peacock Blue		B	Peacock Blue
	D	Starlight Blue		D	Ming Green Met		D	Ming Green Met
	E	Laurel Green		F	Baffin Blue		E	Viking Blue Met
	F	Desert Gold		H	Oxford Blue Met		H	Oxford Blue Met
	H	Chesapeake Blue Met		I	Castilian Gold Met		I	Champagne Met
	J	Monte Carlo Red		J	Rangoon Red		J	Rangoon Red
	K	Algiers Bronze Met		M	Corinthian White		M	Corinthian White
	Q	Sherwood Green Met		P	Silver Moss Met		P	Silver Moss Met
	R	Cambridge Blue Met		Q	Silver Gray Met		T	Sandshell Beige
	S	Mint Green		R	Tuscan Yellow		V	Chestnut Met
	W	Garden Turquoise Met		T	Sandshell Beige		W	Rose Beige Met
				V	Chestnut Met		X	Heritage Burgundy Met
				Z	Fieldstone Tan Met		Y	Glacier Blue
1964	A	Raven Black	1965	A	Raven Black	1966	A	Raven Black
	B	Pagoda Green		C	Honey Gold Met		F	Arcadian Blue
	D	Dynasty Green Met		D	Dynasty Green Met		H	Sahara Beige
	F	Guardsman Blue Met		F	Arcadian Blue		K	Nightmist Blue Met
	G	Prairie Tan		H	Caspian Blue Met		M	Wimbledon White
	J	Rangoon Red		J	Rangoon Red		P	Antique Bronze Met
	K	Silver Smoke Gray Met		K	Silver Smoke Gray Met		R	Ivy Green Met
	M	Wimbledon White		M	Wimbledon White		T	Candyapple Red
	P	Prairie Bronze Met		O	Tropical Turquoise Met		U	Tahoe Turquoise Met
	R	Phoenician Yellow		P	Prairie Bronze Met		V	Emberglo Met
	S	Cascade Green Met		R	Ivy Green Met		X	Vintage Burgundy Met
	T	Navajo Beige		X	Vintage Burgundy Met		Z	Sauterne Gold Met
	V	Sunlight Yellow		Y	Silver Blue Met		4	Silver Frost Met
	X	Vintage Burgundy Met		5	Twilight Turquoise Met		8	Springtime Yellow
	Y	Skylight Blue		7	Phoenician Yellow			
	Z	Chantilly Beige Met		8	Springtime Yellow			
1967	A	Raven Black	1968	A	Raven Black	1969	A	Raven Black
	B	Frost Turquoise		F	Gulfstream Aqua Met		B	Royal Maroon
	D	Acapulco Blue Met		I	Lime Gold Met		E	Aztec Aqua
	F	Arcadian Blue		M	Wimbledon White		F	Gulfstream Aqua Met
	I	Lime Gold Met		N	Diamond Blue		I	Lime Gold Met
	K	Nightmist Blue Met		O	Seafoam Green		M	Wimbledon White
	M	Wimbledon White		Q	Brittany Blue Met		Q	Brittany Blue Met
	Q	Brittany Blue Met		R	Highland Green Met		S	Champagne Gold Met
	T	Candyapple Red		T	Candyapple Red		T	Candyapple Red
	V	Burnt Amber Met		U	Tahoe Turquoise Met		W	Meadowlark Yellow
	W	Clearwater Aqua Met		W	Meadowlark Yellow		X	Presidential Blue Met
	X	Vintage Burgundy Met		X	Presidential Blue Met		Y	Indian Fire Met
	Y	Dark Moss Green Met		Y	Sunlit Gold Met		Z	New Lime
	Z	Sauterne Gold Met		6	Pebble Beige		8	Dresden Blue
	4	Silver Frost Met						
	6	Pebble Beige						
	8	Springtime Yellow						
1970	A	Raven Black	1970 (ctd)	W	Yellow			
	B	Dark Maroon		X	Dark Blue			
	C	Dark Ivy Green Met		5	Ginger Met			
	K	Bright Gold Met		6	Acapulco Blue Met			
	M	Wimbledon White		9	Light Ivy Yellow			
	N	Diamond Blue						
	P	Medium Ivy Green Met						
	Q	Medium Blue Met						
	S	Champagne Gold Met						
	T	Candyapple Red						

A Note About "Standard" and "Not Available"

There was a time when customers could special-order their car with unusual features, despite the requested color or equipment not being officially offered for a particular model. A number of unusual Fords were built as a result. Examples include a 1957 Fairlane 500 painted in University of Texas colors, 1962 Galaxie two-door sedan painted Golden Rod Yellow (a 1955 Ford color), 1963 Country Squire powered by a 427-ci, 1966 Galaxie 500/XL with a column-mounted shifter, 1966 LTD two-door hardtop with bucket seats and console, 1967 Country Squire with a 4-speed and XL interior, etc.

The DSO (District Sales Office/Domestic Special Order) code had extra digits after the two-digit code for the district when special equipment was ordered. DSO codes have been stamped into truck patent or VIN (vehicle identification number) plates since the mid 1950s and were stamped on car plates from the mid 1950s through the 1957 model year. Starting about March of 1962, Ford Motor Company's DSO codes were again stamped on VIN plates with fairly consistent regularity. On the VIN of many 1962 Fords, however, the DSO field is blank. It is not especially uncommon to see some 1963 and even 1964 models without a DSO code.

A two-digit DSO code indicates that the car was ordered by a dealer for stock or for a specific customer without any special equipment or features. A DSO code that is more than two digits indicates the car was ordered with special equipment or features that were not normally available for that model. The first two digits still represent the District Sales Office from which the order was made.

Additional books that may interest you...

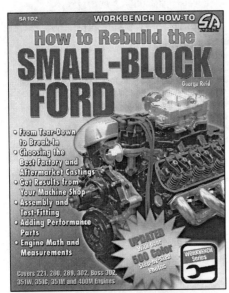
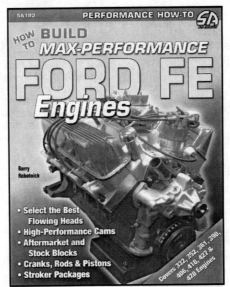